How Effective Is Schooling?

A Critical Review of Research

A Rand Educational Policy Study

How Effective Is Schooling?

A Critical Review of Research

Harvey A. Averch,
Stephen J. Carroll,
Theodore S. Donaldson,
Herbert J. Kiesling,
John Pincus

Foreword by H. Thomas James

Educational Technology Publications
Englewood Cliffs, New Jersey 07632

Library of Congress Cataloging in Publication Data

Rand Corporation.
    How effective is schooling?

    (Its Rand educational policy study series)
    Originally prepared for the President's Commission on School Finance.
    Bibliography: p.
    1. Educational research--United States. 2. Education--United States. I. Averch, Harvey A.
II. United States. President's Commission on School Finance. III. Title. IV. Series.
LB1028.R26   1974   370'.78'073   74-2165
ISBN 0-87778-071-4

Copyright © 1974 The Rand Corporation.

All rights reserved. No part of this book may be reproduced or transmitted, in any form or by any means, electronic or mechanical, including photocopying, recording, or by any information storage and retrieval system, without permission in writing from the Rand Corporation and the Publisher.

Printed in the United States of America.

Library of Congress Catalog Card Number: 74-2165.

International Standard Book Number: 0-87778-071-4.

First Printing: June, 1974.

A RAND EDUCATIONAL POLICY STUDY

PREFACE

This study, the first volume of a forthcoming series of Rand studies in educational policy, assesses what is known at present about the determinants of educational effectiveness. The work was sponsored initially by the President's Commission on School Finance as part of its inquiry into alternative financial arrangements for primary and secondary education. One policy question that arose early in the Commission's work was, finance for what? Do the resources, processes, and organizations now being employed in primary and secondary education appreciably affect student achievement, defined broadly? To answer this question, the Commission sponsored a small interdisciplinary study at The Rand Corporation beginning in January 1971. Because of the potential interest in the work, Rand supplemented Commission funding with its own corporate research funds. This study presents the results of that analytical effort. It represents, in the authors' view, a first step toward increasing the potential effectiveness of interdisciplinary research in education.

Answering the question posed by the Commission required an examination of many strands of research. In terms of traditional disciplines, research on educational effectiveness covers political science, economics, econometrics, psychology, psychometrics, sociology, and sociometrics, as well as the discipline of education proper. Because our inquiry was concerned with implications of research for policy, the analysis has been organized according to questions about educational effectiveness and methods used to get results rather than by discipline. The authors set forth the assumptions underlying each approach, giving the reader some sense of what he should look for when he encounters research claims about the effectiveness of educational instruments. The latter is particularly important, because it is impossible to cover every single study, and new results appear incessantly.

The volume of published educational research relating to effectiveness is so great that we could not attempt to provide exhaustive coverage in the earlier version of this review, which was largely prepared during 1971, under deadlines imposed by the schedule of the President's Commission on School Finance. In fields where the volume of publication is modest (input-output approach, organizational approach), we did attempt to provide exhaustive coverage. In fields where literature is very extensive (process approach, evaluation approach), we relied heavily on published review articles with frequent reference to original articles to verify the findings of the more important research studies.

We have tried to make sure that the literature we did review is genuinely representative of the body of published work since 1950. In revising this study for publication, we have included works published since our original report to the President's Commission in December 1971. Relevant books and articles published in 1972 and 1973 are also reviewed herein. In general, the findings of this recent literature have not altered the conclusions we reached earlier. If anything, the recent literature, such as Jencks' *Inequality* and Mosteller and Moynihan's *On Equality of Educational Opportunity*, strengthens the support for these conclusions. Therefore, we believe that our principal conclusions accurately summarize the current state of research knowledge about the determinants of educational effectiveness. In addition to summarizing the findings of existing research, in Chapter VIII we give recommendations for future research.

The study is organized according to the five approaches to educational effectiveness discussed in the introductory section. The reader who wants details on the findings of individual studies should use Appendix A and the Bibliography.

ACKNOWLEDGMENTS

The authors wish to express their gratitude for comments received on an early draft to Professors Richard Snow and Henry M. Levin of Stanford University; Professor Alex M. Mood of the University of California, Irvine; Joseph C. Kennedy and S.L. Sklar of the President's Commission on School Finance; and Stephen M. Barro of the Rand staff. Professor Robert Stake of the University of Illinois and Marian Sherman Stearns of the Stanford Research Institute also provided valuable comments on the final draft.

FOREWORD

A perennial complaint from educational practitioners and policymakers, at all levels, is that research is not helpful to them. Yet research in education goes on, indeed is accelerating, as more scholars from more disciplines turn their attention to phenomena, processes, and problems related to education.

The apparent lack of communication between the scholar in education and the decisionmakers responsible for educational institutions is puzzling unless one recognizes how different are their two worlds of work. The practitioner is concerned with policymaking and with decisions. He decides what will be done to maintain and improve the services of educational institutions. The atmosphere of this domain is urgent, the problems immediate. The decisionmaker is constantly drawing on two great banks of data, the technical knowledge he can obtain and the social values of the community he serves, to determine what will and what will not go in the circumstances he faces. The scholar, on the other hand, studies the variables that may eventually shape policy, but he deals with them one by one. He works in the relatively quiet domain of the researcher, the investigator, the man who asks *why*; he bargains for time to test his answers. The questions he asks are rarely the questions the decisionmaker wants answered; he is distracted by urgency. His preliminary studies often yield results that conflict with one another, thus adding to the confusion of the practitioner who can not wait for the testing. The researcher looks long and diligently for the additions to tested knowledge that are his occasional reward.

Nevertheless, the great universities continue to produce new and verifiable knowledge about education. Unfortunately, this knowledge does not yet accumulate in the useful patterns we have come to expect from the hard sciences. When the scholar does attempt to integrate the knowledge he obtains from his inquiries, he does so in theoretical formulations that are more likely to aid further research than to have immediate application or to be useful to the decisionmaker.

Obviously, educational practitioners facing grave decisions would benefit from access to accumulated knowledge of likely usefulness to them. Since scholars find it difficult to provide such knowledge on call, the need is evident for some kind of service that performs the function of broker between the scholar and the decisionmaker. This book is an example of how such a brokerage service works. Scholars from several disciplines, working together, analyze and elaborate the questions posed by decisionmakers and rework them into forms that can be dealt with in the scholarly world. They then accumulate whatever casts light on the practical problems calling for solutions and feed back the evidence to the policymakers. In the process they are also able to report on great gaps in knowledge in particular areas, and so alert scholars to possible areas for further study. This kind of brokerage service should have a salutary effect on both scholarly inquiry and decisionmaking, and it should enhance their fruitful interaction.

H. Thomas James
President
The Spencer Foundation

TABLE OF CONTENTS

PREFACE vii

ACKNOWLEDGMENTS. ix

FOREWORD by H. Thomas James xi

Chapter
I. INTRODUCTION. 3
    Educational Effectiveness: The Background for Policy. 3
    Educational Research and Educational Policy 9
    Five Research Approaches 12
        The Input-Output Approach 12
        The Process Approach 13
        The Organizational Approach 15
        The Evaluation Approach 16
        The Experiential Approach 18
    Scope and Limitations of the Analysis 21

II. MEASURING EDUCATIONAL OUTCOMES 25
    Teacher Grades and Essay Examinations 27
    Standardized Achievement Tests 28
        Derivation and Meaning of Normative Scores 29
        Sampling Bias. 29

	Educational Objectives and Test Content	30
	Test Validity	31
	Statistical Problems	32
	Criterion-Referenced Tests	33
	General Intelligence Tests	35
	Summary	36
III.	THE INPUT-OUTPUT APPROACH	39
	Objectives and Methods	41
	Variables	43
	Analytical Problems	44
	Results	46
	Overall	46
	Peer Group Influence	47
	School Resources	50
	Background Factors	51
	Research Problems	52
	Summary	53
IV.	THE PROCESS APPROACH	56
	The Effects of Teachers	58
	Teacher Characteristics and Student Achievement	59
	Teacher Skills and Effectiveness	61
	Teacher Expectations	63
	Student-Teacher Interactions	64
	The Effects of Instruction	65
	Classroom Instruction	66
	Instructional Psychology	72
	Transfer of Learning	75
	Reinforcement and Feedback	77
	Attention Factors in Learning	79
	Retention of Learned Material	80
	Student Characteristics	81
	Abilities and General Intelligence	82
	Aptitude-Treatment Interaction: Special Abilities	84
	Aptitude-Treatment Interaction: General Ability	85

Table of Contents xv

	Student Characteristics and Programmed Instruction	87
	Student Characteristics and Meaningfulness	88
	Concept Attainment	89
	Personality Differences	91
	Early Development and Learning	94
	Summary	96

V. THE ORGANIZATIONAL APPROACH 100
  Introduction 100
  Research Problem and Methods 101
  Results from the Case Studies 105
  Results from Performance Contracting Studies 110
  Evaluation Problems in Performance Contracting 112
  Summary 112

VI. EVALUATION OF BROAD EDUCATIONAL INTERVENTIONS 116
  Findings from Large-Scale Evaluations 117
    ESEA Title I 118
    Head Start 119
    Follow Through 120
    Higher Horizons 121
    Evaluation of the Evaluations 121
    Sesame Street 123
  Findings from Small-Scale Evaluations 126
  Interventions Designed Basically for Research 128
    Stanford University: Computer Assisted Instruction 128
    Gordon: Early Child Stimulation Through Parent Education 129
    Karnes: Ameliorative Preschool 129
    DiLorenzo: Pre-Kindergarten Programs in New York State 130
    Project Conquest, East St. Louis, Illinois 130
  Longitudinal Analysis 131
    Intelligence Test Findings 131
    Achievement Test Findings 134

Summary of Longitudinal Findings 135
Program Characteristics Associated with Success 135
Cost of Compensatory Education. 139
Summary of Findings............................. 142

VII. THE EXPERIENTIAL APPROACH. 146
Introduction: The Approach Defined............... 146
Objectives and Methods 147
Variables 148
Limitations of Research.......................... 151
Results.. 152
Social Values and Educational Objectives 152
The Learning Environment 155
Reformation: Prescription for Education......... 159
Conclusions and Policy Implications 163

VIII. CONCLUSIONS 166
Summary and Discussion of Findings................ 166
The Input-Output Approach 166
The Process Approach 167
The Organizational Approach 168
The Evaluation Approach. 169
The Experiential Approach 169
Limitations of Available Research 170
Conclusions and Policy Implications 171
Where Do We Go from Here? The Substantive
Issues 175
Non-School Factors 175
Interaction................................. 177
Different Forms of Education 178
Where Do We Go from Here? The Methodological
Issues 179

Appendix
A. INPUT-OUTPUT STUDIES 185

BIBLIOGRAPHY... 233

INDEX.. 253

How Effective Is Schooling?

A Critical Review of Research

I. INTRODUCTION

EDUCATIONAL EFFECTIVENESS:
THE BACKGROUND FOR POLICY

This is a study of what research tells us about educational effectiveness in American public schools. The quest for effectiveness implies that it is possible to define the functions of schooling, whether or not it is possible to reach consensus about the relative importance of these functions.

For most of this century, public schools in the United States have been viewed as carrying out five important functions: *socialization*, a unifying and disciplinary force in a society of diverse origins; *sorting*, identifying people's future socioeconomic roles; *custody*, the child-sitting function; *knowledge and skills training*, developing a literate population, with at least a minimum of job-related skills; and encouragement of such individual attributes as *creativity and self-reliance*.

Today, despite the substantial public support that through the forces of tradition and ideology the schools still retain, each of these functions is being called into question. The *socialization* and *sorting* functions are often viewed as supporting politically and socially conservative forces. Because there is a close association between years of schooling and socioeconomic status, and between test scores and years of schooling, the current system, it is alleged, perpetuates the existing social order (Bowles and Gintis, 1972; Jencks et al., 1972). Furthermore, the system lends the cloak of legitimacy to that order by treating the years of schooling and test score results as "objective" determinants of merit. In fact, according to these critics, test scores and years of schooling are largely determined by nonschool factors of heredity and environment, so that merit as defined by the student's own effort has little to do with the outcomes. In this view, schools socialize students to accept the legitimacy of the existing system, and its discipline, providing only the illusion of quality without in any sense providing equal opportunity (Milner, 1972; Spring, 1972).

The *custodial* function is under even more widespread attack. Silberman (1970) and Kozol (1968) are representative of the critics who find that the schools operate in a joyless and mindless atmosphere, stifling children's initiative and creativity to the objective of a disciplinary and instructional lockstep. The custodial function is often overlooked in discussions of school effectiveness, because it is not part of the ideology of education. Yet it is evident that in recent decades, with the progressive elimination of minors from the labor force, the custodial function is increasingly important as a way of supervising the activities of the 5-18 age group. (According to 1970 census data, nearly half of the 18-21 age group was also subject to some degree of supervision in institutions of higher education.)

In the traditional ideology, provision of *knowledge and skills* is considered as the principal element of schooling. Criticisms of the schools' effectiveness in these roles are buttressed by both statistical analyses (Coleman *et al.*, 1966; Jencks *et al.*, 1972) and by observation (Herndon, 1968; Holt, 1967; Kozol, 1968; Silberman, 1970). Although it seems likely that on average the United States is not behind most other developed nations in the levels of knowledge and skills at any given age level, there is widespread belief that American schools consistently fail to serve the poor and minority groups in this respect.

The fifth function, development of such personal attributes as *creativity and self-reliance*, is also called into question for a variety of reasons. Many critics (Friedenberg, 1963; Goodman, 1965; Herndon, 1968, 1971; Holt, 1967) claim that the schools are far more likely to stifle these qualities than to promote them. Others believe that the schools have very modest roles to play in developing these qualities, that the schools neither promote nor retard such qualities, but are largely irrelevant. Finally, many of those who conduct research in child development, while agreeing that such qualities are not only important but also capable of being affected by what happens in schools, nevertheless find themselves at a loss to devise generally acceptable measures of how the schools in particular affect such attitudes or behavior.

The schools, therefore, play multiple roles. In the absence of general consensus on the relative importance of the different aims, and agreement in some instances in the absence of appropriate performance measures, it is impossible to answer the question, "How effective is schooling?" We can look at each dimension, but there is no agreement on how performance along different dimensions should be weighted to arrive at a single "effectiveness score."

There is then no consensus on the relative importance of the various aims of schooling, and often no generally accepted measure of progress toward each of these several aims. General agreement about what constitutes effective schooling is likely to remain elusive. This means that no single measure will provide a definition of effective schooling. Instead, if people are to make rational judgments about educational policy, they will need a variety of measures, each related to some specific dimension of schooling. This is not an academic point. If there is persistent discontent with school performance, it becomes important to find out how the schools could perform better along any of the relevant dimensions. In response to this discontent, the various levels of educational governance in the United States—school districts, state legislatures, and state and federal education agencies—have attempted to introduce a variety of reforms and innovations. So far, there seems to be no public or professional accord about whether these changes, as actually carried out in the schools, represent more effective schooling as compared with traditional methods. All too often these judgments are based on a single measure, scores on standardized tests, which are well known to be resistant to efforts to change them and may be irrelevant to most of the dimensions of schooling discussed above.

The stakes are high in any large-scale effort to introduce changes into public education. First, in the United States education is traditionally regarded as a means of promoting upward social mobility; and in an era more than ever concerned with issues of poverty and discrimination, the schools' present ability to carry out that function is under challenge. The demand for equal educational opportunity is in fact a demand for new concepts of socialization and for a sorting out system that will provide chances for a better life for those whom our society has regarded as underdogs. Second, the schools are a major industry—the costs of public elementary and secondary education now exceed $50 billion annually. Changes in the way schools do business affect the lives of nearly everyone, whether as consumers or suppliers of education, or as members of a society with symbiotic relations with the school system. The rapid rise in per capita costs of schooling over the past quarter-century has turned school finance into a major political issue. These two issues have affected the policies of federal, state, and local agencies and are currently working a gradual transformation in the relations of each to public education. The effort by all levels of government to promote educational reform has led to demands for research that will improve educational effectiveness and illuminate the present state of research knowledge as an aid to policymaking.

The *federal government*, traditionally relatively passive in its relations with public education, has tried over the past decade to introduce major change in the public education system, which has always been highly decentralized and reserved in constitutional law to the states and in practice largely to localities. These interventions have been based primarily on three grounds:

- The existing system fails to provide equal educational opportunity for the poor and the racial minorities. Titles I, VII, and VIII of the Elementary and Secondary Education Act of 1965 are responses to this perception, providing funds to help school districts where there are large concentrations of poor children.
- The educational system is generally less effective than it might be if innovation and dissemination of best practice were encouraged. Title III of the Elementary and Secondary Education Act, providing funds for innovation, and the USOE experimental schools program are responses to this perception.
- The educational system fails to generate on its own either appropriate quality or quantity of research, development, and dissemination of results; therefore federal aid for these purposes to improve the quality and productivity of American education is called for. Federal support of educational research and development has expanded sharply since 1965, both for university-based research and through the creation of a network of research and development agencies around the country. The establishment in 1972 of a new HEW agency, the National Institute of Education (NIE), indicates

that the government is still willing to back educational research and development despite its unimpressive contributions to practice so far.

The *state governments* are the principal source of external financing for school districts. In the face of persistent increases in the cost of schooling, they have been forced to pay the ever-increasing price of public education without, in general, satisfying state legislators that the benefits received have merited the additional costs. State education agencies characteristically have small staffs and are not often renowned for their ability to lead or to innovate. Consequently, the states have generally turned to the federal government for leadership in school reform and have in turn received substantial federal support for enlarging staff and strengthening staff quality. Their role in educational reform outside of the fiscal field remains unclear, despite federal efforts to bolster their role in compensatory education, innovation, and research.

It is hard to generalize about the posture of 16,000 *local school districts* toward educational reform, because their stances are so varied. In general, the offer of federal funds has tempted them toward at least some gestures of reform in the shape of compensatory education and Title III programs. Some districts, however, have long had reputations as innovative districts. They have been joined in recent years by districts finding themselves under successive political pressures stemming from such diverse sources as Sputnik, "Johnny can't read," racial protest in the schools, pressure from radicals of the new left and new right, and the growth of activist teacher organizations. Generally, these innovations have been in school districts with high levels of per student spending (Mort and Cornell, 1941) or those faced by substantial political pressures. However, for locally as well as federally sponsored programs, it has not been clear whether the reforms, either as adopted or as implemented in practice, have led to significant improvements in the schools, although they may sometimes succeed in reducing political tensions. At the local level, then, we observe an effort to seek remedies that will not unduly upset the schools' traditional ways of doing business.

Contemporary critics of the schools reject this approach, which is based on combining reform with the conservation of bureaucratic values. Their criticisms generally take one of two lines; a denial that innovation in the schools *can* have important effects on equal educational opportunity; or an affirmation that only radical change in the governance of schools will improve their performance. The first approach, based on statistical research of the input-output type (see Figure 1, page 13), is most thoroughly developed by Jencks *et al.* (1972). It states that educational effectiveness, as measured by standardized test scores, is largely determined by the student's heredity and environment. Variations in school resources account for only a minor fraction of variations in test scores. Furthermore, variations in people's career outcomes as measured by income and job status are even more weakly related to school factors than are test scores. Therefore, the argument runs, if society wishes to provide "equal educational opportunity," the remedies lie largely outside the educational sector, and the principal argument for increasing or equalizing spending is in order to make the schools more agreeable places to spend the student years.

The second line of criticism, based on observation and experience (see Figure 5, page 18), advanced by such writers as Friedenberg (1963), Illich (1971), and Kozol (1972), rejects the contemporary organization of schools in the United States. It asserts that schools are too structured, too much committed to disciplining people for the requirements of industrial society, and mindless in their emphasis on order as distinguished from individual development. These critics believe that if schooling could be restructured to be more open (the British infant schools are often cited as exemplars in this regard) or even eliminated entirely as formal institutions in order to be incorporated more closely into other social institutions, then student perceptions of themselves and of their appropriate roles, and therefore their self-esteem, would be vastly improved. Since these writers, although of widely varying political and social persuasions, do agree that appropriate educational approaches could benefit children emotionally, intellectually, and socially, they find themselves at least somewhat at variance with the implicit policy recommendations of Jencks *et al.*

According to another group of critics, substantial increases in learning and in educational opportunity can come from applying new educational technologies, without substantial changes in educational organization other than those required for the necessary bureaucratic adaptation to technological requirements. Those who envision technology as the solvent for current dissatisfaction point to a wide range of possibilities within the schools—computer-assisted instruction, cable television, programmed instruction, improved methods of audio-visual reinforcement, and a range of technologies not specifically instructional that can enhance learning abilities (improved nutrition, biochemical aids to mentation, genetic manipulation, and improved psychometric methods that detect individual differences affecting learning styles). So far, with dramatic exceptions like *Sesame Street* or some computer-assisted foreign-language training, these developments are largely prospective. But in principle they present alternative paths to more effective schooling, at least in cognitive domains.

With a world of competing hypotheses about the role of schooling, and a world of suggested alternatives to improve its effectiveness, it seems rational as an aid to policymaking to turn to the body of research on education for evidence about differential effectiveness of various approaches. But each discipline that studies education—psychology, economics, sociology, political science, and so on—has its own perspective, its own paradigms of the nature of educational systems and processes. To make our way through this confusing terrain, we have gone through a two-stage mapping process, first constructing a set of relief maps, each one showing how a particular discipline or set of related disciplines views the functioning and effectiveness of the schools; and second, trying to develop some synthetic view or reconciliation of what each map tells us about how the schools operate under the various resource levels, instructional processes, organization structures, social priorities, and political pressures that characterize them. This second task—to place each research approach in its appropriate dimensions as an element of a synoptic view of the research on educational effectiveness—is more demanding, and so more elusive. We have tried in Chapter VIII of this study to present a sketch of what might be encompassed by such a view of educational research, but this territory remains largely unexplored.

EDUCATIONAL RESEARCH AND EDUCATIONAL POLICY

This study, then, presents the results of an analysis of the research on educational effectiveness, as conducted by a variety of research disciplines. The objective of this analysis was to assess the current state of knowledge regarding the determinants of educational outcomes. We attempted to accomplish this task by conducting a *critical* survey of the research.

Each year literally thousands of educational research efforts are reported. New results are constantly being presented. The vast body of literature on educational effectiveness should provide a firm foundation for the formulation of educational policy. Thus far, it has not done so.

There are a number of reasons for the gap between educational research and educational policy. First, there are many diverse streams of educational research. In terms of traditional disciplines, research on educational effectiveness appears in economics, econometrics, political science, psychology, psychometrics, sociology, and sociometrics, as well as the discipline of education proper. Researchers have tended to follow relatively narrow, intradisciplinary paths. There have been few attempts to connect these paths; nor is there a clear map down any given path. Policymaker and researcher alike, therefore, find it very difficult to draw policy implications from these various disciplines.

Second, the sheer magnitude of the literature on educational effectiveness makes it impossible to keep up to date on the research being conducted in any one field, let alone to keep up with what is being produced across the entire range of educational research.

Third, educational research has seldom been explicitly policy-oriented. A considerable volume of research has been aimed at increasing understanding of how, and under what conditions, learning takes place. But the basic research has rarely been framed in the language of decisionmaking.

Fourth, and perhaps most important, the research is full of contradictory or inconsistent findings. The policymaker thus finds himself constantly basing his decisions on controversial and disputed research results.

This analysis is directed toward the needs of the educational policymaker. We believe that what is important for the inquiry at hand is to extract the policy-relevant findings from the research and to derive from them broadly based conclusions as to what we now know about educational effectiveness. The analysis is based upon comprehensive reviews of the many streams of educational research. Throughout the analysis, we have attempted to examine the validity and credibility of research results. In the case of each research effort reviewed, we tried to discover whether the study was internally valid (did the researcher pursue proper methods for the questions he addressed?); and, if it was, we asked if the results were credible in the light of accumulated knowledge (were the findings consistent with those of other studies in the area?).

The need for examination of internal validity is clear. We cannot base policy on incorrect or misleading research results. Accordingly, we must ask whether the results of any particular study were generated by a proper method of analysis.

Just as important is the issue of credibility (external validity). There is always some chance that a particular variable, or a particular set of variables, that appears to have a significant effect upon achievement is in fact unrelated to educational outcome. For this reason, educational policy cannot rely on the results of any one study. Whether studies say anything about actual educational outcomes depends, then, on results that appear consistently throughout a number of studies. If an educational resource or procedure shows up as important in a large number of studies, then we should be able to state with considerable confidence that this resource or procedure should be selected by policymakers (allowing for the relative costs of resources and procedures).

Note that an examination of credibility serves three distinct purposes: First, it provides a way of summarizing numerous disparate studies. Second, it addresses the question of what should be believed in the face of inconsistent or conflicting results. We resolve such conflicts by "adding up" the evidence on each side of a dispute. Third, consideration of external validity enables us to deal with the avalanche of research results. No review, this one included, could possibly consider every single educational research study. But, if a large number of internally valid studies yield consistent results, then we can be fairly sure that any omitted study would not have substantively changed our conclusions.

None of the many ways of accumulating evidence from dissimilar studies to reach a conclusion as to the results of the body of research[1] is entirely satisfactory. Each research report we review can be considered as a witness presenting testimony. Our test of internal validity can be compared to cross-examination. Interstudy consistency is determined subjectively, our judgment being based upon the accumulated evidence presented by many diverse research reports. We do count the number of studies in which an independent variable is examined and calculate the proportion that finds that variable to be significant, but we do not simply weigh each study equally. Rather, we are more persuaded by studies that use larger samples or more replications, better designs, a greater number of controls for intervening variables, or more accurate measures of the variables in question. In general, then, what follows is not a classical review of research, listing findings without much evaluation of the results. Rather, it is our answer to the question, "What does the research tell us about educational effectiveness?"

Accomplishing our objective required that this vast body of literature be organized and evaluated on the basis of some analytical structure. Our discussion of the research on educational effectiveness is organized according to five basic research approaches—that is, *according to the aspect of education that is examined in the analysis, the questions being addressed, and the method deemed appropriate to answer the questions.*

FIVE RESEARCH APPROACHES

The five approaches provide a way of collecting studies that share a similar focus and purpose and use similar analytical techniques. We can thus identify the similarities and differences among the many streams of educational research. Individual studies or groups of similar studies are placed in perspective. Moreover, common standards of internal validity apply to studies within each approach. This simplifies the task of evaluating the results of individual research efforts. Finally, because studies in an approach tend to have a common orientation, the relationships among their results are more easily observed.

The Input-Output Approach

Much of the research produced in the input-output approach has been prominent in recent policy debates—for example, the *Equality of Educational Opportunity* survey (Coleman et al., 1966) and its various reanalyses. Research in this approach views the school as a black box containing students (Figure 1). Resources are applied to the students in the box, and from this application some output flows. Output is usually defined in terms of cognitive achievement as measured by standardized achievement tests. Some studies define as outputs such variables as dropout rates or percentage of students going on to college. School resources, or inputs, generally include a broad range of factors describing teachers' characteristics (experience and verbal ability are two examples) and physical attributes of the school (the number of library books per student, age of building, class size, and the like).

Introduction

Figure 1—The input-output approach

Research is directed toward the question, "To what extent are variations in educational outcomes due to variations in resource levels?" Ideally, the research is supposed to identify the extent to which each resource contributes to educational outcomes. Policymakers should then be able to identify those resources that are most effective and restructure the current use of resources toward the more effective configurations discovered by research.

The empirical problem is to establish the relation between input and output. In practice, statistical analysis is applied to *ex post*, cross-sectional data, although the desire for longitudinal data is often asserted. In other words, the analyst collects a body of data at a point in time—usually survey data—applies various statistical techniques—usually multiple regression—and tries to make statements about the effects of inputs.

The confidence we can place in research results depends upon (1) the internal validity of particular studies—the logic and design of the analysis; and (2) the external validity—the consistency of findings across studies. With respect to internal validity, one asks: Were the procedures generally accepted for this approach carefully followed? And, if so, are the results consistent with the underlying model? For the input-output approach, internal validity is measured by tests of significance and goodness of fit.[2] External validity concerns whether studies say something about the real educational world. Do they say something about the schools? Here the test is interstudy consistency. Are the resources identified as effective in one study also found to be effective in other studies?[3]

The Process Approach

The second approach—education as a process—is based on a quite different fundamental assumption about what determines educational outcomes (Figure 2). Here the researcher focuses on the "inside" of the box. Resources are assumed to be predetermined or given. What matters here are the processes by which the resources are applied to the students and the response of the students to the processes. If we can correctly identify processes of education or learning, *they* will determine the quantities of resources that the schools require. The processes of concern can be those connected with teachers, students, or instruction, or the interactions among them. Educational outcomes for the most part are limited measures of cognitive achievement. In a few cases noncognitive achievement is examined.

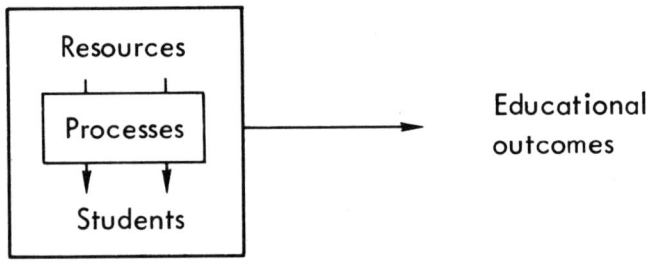

Figure 2—The process approach

In most cases, the main purpose of this approach is to extend our knowledge about educational processes. In general, there has been much less orientation toward concrete policy action among researchers here than among those who pursue the input-output approach. The policy applications have so far been secondary. To illustrate, when conducting an experiment, psychologists lay great stress on experimental control of confounding variables. Sometimes, to minimize the extent to which a student's previous learning experiences affect the outcome of an experiment, they deliberately examine learning tasks that are very unlike the learning tasks encountered in the classroom— memorizing lists of nonsense syllables, for example. Consequently, the results of the experiment offer little direct policy guidance.

Research here usually consists of small-scale experiments or variations of treatments, often performed in a laboratory. The problem thus becomes one of putting together the experiments or treatments

Introduction

that bear on the same process to see whether they are consistent. The experiments are collated through review articles varying greatly in quality. Here internal validity depends upon whether the studies have proper experimental design, whether they controlled for everything that could confound the results; external validity, again, depends upon consistency among studies. Do the same processes appear to affect academic achievement in the same way across a number of studies?

The Organizational Approach

In the organizational approach to the issue of educational effectiveness, what is done in the schools is viewed as being not the result of a rational search for effective inputs or processes but a reflection of history, social demands, and organizational change and rigidities. In Figure 3 we distort the shape of the "box," because its structure matters here (the school system as a whole). The inputs are the rules, the procedures, the incentives that are set up within the system. The approach is more concerned with the people in the system—teachers, administrators, appointed and selected officials—than are the previous two approaches. The measure of responsiveness to change is the ability to adapt to a changing clientele. The assumption is that responsive schools will deliver satisfactory academic outcomes, but not necessarily the maximum feasible outcomes.[4] Why? Because in this approach the schools have multiple objectives, not just academic

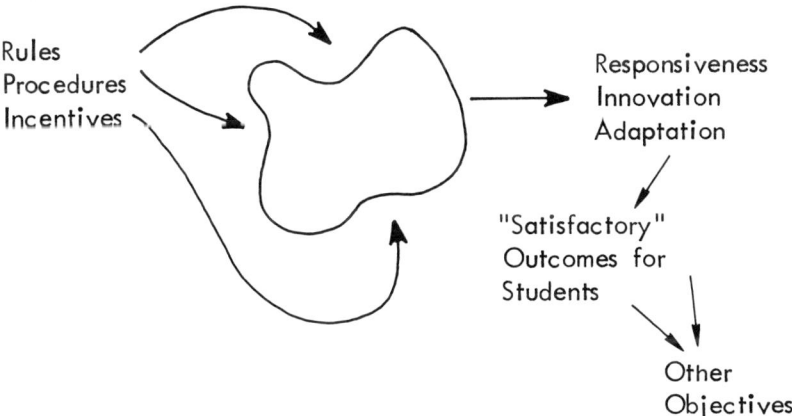

Figure 3—*The organizational approach*

outcomes; they do many things. And the schools are doing well if they get satisfactory achievement along with the other goals that have to be satisfied. The perceived crisis of the classroom is caused by an inflexible stand in the face of changing demands by students, parents, the immediate community, and the government. The purpose, then, is to understand the behavior of the whole system and describe the shape of the box and how and what happens to the people in it—not just the students, but the teachers, the administrators, and the community as a whole.

Research here primarily uses case-study methods. There are no formal tests of either internal or external validity; in fact, it is rare in these case studies to find much concern about such matters.[5] There are no statistical tests, almost by definition; interstudy consistency is hard to determine, since the point to be illustrated rarely recurs. Nevertheless, we try to apply "reasonable" criteria of our own to assess these studies.

Although the organizational approach is relatively undeveloped (as compared with the previous two approaches), we believe that it is closely related to schools' finances. The leverage of alternative financial schemes seems greater on organizational structures than on resources or processes. It is hard to see how overall financial schemes could be tied to the internal use of resources or processes of school systems without creating massive problems of administration and control. It is possible that alternative financial schemes, if they can be found, could affect the shape of our educational box to make it more receptive to effective resources or processes.

The Evaluation Approach

Studies within the evaluation approach attempt to analyze the effectiveness of broad educational interventions that are directly related to large issues of social policy. These studies are analyses of programs in which treatments are devoted to "groups of children as a whole in diverse programs, taken as a whole" (Stearns, 1971a, p. 6). In such interventions the resources devoted to each child are increased substantially. *Since any number of educational inputs or processes are changed at the same time, it is difficult to tell precisely which program features are responsible, even where there is demonstrated success.* Researchers using this method tend to address the question, "To what extent did a generalized intervention affect educational outcomes?"

Research focuses on school systems in which there have been interventions on a large scale (Figure 4). The primary concern is to identify the relationship between the existence (or magnitude) of an intervention and educational outcomes. These analyses seldom attempt to determine why or how an intervention affected outcomes.[6] This contrasts to the other approaches in which the analyst focuses on the effect of a particular educational practice.

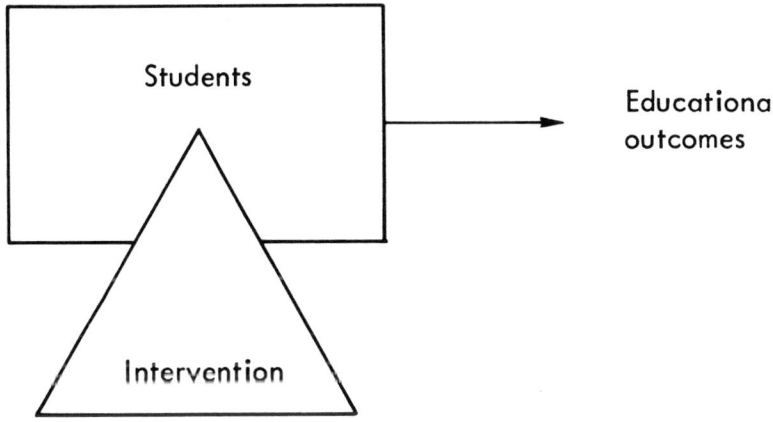

Figure 4—*The evaluation approach*

These studies tend to be more policy-oriented than those included in any other approach. Their general purpose or goal is to discover what "works." The implication is that if we can discover what "works," we can replicate the intervention elsewhere.

The analytical technique used to discover whether an intervention was successful is *ex post* examination of the outcomes of students upon whom the intervention was focused. The evaluator typically attempts to identify a group of students who, although not themselves targets of the intervention, resemble the students who were. He then compares the outcomes of the target group of students with the outcomes of the non-target, or control, group of students. Any differences in outcomes are presumed to be reflections of the intervention's effect.

In evaluations, the researcher usually chooses the members of the control group after the program has begun rather than by some random process, and there is always the possibility of some systematic difference between control group members and target group members. If there is, differences in outcomes between the two groups may reflect the difference between the groups and not the effect of the evaluation. Accordingly, the question of internal validity hinges on the method by which a control group was chosen.[7]

The Experiential Approach

The experiential approach is concerned with what happens to students in schools as an end in itself. The school is viewed as an institution containing students and having an effect on them (Figure 5). It is generally (but not always) acknowledged that the influence of the school may affect educational outcomes. But this is not viewed as being the primary concern. Rather, considerable importance is placed on that influence as an outcome in itself. The primary emphasis is on the effects of school experiences on students' self-concepts and on their relation to other people and to social institutions.

The purpose of these studies is to show how the system works and its effect on those within the system. The central question addressed is, "What does the school do to students?" The research is conducted by "on-the-spot" observation. That is, research reports in this approach are frequently provided by participant observers in the form of descriptions of their experiences. Others are done by people outside the formal education system who are proponents of educational reform.

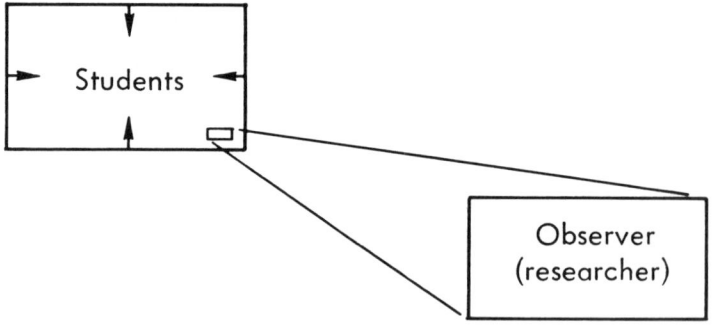

Figure 5—*The experiential approach*

Introduction

It is always difficult to examine the internal validity of case studies, which are often used in the experiential literature. And case studies by participant observers are usually the most difficult. The participant observer reports and interprets what he has seen, but what he has seen is in large part his own behavior and the response of others to his behavior. In fact, one of the presumed advantages of participant observations is the insight obtained by engaging directly in the activities being studied. The objectivity of the researcher becomes a major issue. Further, the majority of studies we reviewed in this approach were not conducted by professional researchers. Rather, they were provided by persons who entered the system intending to be teachers but who were so incensed at what they observed that they felt compelled to communicate their observations to others. Accordingly, their personal feelings are an important aspect of what they report.

We have attempted to examine the internal validity of these reports by asking whether they are internally consistent. (Does the author seem to interpret what he observes in a consistent manner?) We have also tried to discover whether his observations seem to be based on circumstances peculiar to his situation. (Do his observations concern his particular class, school, or system; or do his observations concern aspects of education in general?)

From each work reviewed we have tried to derive a set of propositions about the influence of the educational system on students. External validity was checked by comparing these sets of propositions to discover which seemed to be supported by a number of persons in different circumstances.

The formal procedure we used in our analysis is outlined in Figure 6. We examined individual studies in each approach and attempted to determine whether they were internally valid. Did the researcher use methods appropriate to the problem he addressed? Did he interpret his results correctly in view of the advantages and limitations of the analytical techniques he used? We discarded those studies that did not satisfy minimum requirements of internal validity. We also made the maximum possible use of previous reviews. However, for particularly important studies we returned to the original source, even when the results of these studies were already included in one or more review articles.

The next step was to bring together the results of the individual studies and of the previous reviews. We attempted to derive general conclusions as to what were the overall results of the many research efforts. Our primary criterion was inter-study consistency. Did the results tend to support or reinforce one another? Or did we find that roughly similar studies, asking basically the same question and using basically the same methods, yielded substantively different results? This procedure was followed for each of the five approaches.

Finally, we combined these five sets of results to derive overall conclusions as to what is now known about educational effectiveness. It was from these conclusions that we drew our policy implications.

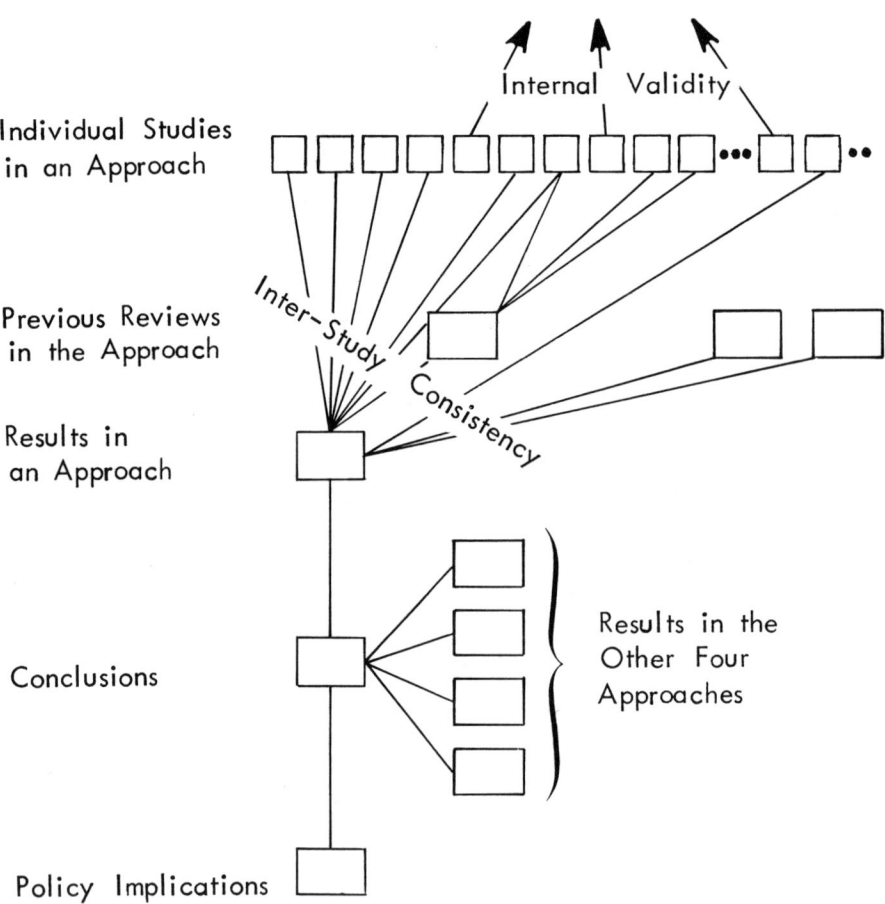

Figure 6—Formal procedure used in analysis

Introduction 21

SCOPE AND LIMITATIONS OF THE ANALYSIS

A large volume of educational research is based on *a priori* reasoning. That is, the researcher begins with some general propositions about learning that he believes to be true. From an analysis of these general propositions the researcher derives specific propositions regarding the effectiveness of particular educational practices—instructional methods or materials, characteristics or skills of teachers, and so on. Activities such as this are a vital part of the research process; but they are only a part of the research process. We know very little about the nature of learning. Our theories and models of learning have many gaps and should be regarded, at best, as crude approximations to reality. Accordingly, the specific propositions derived from general theories of learning can be viewed only as hypotheses. They may be true, but it is quite possible that they are false. Until they have been subjected to empirical test they must be viewed as unproved. Accordingly, we have considered only studies in which some substantive, empirical evidence is presented in support of the researcher's claims.

An education system has many functions and many outputs. Some outputs relate directly to the student, others hardly involve him at all. For example, the school system must interact with the community and must provide a number of outcomes relevant to the community. In doing so, the school may sometimes act in ways that seem to operate against desired outcomes for the student. The school also has a political role and must provide outcomes that allow it to compete within a political system for power, money, and position. Whatever importance one assigns to political and social functions, it seems to us that they are not the school's primary objective, which is to educate students. Throughout this report we focus on research into the determinants of student learning.

What exactly does student learning mean? The easiest and perhaps the first definition that comes to mind is to interpret learning as the acquisition of knowledge and cognitive skills. In practice, this has mainly been reduced to using standardized tests for measuring retention of specific subject matter; higher cognitive processes (abstract reasoning, problem solving, and creative thinking, among others) are seldom measured (Klein, 1971). Teacher grades and essay examinations are sometimes used as measures of broad cognitive abilities, but these measures are extremely unreliable. Along with the general failure to measure cognitive achievement adequately, there is an almost total failure to evaluate and identify "noncognitive achievement."[8] Thus, of the many and diverse kinds of student learning, almost all of the educational research that examines student learning is based on a narrow range of cognitive skills as measured by standardized tests.

By and large, researchers have not used broad measures of student learning nor have they resolved the important problem of individual priorities of educational outcomes. However, one does find that many of these same researchers who have not been able to resolve this problem analytically frequently discuss the importance of priorities and individual differences in priorities. It is becoming increasingly clear that there are different educational objectives and values as well as individual differences in types and levels of ability. We must therefore realize that research based on limited measures, and accounting for relatively few objectives, cannot lead to conclusive generalizations about educational outcomes.

In this study we have avoided extensive discussion of the aims of education (although implicit criteria are inevitable whenever effectiveness is discussed). Nonetheless, certain issues are necessarily raised:

- To what extent should education be an agent of social reform as compared with a force for social stability?
- To what extent should education be oriented toward vocations, to personal development, to the pursuit of knowledge, to screening people by ability categories?

We are reluctant to address the aims of education because the researcher is no more competent to solve these issues than is any other citizen. The question is one of values. In any case, we have had to recognize these issues because they are inescapable in consideration of any social policy.

There are additional limitations on the scope of our work. Because we did not have time and resources enough, we could not cover all the existing research. In particular:

- We reviewed very little of the pre-1950 literature on educational effectiveness. This meant excluding such classics as the Progressive Education Association's Eight-Year-Study and Terman's work on gifted children.
- We reviewed very little research by sociologists and political scientists on educational effectiveness, except as it related to the organizational and experiential approaches. We have not reviewed the findings of educational philosophers, except, to a limited extent, in the experiential approach.

Introduction 23

Because the measurement of educational outcomes is a central issue in research on educational effectiveness, we discuss measurement problems in detail in Chapter II. Chapters III through VII are devoted to reviews of the research in each of the five approaches. Chapter VIII summarizes the results and presents our conclusions and policy implications.

NOTES TO
CHAPTER I

1. See, for example, Light and Smith (1971).
2. These terms are defined below. See Chapter II.
3. In theory, external validity could rest on acquiring new, unanalyzed data on exactly the variables considered in any given study. In practice this would be very costly. For example, few would now advocate a replication of the Coleman survey. So the test of inter-study consistency becomes *ad hoc*. Do studies that address the same question with somewhat different variables and somewhat different data suggest that the same inputs are important? If so, then those who use the input-output approach say there is a case that the same kinds of resources determine the same kinds of outputs. But they can never be sure. See Chapter III.
4. We emphasize that this is an assumption. We are aware of no empirical evidence that students' outcomes are related to the responsiveness of their school. It does, however, seem a reasonable thing to believe.
5. Although case studies flourish in educational research and elsewhere, evaluations of the methods are very difficult to find. But see Bock (1962).
6. The why or how of an intervention is often presumed in that the intervention was originally justified by a hypothesis as to why the intervention could be expected to "work." If it then does (or does not) "work" there is a tendency to assume that the hypothesis was (or was not) valid.
7. Note that we do not ask whether a study has a proper experimental design. If it had, it would have been included in the process approach.
8. This expression is used because it is becoming the vogue in

education literature, although "achievement" is not the best term to use in this regard. It would be more accurate to talk about noncognitive growth, but debate over terms seems relatively unproductive as long as it is generally understood what the term "noncognitive achievement" means. In particular, we include the concepts traditionally described by the term "affective domain" in "noncognitive achievement."

II. MEASURING EDUCATIONAL OUTCOMES

Students' educational outcomes are generally divided into two categories—cognitive and noncognitive.[1] Noncognitive factors include motivation, attitudes, learning styles, social skills, self-awareness, and even such vague but important concepts as happiness and quality of life.

Interest in the improvement and measurement of affective conditions has steadily increased in recent years, motivated in part by the lack of success in modifying cognitive achievement through "standard" educational innovations. One view of the importance of affective growth maintains that affective factors are the major determinants of cognitive achievement, and there is considerable experimental evidence supporting this view. Generalization[2] of cognitive ability results not only from the transfer of specific skills but also from the effects of such noncognitive factors as the establishment of learning styles, learning sets, motivation for learning, and attitudes about learning. The other view holds that growth in affective rather than cognitive factors is the more relevant goal of education. These views are certainly not mutually exclusive, and most educators agree that noncognitive factors are important for both reasons. In fact, the distinction between affective and cognitive achievement is rather artificial: attitudes, motivation, and so on, have strong intrinsic cognitive components, and cognitive skills have strong intrinsic affective components.

Noncognitive factors undoubtedly outweigh the importance of specific cognitive skills for future learning, although acquiring cognitive skills may itself considerably affect noncognitive factors such as motivation, self-awareness, and the like. In their book on evaluation of learning, Bloom, Hastings, and Madaus (1971) devote an entire chapter to measuring affective behavior and include affective goals in stated educational objectives. Recent research literature, especially that related to compensatory and preschool education, repeatedly comments on the importance of noncognitive factors in determining cognitive achievement and the necessity of identifying, measuring, and shaping these factors at an early age (for example, Denenberg, 1970).

Noncognitive factors have even greater significance in the light of recent evidence showing low correlation between cognitive achievement (measured by grades and standardized tests) and later life success. Cohen (1970), Gintis (1971), and Holtzman (1971), cite evidence indicating that achievement in terms of job, social class, and general life expectations is apparently only incidentally related to school achievement. It is true that a high correlation exists between amount of education and amount of income, but there is some evidence that the relationship results from factors unrelated to the content of education (Berg, 1970). Moreover, Gintis promotes the thesis that noncognitive factors have a strong influence on worker earnings and productivity. He reviews evidence in support of this thesis and shows that important dimensions of noncognitive achievement are not promoted or rewarded in most conventional schools. Schools need to include noncognitive factors in their education objectives and develop better methods for their evaluation.

Despite growing discourse among educators about the importance of affective growth, the successful implementation and measurement of affective objectives in the schools remain disappointing. Affective objectives must be stated in the development of curricula, then translated into classroom activities. This process is a difficult one; authorities do not agree on definitions, nor do they agree on the relative importance of affective objectives. Even where this hurdle is overcome, the status of affective measuring instruments is quite primitive.

Partly as a result of the difficulties in measuring affective achievement, educational effectiveness research is directed almost entirely toward explaining cognitive achievement, as measured by standardized achievement tests.[3] Also, as a result of the increasing interest in accountability, student achievement is being measured more and more by standardized tests,[4] with test scores based on national norms. Although this practice allows a school to assess itself relative to other schools, these tests introduce a number of liabilities and hazards. Foremost among these is the danger of suppressing desirable outcomes that are not conventionally measured by standardized tests (abstract reasoning, creativity, and so on).

Although it certainly is necessary and important for children to acquire basic reading and math skills, focusing on teaching these skills may be less important than is often believed. It is generally assumed that achievement in basic math and reading skills as measured by standardized tests is correlated with, and perhaps responsible for, achievement in other subject matters and cognitive areas. However, special programs have not been able to demonstrate the generalization of improvement in basic reading and math skills; in view of the rather temporary nature of many of the gains obtained in these programs, the lack of generalization is not surprising. Undoubtedly, these skills do generalize under some conditions, but the conditions are not known.[5]

Proponents of the view that basic skills can be acquired when they are needed, and that a fixed curriculum, graded approach to teaching these skills is wrong, would attach little significance to the results of standardized reading and math tests, nor would they support programs aimed at bringing all students up to "grade level." Certainly there is room to question the basic intent of standardized tests—that is, to measure amount of learning in specific skills. Even if one believes standardized tests adequately measure important educational outcomes, many problems remain with test design, scoring, and especially interpretation. In the rest of this chapter we discuss the major technical issues involved with standardized tests. First, however, we briefly consider the problems associated with two widely used alternative measures of cognitive achievement—teacher grades and essay examinations.

TEACHER GRADES AND ESSAY EXAMINATIONS

Teacher grades of students' performance are extremely unreliable; they do not always correlate with standardized test scores, and teachers do not correlate with each other in grades assigned to the same student (Cronbach, 1970). Teacher grades are greatly influenced by student characteristics not associated with cognitive performance (docility, social class, and so on), and criteria vary from teacher to teacher.

Grades are further influenced by school policy factors such as "grading on the curve," or community pressure from parents who do not like to see their children fail. The technical problems associated with grades as a subjective rating system are complex, but they need not be discussed here. Grades have played almost no part in the research on evaluation of educational outcomes.

Essay examinations are widely used in education, sometimes because objective tests cannot be designed to measure many criteria of learning. In spite of their advantage in being able to measure broad kinds of cognitive ability, test scores are generally not reliable. Answers to essay questions vary in vocabulary, style, thought, originality, neatness, and many other factors. A single score is a complex weighted sum of the scores on each dimension. Moreover, since subscores are rarely worked out by the grader, the relative weights vary among graders, for the same grader over time, and depending on the situation. In reviewing the research on essay examinations, Coffman (1971) points out that much research is still needed in the development of rules for writing and scoring essay questions. None of the research reviewed in this study uses essay scores as a measure of educational outcomes.

STANDARDIZED ACHIEVEMENT TESTS

The development of standardized tests has a long history, and the current state of the art is highly complex. Writing test items, which at first thought may seem simple, is in fact exceedingly difficult (see Anderson, 1972; Bormuth, 1970; Wesman, 1971). After items are written, a long and repetitious process of statistical analysis follows. Although this is an important area, in this chapter the topic of test item development is mostly omitted; instead we focus on problems originating after a test has been developed. Many of these problems, such as scoring and interpreting tests, have little to do with the sophistication of items; other problems, such as test validity and reliability, are closely related to item content.

Achievement tests are severely criticized in the following sections. However, we emphasize that these tests, when properly used and interpreted, do measure group achievement in subject matter areas as conventionally conceived. These tests are far less adequate for indicating individual student achievement (rather than a group average).

Derivation and Meaning of Normative Scores

Assuming test items actually measure the amount of learning that has taken place in a course of instruction, normative scores are necessary to determine what a "raw" test score[6] means (cumulated over all items). For example, how much "better" is a raw score of 70 than one of 60 (that is, how much more about the course does the student know)? How high a score should be "expected"? Normative scores are one approach to answering these questions.

A normative score indicates a student's position in a distribution of scores. To determine the reference distribution, a sample from a specified population is selected and given the test (for example, fourth-grade children in California). A given individual's raw score can then be represented as higher than x percent of the sample scores or as being at the xth percentile. If it is assumed that the sample distribution is "close" to the population distribution, the percentile score represents the student's position in relation to the general reference population. Percentile scores can be transformed into grade equivalent or other types of normative scores.

Although grade and age equivalent scores are widely used, they have been severely criticized (Angoff, 1971; Cronbach, 1970).[7] Cronbach (1970, p. 98) comments on equivalent scores:

> In the writer's opinion, grade conversions should never be used in reporting on a pupil or a class, or in research. Standard scores or percentiles or raw scores serve better. Age conversions are also likely to be misinterpreted. A 6-year-old with mental age 9 cannot pass the tests a 12-year-old with mental age 9 passes; the two simply passed about the same fraction of the test tasks. On the whole, however, age equivalents cause less trouble than grade equivalents, if only because the former are not used for policy decisions in education.

These comments represent only the highlights of the problems inherent in equivalent scores. For a detailed treatise, the reader is referred to Angoff (1971).

Sampling Bias

An important issue in deriving standardized scores concerns the choice of the normative population. A test with national norms is supposedly based on a sample representing the normative population across the nation. To be accurate, the sample population must be stratified in the same proportions as the overall population that is, blacks and whites, poor and rich, and so on, must appear in the sample in the same proportion that they appear in the general population. This means that any nationally normed test primarily reflects the characteristics of white, middle-class America, simply because there are so many more white, middle-class Americans than anything else.

Sample bias arises when a test is normed on one population and used to test people from another population. A special case of sample bias, called cultural bias, arises where the normative population is culturally different from the tested one. These biases can be subtle and may lead to gross misinterpretations of data. For example, a nationally normed test of concept ability might be given to children from a Mexican-American ghetto. If the test uses written test items and instructions, the children's scores are affected by their ability to understand the language, and if they have language problems, their concept ability scores will be poor. Their "true" concept ability remains untested. Attempts to develop tests that are unconnected to language ability have not been very successful; even "nonverbal" tests are frequently found to correlate with language ability.

A more subtle influence of the normative population occurs through the operation of the values of that population. Standardized tests necessarily (because of method of construction) reflect what the normative population feels is important. Without great exaggeration, one may state that these tests indicate how well students have achieved white, middle-class goals. The problem of cultural bias in testing and in emerging social issues is discussed by Holtzman (1971, p. 551):

> The emergence of black culture, the Chicano movement, and the stirring of the American Indian as well as other forgotten groups in the wake of desegregation and civil rights legislation have forced white America to re-examine its soul. The result in the field of mental measurement has been a recognition and acceptance of cultural variability, a search for new kinds of cognitive, perceptual, and affective measures by which to gauge mental development, and a renewed determination to contribute significantly to the task of overcoming educational and intellectual deprivation.

In general, tests designed for normative use lend themselves to gross misinterpretation of the abilities of those who are culturally different from the majority.

Educational Objectives and Test Content

The apparent failure of many innovative educational programs is often attributed to the fact that standardized tests used to evaluate the programs do not measure outcome in terms of some or all program objectives (for example, Cohen, 1970; Klein, 1971; Lennon, 1971). Part of the problem is that objectives are rarely stated with sufficient clarity; but even overlooking this liability, the match between program and test objectives is often poor. In the first place, as Klein (1971) points out, valid tests covering all of the objectives a school might like to attain do not exist.

Second, tests may cover some program objectives, but there is usually poor agreement between the specific objectives and the test content. For example, a test may measure reading ability in terms of, say, eight areas. A specific program might be aimed at only six objectives, with no interest in the other two. Most tests, however, only report a *single* score averaged across all areas, and this score indicates achievement on all eight objectives. A score would be a combination of how well a student did on the six reading program objectives, plus how well he did on the other two, making it impossible to evaluate the program. Tests are not designed with specific programs in mind, and poor overlap is to be expected between the objectives a test measures and those an education program aspires to. Another complication occurs when the test does not represent test objectives equally. Some of these problems would be eliminated if the tests reported separate scores for each area or objective.

Test Validity

Test validity generally means, "Does the test measure what it is supposed to measure?" It is formally determined by a number of techniques.[8] One, a complex process called *construct* validity, determines how well tests that supposedly measure the same thing correlate with each other. Low correlation indicates that one or all of the tests do not validly measure the construct being considered. In *predictive* validity, the test is correlated with an external criterion. For example, a test of reading readiness might be validated by using success in a reading course as a criterion. The assumption is that better readiness leads to better achievement. In practice, both kinds of measures are necessary for test validity. A third type, sometimes referred to as *face* validity, simply asks if the items in the test appear to measure what the test is designed to measure. Although this method lacks the sophistication of the first two, many standardized tests fail even on face validity. Klein (1971) points out several examples in which it is obvious that the test items have little to do with what the test purports to measure. There are, in fact, many tests purposely designed without consideration of face validity, although they are not widely used in education. Finally, a test is said to have *content* validity if it measures something that some authority asserts that it measures. Much of the foregoing discussion on the relationship of objectives to test content relates to content validity. Generally, several of these methods are used in determining the validity of a given test.

As previously mentioned, tests often do not adequately overlap program objectives, and generally they are not valid even when they do appear to overlap. In a book on the theory and design of test items, Bormuth (1970) criticizes current methods of test construction on the grounds that the item generation techniques lead to tests of low validity. An item represents the test writer's response to instructional material; the student's score is thus a function of the test writer and has no known relationship to instructional content.

The UCLA Center for the Study of Evaluation reviewed over 1,500 standardized tests used in elementary schools (Hoepfner, 1970). Results indicate the tests are unsatisfactory in almost every respect. Klein (1971) has written a strong criticism of standardized tests and their misuse:

> So far, the discussion has painted a pretty bleak picture regarding the utility of standardized tests for accountability. The major problems involve questionable test validity, poor overlap between program and test objectives, inappropriate test instructions and directions, and confusing test designs and formats. In short a VOID exists between the demands of accountability and the present stock of standardized instruments. Further, this void will probably only widen as the pressure for accountability increases unless we start improving the methods of test construction and use. (Emphasis in original.)

Klein's comments are applied to accountability, but they are also true for educational research based on standardized achievement tests in general. The first step in research is accurate measurement; and, in this respect, achievement tests are too often misused or misinterpreted. As Anastasi (1967), among others, has pointed out, improvements are needed more in the interpretation of scores and orientation of users than in the actual construction of test instruments.

Statistical Problems

Inadequacies in the use of achievement test scores in educational research are partly attributable to the frequent use of faulty statistical analyses. By far the majority of studies on compensatory programs report data on achievement gain over some period, and performance contract agreements are almost exclusively written in terms of achievement gain scores.[9] Gain scores are extremely biased estimates of true gain (for example, see Harris, 1963). An article by Cronbach and Furby (1970) offers some refinements on techniques for estimating true score; however, the important message is that the authors see no advantage in using gain scores in the first place. Status scores (scores at any point in time) contain all the information given in change scores, at least for the situations in which change scores have traditionally been used. For example, if it is necessary to evaluate the improvement produced by an innovative program, this is best accomplished using a control group. In both treatment and control groups, only the final status or achievement score need be used. Pre-test scores can be involved in the statistical analyses but not in computing gains. The groups are not compared with respect to each other. In many instances, it is unnecessary actually to use an experimental control group. Instead it is possible to use the past history of the system as a benchmark.

Criterion-Referenced Tests

Standardized (normative) tests are sometimes criticized because their scores do not indicate the specific skills a student masters. They only place him relative to other students, and not relative to instructional content. For example, two students scoring at the fiftieth percentile on a reading test could have answered different questions correctly and have acquired different reading skills. This is true even if the test gives percentile scores for a number of subskills; they are still normative scores. This problem is being attacked through the design of so-called *criterion-referenced tests* (Cronbach, 1970; Glaser and Nitko, 1970; Nitko, 1971; Popham *et al.*, 1971). Each item on a criterion-referenced test is designed to measure or indicate the accomplishment of a particular skill. The important factor is which items are passed, not the number. Test scores are for advancing the student, not generally to summarize achievement. The student is not allowed to proceed to advanced instruction until he acquires prerequisite knowledge.

A key feature of criterion-referenced tests is their relationship to the specific goals and subject matter of a course. Test items are designed to indicate success on the learning tasks necessary to cover the subject matter and to meet the course objectives. This requires a detailed analysis of course material. Few general procedures for this analysis have been developed, although Gagné's work on hierarchical organization (1962) shows promise. Chapter IV discusses research on the organization of instructional material; there we point out that skills and knowledge required for a course can be arranged in a hierarchy such that success at a higher level depends upon acquisition of skills at a lower level.

The distinction between normative and criterion-referenced tests is made primarily on the basis of the purpose for which the test was constructed and how information obtained from it is used. The purpose of a criterion-referenced test is to indicate a student's status on a set of specific tasks necessary for the completion of a course of instruction. The test information not only assesses his accomplishments but is also used to determine what tasks the student is ready to undertake. Normative-referenced tests indicate a student's relative position in a population, and the information from these tests is used to evaluate his achievement relative to other students, in terms of overall achievement. The use of criterion-referenced tests for this purpose is not clear, since such tests indicate which instructional tasks the student has accomplished; essentially, he passes or he does not for each task. The *number* of tasks cannot be meaningfully added for a total test score. Criterion-referenced tests serve diagnostic and prescriptive functions in evaluation, which aims at special information for student remediation or course improvement.

Much work remains to be done in developing criterion-referenced tests, but they appear to have great promise. Their greatest potential value is that they focus on instructional content, yield information for remediation, and allow for individual differences in performance. There are, however, many hazards inherent in the use of criterion-referenced tests deriving from both theoretical and practical sources (Glaser and Nitko, 1970; Stake, 1971). These tests are designed to evaluate specific course objectives, and objectives are not always agreed on, nor can complex subjectives be clearly stated. The result can easily be an oversimplification of course objectives in order to facilitate agreement and item construction. Criterion-referenced tests are often criticized on the grounds that they promote teaching to the test, because each course objective is measured by specific items. Of course, as Stake (1971) points out, if the test items comprehensively cover the universe of material taught (or skills required), then teaching to the test is exactly what is required. In addition, criterion-referenced tests are costly to develop and cannot be developed for standard or wide applications. The domain of tasks included in an advanced course curriculum may become too large and complex to cover with any reasonable number of items.

GENERAL INTELLIGENCE TESTS

General intelligence tests are standardized achievement tests. They have been developed over a longer period than most standardized achievement tests, and more research has been directed toward their improvement. They are more valid when properly used, they usually report subscores on various test objectives, and directions for administration are generally better. Sometimes changes in IQ scores are used to measure student achievement, and many attempts have been made to improve IQ scores through compensatory school and preschool programs. Failure to find consistent evidence that IQ can be modified (for example, Butler, 1970) led Kohlberg (1968), among others, to argue that IQ is not a good measure of the efficacy of these programs. For years, psychologists have stated that many IQ tests are mostly achievement tests. They measure what the person has learned, not primarily his capacity for learning. The scores reflect environmental influences and past learning as well as innate ability. The belief that IQ can be affected by environment has been confirmed many times in studies of identical twins, but many factors contribute to this effect other than those present in the school environment (Vandenberg, 1966). On the other hand, Jensen (1969) reports evidence that IQ is largely determined by genetics and can be modified by environment only in a relatively small degree. This conclusion is highly debated; the arguments, pro and con, are extremely complex and involved (Hunt, 1972; Scarr-Salapatek, 1971).

The various uses of IQ tests in recent education programs has brought about a reemergence of debate and inquiry into the validity and meaning of general intelligence test scores. The crucial factor in determining the appropriateness of their use (or of the use of any achievement test) depends on the goals and objectives the test is being used to evaluate. This is never an easy task. It is made even more difficult by the interaction of social values and subtle and nonverbalized goals that exert profound influence on test content, scores, and interpretation. This has been well stated by Jensen (1970):

> It should not be forgotten that intelligence tests as we know them evolved in close conjunction with the educational curricula and instructional methods of Europe and North America. Schooling was not simply invented in a single stroke. It has a long evolutionary history and still heavily bears the imprint of its origins in predominantly aristocratic and upper-class European society. Not only did the content of education help to shape this society, but, even more, the nature of the society shaped the content of education and the methods of instruction for imparting it. If the educational needs and goals of this upper segment of society had been different, and if their modal pattern of abilities—both innate abilities and those acquired in these peculiar environmental circumstances—were different, it seems a safe conjecture that the evaluation of educational content and practices and consequently the character of public education in modern times would be quite different from what it is. And our intelligence tests—assuming we have them under these different conditions—would most likely also have taken on a different character.

Intelligence tests are, of course, also subject to all of the other problems associated with normative tests, and errors of interpretation are common. The standard use of general intelligence tests in education is probably best discouraged. The relationship of measured intelligence to education is discussed in Chapter IV.

SUMMARY

Using standardized tests to evaluate student achievement has become a major enterprise in the schools; but in spite of the wide use and reliance on these tests, they are generally inadequate. This is alarming in light of the growing activity in evaluation of educational outcomes based on standardized test scores. Standardized tests, even when properly used and interpreted, evaluate only a limited number of educational objectives. At best, generally used tests measure only limited aspects of cognitive performance; higher cognitive abilities and achievements go untested. Noncognitive achievement is sometimes talked about, but the evaluation of these factors is still in a very crude state. Inasmuch as schools and innovative education programs are being evaluated in terms of such limitations, there is a crucial need for immediate improvements in test design, concept, scoring interpretation, and administration.

NOTES TO
CHAPTER II

1. Sometimes referred to as affective.
2. Generalization is the spreading of acquired skills to areas in which the student has had no specific practice. For example, generalization (or transfer) occurs when an improvement in basic reading skills leads to (1) an improvement in concurrent school achievement, such as proficiency in social studies or science; and (2) an improvement in future school achievement, including reading.
3. In Chapter VII we discuss and review the "reform" literature in education. It should not be surprising that most of the reform authors consider high level cognitive and noncognitive factors to be the more important indicators of student learning, and their conclusions are rarely based on the results of standardized tests. However, reliable measures of these factors do not exist, and conclusions are mostly argumentative and based on personal experience.
4. The most widely used standardized tests measure achievement in subject matter areas, although there are also many tests for math and reading readiness, concept attainment, psycholinguistic performance, and other general and specific ability tests. In the elementary grades, the current programs of performance contracting and accountability have focused almost entirely on measuring these skills.
5. See Chapter IV for a discussion of research on generalization.
6. A raw score is a measure of the actual number of correct responses. The score may be a simple frequency count or it may be the sum of test points, with each test item given some arbitrary assignment of possible points.
7. Age equivalents are most often used with mental abilities tests, and they report a "mental" age score. The score represents age level relative to mean performance on a regression line. Equivalent scores are obtained by administering a test to samples of children over the range of desired grades (or ages). The average for a grade (or 50th percentile score) determines the grade level score. A line is then plotted between the mean score obtained by each grade across all grades. This regression of score on grade is used to determine a child's grade equivalent score by the simple procedure

of noting where his score falls on the regression line. If the regression of grade on score (rather than score on grade) had been used, a different regression line would have resulted, and scores would have different grade equivalents. This basic ambiguity is further clouded by the fact that the interpretation of the equivalent score depends upon the variation of scores about the mean for each grade in the original sample (that is, the variation about the regression line). A child who is two grades advanced on a test of high reliability (low variability about the regression line) is also high in his percentile rank (say 95). But, if the test were of low reliability (high variability), the same two-year advanced status would be associated with a much smaller percentile rank (say 70). Further, a sixth grader with a ninth-grade equivalent score does not possess the skills of a ninth grader, nor is he psychologically the same.

8. For a detailed discussion, see Cronbach (1970).
9. A student's best performance is determined by many factors other than his "true" knowledge or ability. Because these other factors vary over time, a person's test score will also vary, so that any given test score is an estimate of the true state of his knowledge or ability. The achieved test score may be a percentile, an age equivalent, or a simple sum of correct items. A gain score is obtained by subtracting a student's score on a test from his score on the same test taken at a later time.

III. THE INPUT-OUTPUT APPROACH

In this chapter we review the results of a number of studies of educational effectiveness in what we have called the input-output approach. These studies are distinguished by a view of the educational process that holds a student's educational outcome is determined by the quantities of resources his school makes available to him; by the personal, family, and community characteristics that influence his learning—typically grouped under the term "background factors"—and by the influences of his peers. In this approach the school in which the student is enrolled affects his outcome only to the extent that it serves as the channel through which resources flow to him. In particular, the structure and organization of the school and classroom are neglected.

The educational "production function" is a formal representation of the relationship between school resources and background factors on one hand, and student outcomes on the other. It is commonly expressed in the form of a mathematical relation or equation:

(1) $$O = g(r_1, \ldots, r_n, f_1, \ldots, f_m, p_1, \ldots, p_k)$$

where there are assumed to be n relevant school resources, m relevant background factors, k relevant peer group influences, [1] and:

O = a student's output for example, his score on a standardized achievement test;

$r_1, \ldots, r_n$ = the amounts of school resources 1 through n, respectively, that he received—for example, resource 1 might be the ability of his teacher, resource 2 the size of his class, and so on;

$f_1, \ldots, f_m$ = the amounts of background factors 1 through m, respectively, that the student has been exposed to—for example, f_1 might denote his family's income, f_2 his father's occupation, and so on;

$p_1, \ldots, p_k$ = the amounts of peer group influences 1 through k, respectively, that the student has been exposed to—for example, p_1 might denote the proportion of his classmates that intend to go to college, p_2 the proportion of his classmates that are members of minority groups, and so on.

The educational production function is expressed in its most general form in Eq. (1), which merely states that for any particular student, described in terms of his background factors, the amounts of school resources he receives and the influences of his peers determine his outcome. In order to make a quantitative estimation of the impact of any particular resource upon outcomes, the precise relationship between inputs—resources, factors, and peer group influences—and outcomes must be specified. Conceptually, any one of an infinitely large set of possible relationships can be specified. In practice, however, only one functional form—the linear one—has thus far been used in educational production-function studies. But this is more a reflection of the limitations of current statistical techniques than the result of any consensus about the underlying nature of the educational process.

The linear production function assumes that each unit of a particular school resource or background factor or peer group influence contributes a *constant* amount to student outcome. The unit contribution of any one input does not vary with the amount of that input the student receives, nor with the amounts of any of the other inputs the student receives. This specification of the production function can also be expressed as an equation:

(2) $\quad O = a + b_1 r_1 + \ldots + b_n r_n + c_1 f_1 + \ldots c_m f_m + d_1 p_1 + \ldots d_k p_k$.

As before, O denotes the student's outcome, r_i denotes the amount of the ith school resource the student received (i = 1, ..., n), f_i denotes

The Input-Output Approach

the amount of the ith background factor (i = 1, ..., m), and p_i denotes the amount of the ith peer group influence (i = 1, ..., k), b_i is the unit contribution of the ith school resource, c_i the unit contribution of the ith background factor, and d_i the unit contribution of the ith peer group influence.

Equation (2) can be interpreted as follows. Suppose a student were to receive r_1 units of the first school resource. If each of these units contributes b_1 to his outcome independently of the quantities of any other inputs he receives, the total contribution of the first school resource to his outcome is b_1 times r_1. An identical argument would show that the total contribution to outcome of any other school resource, say the ith resource, is b_i times r_i. Similarly, if the student is exposed to f_i (p_i) units of the ith background factor (peer group influence), the total contribution of that factor (influence) to his outcome will be c_i times f_i (d_i times p_i). Since the contributions are independent of one another, and every input that influences a student's outcome is presumably included in Eq. (2), we need simply add them together to determine a student's outcome. (The first term on the right-hand side of the equation, a, is a normalizing constant that need not concern us here.) For example, Kiesling (1969) has fitted the following equation:

$$O = 2.26 - .012\ r_1 - .0065\ r_2 + .0013\ r_3$$
$$- .00065\ r_4 + .0017\ r_5 + .127\ f_1$$

where
- O = Composite score on Iowa Test of Basic Skills for an urban school district
- r_1 = Teachers per pupil
- r_2 = Expenditure on books and supplies per pupil
- r_3 = Teacher salary
- r_4 = Value of school-owned property per pupil
- r_5 = Expenditure on principals and supervisors per pupil
- f_1 = Index of occupation of adults in district.

OBJECTIVES AND METHODS

The objective of research, in the present case, is to estimate the numerical values of the b, c, and d parameters in Eq. (2). If we knew these values, we could predict what would happen if we provided students with more or less of any particular school resource. This would allow us to determine whether increasing (or decreasing) the amount of any one school resource would affect students' outcomes more or less than increasing (or decreasing) the amount of any other school input. Taking account of the relative prices of the various school resources, we could then determine how much of each school resource should be purchased to attain any particular goal for student outcomes at minimum cost. In short, we could formulate optimal educational policies.[2] However, the costs of obtaining school resources have not yet been incorporated in empirical analyses. Estimates of educational production functions—the topic to which we devote the remainder of this chapter—are only the first step toward an educational policy.

Multiple regression analysis is used to estimate the values of the coefficients—the b, c, and d parameters—in Eq. (2). Details of the technique can be found in any statistics text.[3] A multiple regression analysis provides for tests of the "significance" of the empirical results. These are formal measures of the accuracy of the results in the sense that they indicate how much confidence can be placed in them. In educational production function studies the analyst is typically concerned with identifying resources or factors that affect student outcomes. In terms of Eq. (2), he is concerned with identifying inputs where coefficients have *non-zero* values. To say that the coefficient of a variable is significant means that the test of significance indicates a small probability that that particular coefficient is zero. Just *how* small is referred to as the significance level.

The basic assumption underlying all studies in the input-output approach is that the production function is an equally accurate description of the educational process for all students, or at least for some identifiable subgroup of students. In other words, the unit contribution of any given resource, factor, or influence to student outcome is assumed to be approximately the same for all, or some subgroup of, students. This assumption implies that if any particular resource or factor does have a great influence on student outcomes, the coefficient of that resource or factor should be significant in any study that examines it. Otherwise, every student must be different or respond differently to the same resources.[4]

There is always some possibility that a variable that appears to influence student outcomes greatly may, in fact, be unrelated to

The Input-Output Approach

outcome. Therefore educational policy cannot be based on the results of any one study. The basic assumption of production function analysis reinforces this point. We do not emphasize the results yielded by any one study. Rather, our primary concern is to identify results that consistently appear throughout a number of studies.

VARIABLES

At one time or another, educational researchers have investigated a large number of student outcomes, school resources, and background factors. It would be futile to attempt to list them all here. To convey some feeling for the sorts of variables that are investigated in educational production function studies, we describe some that appear very often. Appendix A contains complete lists of variables for each of 21 major studies in this approach.

Student outcomes are most often cognitive achievement, measured by scores on standardized reading or mathematics achievement tests. Dropout rates or "holding rates"—the latter is defined as one minus the dropout rate—are occasionally examined. Less frequently included in student outcomes is some measure of college attendance or intention to attend. Recently, researchers have begun to investigate students' attitudes as outcomes of education; but, by and large, the noncognitive domain and much of the cognitive domain remain unexplored.[5]

School resources always include measures of the "quality" of the school's faculty. Average teacher's experience, salary, degree level, and verbal ability are the four most common. Average class size or student-teacher ratios appear often as well. Measures of the physical plant or facilities of the school are also generally included in educational production function studies. The age of the school buildings and the number of library books per student are examples.

Background factors include measures of the socioeconomic status of the students' families or of the communities their school serves. Average family income, father's (or mother's) education, and father's (or mother's) occupation are typical. The racial composition of the community and whether the community is urban or rural are examples of community factors.

Peer group influences include measures of the educational attainment and aspirations, the attitudes and motivations of a student's classmates. The percent of his class that intends to enter college, the proportion of his class whose families own encyclopedias, and the attendance and transfer rates of his classmates are typical measures of a peer group's influence on a student.

ANALYTICAL PROBLEMS

The educational researchers who have worked in the input-output approach have been plagued by many severe analytical problems. Before presenting the results of these studies, we alert the reader to the limitations of this research approach.

The most serious difficulty is rooted in the sorts of data used in the empirical analyses. No production function studies of educational effectiveness have been based upon observation of true experiments. Rather, they have relied upon so-called "natural experiments" for their empirical content.

By a natural experiment we mean a situation created by chance or coincidence, from the researcher's point of view, in which basically similar individuals have been subjected to different stimuli.[6] By analyzing their responses, the researcher hopes to discover how individuals in general will respond to the various stimuli. In education, for example, a natural experiment would occur if students at the same grade level from identical backgrounds and subject to identical peer group influences were to attend different schools and thus receive different amounts of various school resources. An analysis of this situation might reveal whether differences in the students' outcomes were systematically related to differences in the amounts of the resources they received. Another natural experiment would occur if students from differing backgrounds were to attend the same school at the same grade level, be subjected to the same peer group influences, and receive identical amounts of every school resource. Analysis of this situation could show the extent to which differences in their outcomes systematically varied with the differences in their backgrounds.

But students come from a wide variety of backgrounds, attend different schools, and, even within the same school at the same grade level, may receive substantially different amounts of each school resource. Thus the researcher is faced with an extremely complex natural experiment. Subject to important limitations, multiple regression techniques can deal with such a situation, at least so far as the data generated by this convoluted experiment are amenable to analysis. But the data often impose serious limitations on the analysis.

The Input-Output Approach

Individual schools tend to serve relatively homogeneous populations. The students in any one school generally live in the same neighborhood and are subject to the same community influences. Further, their families are apt to be similar in terms of social and economic characteristics. Hence, a student's background is likely to be quite similar to the backgrounds of his peers. The levels of various school resources also vary from one school to another. As a result, we observe that students' outcomes systematically vary with simultaneous variations in school resources, peer group influences, and students' backgrounds. Under these circumstances we generally cannot separate the part of the variation in outcome due to variation in school resources from the parts due to variations in students' backgrounds or peer group influences.

In most cities, for example, new school buildings are located in the urban fringe, serving predominantly middle- and upper-class communities. The older schools are found in the older sections of the city, often in poverty areas. If students in the newer schools have systematically higher outcomes, by some measure, we could observe that students from middle- and upper-class backgrounds who attend the newer schools do better than students from poverty backgrounds who attend the older schools. But we could not determine whether they performed better because they came from more advantaged backgrounds, because they attended schools with new buildings, or because their classmates came from more advantaged backgrounds.

A second major problem that confronts researchers using the input-output approach stems from data aggregation. The researcher would like to examine the relationships among the school resources an individual student receives, his background, and the influences of his peers on one hand and his educational outcome on the other. But data are almost never available in such detail.[7] The researcher generally has data available only in much more aggregated form. For example, a researcher might wish to investigate the extent to which a teacher's experience affects the outcomes of his students. Ideally the researcher would collect outcome data from students who had different teachers and analyze the relationship between student outcome and teacher experience.[8] If the data do not permit him to identify the particular teacher each student had, he cannot, of course, conduct the study. What researchers often do in these circumstances is to collect data from students in a number of different schools (or even districts) and investigate the relationship between a student's outcome and the *average* level of teacher experience in his school (or district).

The problem here is that if a teacher's experience does in fact affect his students' outcomes, a considerable amount of information is lost. *Within* a school there would be considerable variation in students' outcomes caused by variations in their respective teachers' amounts of experience. But this variation is averaged out and cannot be investigated in an analysis that uses aggregate data.

Roughly 30 percent of the variation in students' outcomes is variation among schools. Thus, an analysis of individual students' outcomes that uses school resources or peer group influence data aggregated to the school level can at best account for about 30 percent of the variation in students' outcomes. Analyses that use data aggregated to the district level are even more restricted because the variance in students' outcomes between districts is smaller yet—even more information is "averaged out" of the analysis.

RESULTS

In reviewing educational production function studies, we surveyed the literature in a number of different fields. Education, economics, sociology, and public policy have all included such analyses in their domain. From this literature we selected a number of studies for careful and detailed examination. Two criteria were used in the selection process. First, we chose for detailed review only studies that examined the influence of a school resource, simultaneously taking account of the influences of other school resources and background factors. Second, we avoided studies that misused statistical estimation procedures. The results presented below derive from our examination of the reports that satisfied these criteria.[9]

Overall

Considering first the overall results of these studies, we generally find that estimated production functions seldom explain students' outcomes very well. This finding is based on an examination of what are commonly termed "goodness-of-fit" statistics. Intuitively, we can view goodness-of-fit statistics as estimates of how accurately we could predict a student's outcome using the results of the production function analysis. Suppose we knew no more than a student's grade level and were asked to predict how well he would perform on a standardized achievement test. The best estimate we could make would be the mean score achieved on that test by students at that grade level. Now suppose that we had a complete description of the student's background factors, peer group influences, and the school resources he has received. If we used this information in a production function to estimate his performance on the test, and if our prediction were perfect, we could say that the function was 100 percent accurate. On the other hand, if our estimate based on the production function were no more accurate than the estimate we would make in the absence of that information, we would say that the function was 0 percent accurate. In these terms, production function studies are rarely better than 15-20 percent accurate, and often far less.[10] In sum, although the production functions estimated thus far are helpful in understanding student outcomes, the amount of help they offer is relatively small.

Peer Group Influence

The debate over the importance of a student's peers is illustrative of the analytical problems encountered in production function analyses of educational effectiveness. To demonstrate the sorts of difficulties that stem from these problems we trace the debate chronologically.

Student body effects were not examined in the context of production function research prior to the Coleman Report (1966). That study included the following results:

- A pupil's achievement is strongly related to the educational backgrounds and aspirations of the other students in the school (p. 22).
- There is evident, even in the short run, an effect of school integration on the reading and mathematics achievement of Negro pupils (p. 29).[11]

These results followed from an analysis showing that, in terms of the concepts introduced earlier, a production function that included variables measuring the background of the student body could predict a student's outcome significantly more accurately than one that did not.

Bowles and Levin (1968b) examined the Coleman Report in some detail and disputed many of its findings. In particular, they questioned the two results cited above. Coleman did not have an opportunity to observe the behavior of poor children who attended majority poor schools and then transferred to majority middle-class schools.[12] Instead, he had to rely upon natural experiments. Specifically, Coleman compared the outcomes of poor students who attended majority poor schools with the outcomes of poor students who attended majority middle-class schools. His results stem from the apparently superior performance of the latter, even after controlling for the school resources they received and their backgrounds.

Bowles and Levin point out that predominantly poor schools tend to serve communities that are substantially different from the communities served by predominantly middle-class schools. Thus, poor students who attend predominantly middle-class schools come from families and live in communities that are quite different from the families and communities of the poor students who go to predominantly poor schools. In short, the background factors of students in high-aspiration, high-educational-background schools may cause them to perform better, and not merely the fact that they are in such schools.

Coleman's finding with respect to integration is also questioned by Bowles and Levin. They point out that differences in emphasis exist in various sections of the Report. "And in fact Coleman has emphatically stressed that the survey revealed no unique effect of racial composition on the achievement levels of nonwhites" (Bowles and Levin, 1968b, p. 22). But we note that on this point Bowles and Levin do not refute Coleman. Rather, they argue that alternative interpretations of Coleman's empirical results are as likely to be valid as Coleman's interpretations.

Bowles (1969) has conducted a production function analysis using the Project TALENT data file. He found that "a measure of the social class and achievement levels of the school . . . is not significantly related to black achievement" (p. 72). Bowles also suggests that apparent student body effects are very likely to stem from the difficulty of identifying the contribution of a student's background factors to his outcome in complex natural experiments.

M.S. Smith (1972) has made a complete reanalysis of the Coleman data. Like Bowles and Levin, he disputes many of Coleman's findings. Again, we limit our discussion to Smith's findings with respect to the student body effect. Smith argues that Coleman made a mechanical error in his analysis of the individual's background. In essence, the wrong variables were entered into the empirical study:

The Input-Output Approach

> This mechanical error *affected the strength of the relationship between individual verbal achievement and the Student Body factor more than any other relationship.* ... *The Report's estimates of the amount of achievement variance explained by the Student Body factor are severely reduced when the intended background controls are used.* (Emphasis in original, pp. 63-65.)

Smith goes on to argue that in one of these mechanical errors the percentage of high school students taking college curriculum was erroneously entered into the empirical analysis in place of the percentage who intended to go to college. This variable played an important role in establishing the significance of the student body effect. Coleman interpreted this variable as a measure of the aspirations of the student body. He felt that its significance in explaining student outcomes indicated that students who attend schools where the student body has high aspirations perform better than otherwise similar students who attend schools where the student body has lower aspirations. Hence, there is a student body effect.

Smith points out, however, that Coleman's data were collected from academic, vocational, and comprehensive high schools and that the original analysis did not distinguish among the three. There is a selection process whereby students are assigned to schools on the basis of their presumed ability. And the proportion of a high school's students in college curriculum may simply be a measure of whether high (presumed) ability students are assigned to that school. Hence, Smith argues, the proper interpretation of Coleman's empirical results is that students assigned to schools for pupils of high ability perform better than students not assigned to such schools. Consequently, we are observing the results of an assignment process, not a student body effect. In summary, there is *"no evidence that the characteristics of the student body have a strong independent influence on the verbal achievement of individual students."* (Emphasis in original, p. 76.)

Our review of the evidence as to the existence of peer group influences suggests four main conclusions:
1. There is no strong evidence that student body effects exist. In particular, there is no evidence that the racial composition of a student body affects the performance of individual members of that student body.
2. There is no strong evidence to the contrary. Many researchers have argued that alternative and more likely hypotheses

could have led to the results being interpreted as student body effects. But no researcher has shown that student body effects do *not* exist.
3. There is no evidence in the production function literature that student body effects might be negative.
4. The entire controversy over the existence of student body effects and the absence of conclusive empirical results stems from the data problem described earlier. So long as production function research is based on data generated by natural experiments, it will be difficult, if not impossible, to completely isolate the relative contributions of school resources, background factors, and peer group influences.

School Resources

Our examination of the production function literature suggests two findings with respect to school resources:
- School resources are seldom important determinants of student outcomes.
- No school resource is consistently related to student outcomes.

The first finding can be intuitively expressed in the following terms. Suppose we knew what resources a student had received but nothing about his background or the backgrounds of his fellow students. Using this information in a production function, we could predict the student's outcome with only slightly more accuracy than if we knew only his grade level. In rough terms, knowing what resources a student received would allow us to predict his outcome about five percent more accurately.

On the other hand, suppose we knew both the student's background and the resources he received. Suppose, further, that we "controlled" for the influence of background factors by examining how much more accurately (as compared with knowing only a student's grade level) we could predict his outcome on the basis of his background and then asked how much further accuracy we could get if we added our knowledge of the school resources he received to the prediction. In this case school resources would add roughly one percent to the accuracy of our prediction.

The difference between these two numbers—one percent and five percent—stems from the analytical problem described earlier. There is considerable overlap between students' backgrounds and their school resources. If we consider only school resources, the influence of the overlap is entirely attributed to the resources. If we consider only background factors, the influence of the overlap is entirely attributed to them. Finally, if we consider only background factors and attribute the influence of the overlap to them and then add school resources, the resources are attributed none of the overlap. In short, we can be sure that school resources contribute between one and five percent to our prediction of student outcomes.[13]

Thus far we have focused on the overall contribution of school resources to student outcomes. Almost every study finds one or two or three school resources to be significantly related to student outcomes. But these studies generally examine a large number of school resources. Along with the two or three resources that are found to be significant, many are found to be insignificant. And, when we compare the results of various studies, we find that the same resources do not appear among the lists of significant variables studies have compared. For that matter, it is not unusual to find a research report in which the students have been divided into a number of groups by some stratification rule, with separate analyses yielding distinctly different results with respect to the significance of school resources for each group.

Background Factors

Two results concerning the effects of background factors emerge from the analysis:
- Background factors are always important determinants of educational outcomes.
- The socioeconomic status of a student's family and community is consistently related to his educational outcome.

In terms of the intuitive notion of predictive accuracy we have been using, we could predict a student's outcome roughly 15 percent more accurately if we knew his family's socioeconomic status. Further, in every study, the socioeconomic status of the student's family and of the community in which he lives proves to be significantly related to his outcome.

All in all, then, the production functions estimated thus far enable us to use information regarding a student's background and the services he received from his school to predict his outcome somewhat more accurately. However, this improvement in accuracy comes, for the most part, from our ability to take account of a student's background in making our prediction. Knowledge of the resources the student received has proved to be of minor value. An obvious implication of this argument is that, if knowing the amounts of the various school resources a student has received does not enable us to predict his outcome more accurately, we have little reason to believe that receiving these resources has had much influence upon his outcome.

RESEARCH PROBLEMS

The researcher who attempts to estimate an educational production function encounters problems on many levels. One serious problem is that we may not even be asking the right questions. What is it that we are trying to accomplish? As an example of this sort of problem, consider the concept of out-of-school learning. Many researchers have argued that students spend a relatively small proportion of their time actually in classrooms supposedly learning something. It is quite possible that considerable learning goes on out of school. Thus, schools may be making a tremendous difference; but if this difference is still small in comparison with total learning, it is hard to isolate.

Even if we are asking the right questions, we may encounter serious substantive problems. Consider, for example, the possibility that the production function is student-specific. Suppose that different students have different learning patterns and that the importance of any particular resource varies with the learning patterns of a student.[14] Then these resources could be extremely important to some students. But because the production function essentially averages over all students, this student-specific relationship goes unnoticed.

There are numerous methodological problems. Many researchers have pointed out, for example, that schools aim at more than one outcome. They do not merely aim to teach a student how to perform well on some standardized achievement test. At the very least, they are interested in teaching reading and mathematics, minimizing dropouts, and imparting a number of noncognitive skills. Schools may be using their resources with different emphasis with respect to outputs. Suppose, for example, that we compared four schools and that in one school the teachers spent all their time teaching reading, in another school they were all emphasizing mathematics, in a third they were all behaving as jailers and trying to keep the students out of trouble, and in the fourth they were all looking toward various noncognitive skills.

When we examine the relationship between reading achievement and use of teachers in these schools, we are not apt to find a significant relationship.

The statistical method of handling this sort of problem is termed simultaneous equations. There have been some attempts—a very few—at using these techniques, but they have not been very successful. In general, there is good reason to believe that our statistical techniques have just not been up to the kinds of problems we are addressing. Furthermore, these statistical techniques—in particular, their limitations—are seldom well understood by the people using them.

Finally, there are many straightforward measurement problems. We are trying to measure extremely difficult things in educational research. We may believe that the ability of a teacher to teach influences what his or her students learn. But no studies in this approach have yet used any direct measure of teaching ability. Instead, they have used proxy variables, such as a teacher's salary or verbal ability or experience. But if more experienced teachers are not better teachers, and if higher paid or more verbally facile teachers are not better teachers, then experience or verbal ability or salary will not yield significant results. But that does not mean that teaching ability has no influence upon student outcomes.

SUMMARY

Research into educational effectiveness by means of the input-output approach has not, as yet, yielded consistent results regarding the importance of school resources. Background factors tend to dominate the results. No single resource consistently appears to exert a powerful influence on student outcomes. Some school resources appear to be important in each study, but the same resources appear to be unimportant in other studies. In fact, there is very little evidence that school resources in general make a powerful impression upon student outcomes, even neglecting the question of which school resources are influential.

This body of research has not identified what particular resources should be provided to students. It has yielded one important policy implication. The resources for which school systems have traditionally been willing to pay a premium—teachers' experience, reduced class size, and teachers' advanced degrees—do not appear to be of great value. Inexperienced teachers do not appear to produce students whose outcomes are significantly worse than the outcomes of students whose teachers are experienced, other things being equal. Similarly, students who are in small classes or whose teachers have advanced degrees do not do better, other things being equal, than students attending large classes or whose teachers lack advanced training.

It must also be emphasized that these results should not be interpreted as indicating that school resources *do not* affect student outcomes. We can only observe that these studies have failed to show that school resources *do* affect student outcomes. The difference between these two points is a reflection of the problems encountered in doing research in the input-output approach. There are many fundamental difficulties in this research approach, any one of which could have led to the inconclusive results cited above. And, of course, there is no way to determine whether the absence of results stems from the absence of an underlying relationship between school resources and student outcomes or from a research method that could not find results even if they were actually there.[15]

NOTES TO CHAPTER III

1. Some researchers prefer the term "student body effects."
2. The role of resource prices in the formation of educational policy is often overlooked. Even those researchers who recognize the importance of resource prices in their theoretical discussions do not introduce them into their empirical analysis. But school resources are not free, and school systems do not have unlimited budgets. Consequently, the important questions from the viewpoint of the educational policymaker are not: How much does resource 1 contribute to student outcomes? and so on. Rather, educational policymakers must ask: How much of resource 1 should be purchased? and so on. For a discussion of this issue, see Cain and Watts (1968).
3. See, for example, Wonnacott and Wonnacott (1970).
4. See Chapter IV for a discussion of this possibility.
5. See Chapter II.
6. The situation may have been deliberately caused by individuals or groups of individuals for their own purposes. The point is that the

situation was not brought about specifically to meet the researcher's needs.
7. Hanushek (1970) is the only analysis yet conducted on this level of detail.
8. In such an analysis, variables measuring other school resources, background factors, and peer group influences would have to be included. We neglect these variables to focus on the main issue.
9. Appendix A presents a detailed summary of each report reviewed.
10. Formally, the goodness-of-fit statistic, or "r^2" to use the standard notation, is the percent of total variance in students' outcomes that is attributed to the variance in the explanatory variables—resources, influences, and factors. But, as indicated above, the total variance in students' outcomes *between* schools is about 30 percent of the total variance in students' outcomes. Thus, an analysis that uses aggregate data—as all but one do—may report an r^2 of, say 0.50. That means that 50 percent of the variance in students' outcomes *between* schools is "explained" in the analysis. But that is only 15 percent (.50 x .30) of the total variance in students' outcomes.
11. Note that integration is a particular variant of peer group influence insofar as educational effectiveness is concerned.
12. The awkward term "majority poor" is used here to describe schools where the families of a majority of the students are poor. Related terms such as "majority middle-class" and "predominantly black" are similarly defined.
13. For an extended discussion, see Mayeske *et al.* (1969).
14. See Chapter IV for evidence that this is so.
15. For a general discussion of this point, see Levin (1971).

IV. THE PROCESS APPROACH

The general purpose of research on the process approach is to improve our understanding of the way education takes place and to determine factors affecting educational outcomes. Studies of teachers' characteristics (skills, behavior, personality, and the like) are obviously relevant to understanding the educational process, as are studies of teaching methodology and basic psychological studies of learning (but few results of the last are directly applicable to the classroom). Perhaps most important in the long run are psychological studies of individual differences, child development, personality, and learning in instruction; these studies are beginning to define student characteristics and instructional practices that determine educational outcome.

This review of research covers studies of the educational process as undertaken in the classroom, as well as studies made in the psychological laboratory that appear to bear on the educational process. Laboratory and classroom studies are distinguished not so much on the basis of where the study took place as on the basis of the study objectives, the learning tasks, and the kinds of outcome measures. Some measure of educational outcome is generally used in classroom studies (achievement tests, grades, and teacher or supervisor ratings). Laboratory studies usually have theoretical objectives, such as advancing knowledge about psychological phenomena, testing theory, or investigating empirical relationships between psychological variables. In these studies, measures of outcome are varied and difficult to summarize. They are, however, generally based on the learning or retention of well-defined and highly specific responses. The researcher is not primarily concerned with the amount learned but with the way in which the learning takes place and the factors that affect learning or retention. For example, an experimenter might present pairs of auditory and visual stimuli to children to investigate the different effects of each type of stimulus on learning and retention. The pairs are presented until the child can recall without error the second stimulus in each pair upon presentation of only the first. The measure of learning is the number of presentations necessary before the child has learned the list without error. This measure is studied across age groups to determine whether there are age-related differences in the learning of visual or auditory stimuli.

Classroom and laboratory studies differ greatly in their objectives and approaches. Classroom studies have not generally produced highly definitive results. Laboratory studies, however, have produced many significant and consistent results, but their relevance for classroom learning is often not clear.

To review the thousands of studies on education that are published each year would be impossible. Fortunately, however, a number of review articles and books cover broad areas of research. Some of these reviews merely summarize a large number of studies; others criticize and analyze as well as summarize. Some relate studies to one another and to basic issues in methodology and education. These reviews are easier to read and comprehend, although there is the risk of being swayed by the particular orientation of the reviewer. To cover a wide range of educational research and to give the reader a comprehensive view of the vast area of process research, we have drawn upon the analytical review articles rather than the original studies. In many cases, we read the original studies to check on the reviewer's summary and conclusions, but usually we do not cite original references. In other cases, the same study was discussed in more than one review, especially the more important studies. This redundancy helps our assessment of the amount of "bias" present in a review. By and large, we found reviews to be remarkably unbiased. We have tried to give a general indication of the excellence of various reviews and also to indicate some of the specific studies that are crucial.

In general, we relied upon a review if it summarized findings across studies and gave an evaluation that did not contradict our own evaluation of studies defined as critical. A study was considered good if it provided enough information by which to judge its internal validity, and if it did in fact appear internally valid. We have made frequent use of quotations, mainly to give an impression of the prevailing atmosphere or to clarify a point.

This chapter is divided into three parts. In the first, we present the general results of research on teacher characteristics. We are primarily concerned with research that relates teachers' skills, behavior, attitudes, or personality to some measure of student achievement. The second part presents the results of research on instructional methods. Some of this research has been conducted in the classroom, but most of it is from the psychological laboratory, particularly studies that report positive results. Most classroom studies are at best inconclusive. Finally, we present the results of research that reveals the importance of individual student characteristics to achievement. The basic theme is that students respond differentially to educational factors (teachers and instructional method) depending on their own characteristics—that is, there is a student-teacher-method interaction. We believe that the presence of these interactions is one of the most important factors brought out in this study.

THE EFFECTS OF TEACHERS

Studies of teacher characteristics since the 1930s now number in the thousands. In spite of this large implied expenditure of time and money, little is known about the influence of teacher characteristics on student performance. With the exception of a few recent studies, student achievement has rarely been used as a criterion, and much research is based on the opinion of the experimenter concerning desirable teacher characteristics. Significant differences are often reported between teachers (and schools) in terms of teaching skills, years of education and experience, and the like. It is then explicitly or implicitly assumed that these qualities are essential to student achievement. These assumptions are more often wrong than right. Attempts to use criteria other than achievement, such as supervisor or fellow-teacher ratings, are not successful in that the ratings do not correlate with student achievement (Harris, 1969). This lack of correlation could mean either that the ratings are based on indicators of success other than achievement or that supervisors and teachers do not have a good idea of what constitutes superior teaching.

A large part of past research has focused on measuring various attitudes and personality traits of teachers, with some attempts to

The Process Approach

relate these to supervisors' estimates of classroom success. Often, the studies simply intercorrelate various tests of teacher attitudes, interests, intelligence, and so forth. In the end, either these studies show contradictory results or the results have little practical value, and quite often both are true. A major problem with research based on attitude and personality scales is that obtainable results tend to be superficial and obvious. Getzel and Jackson (1963) make this point:

> For example, it is said after the usual inventory tabulation that good teachers are friendly, cheerful, sympathetic, and morally virtuous rather than cruel, depressed, unsympathetic, and morally depraved. But when this has been said, not very much that is especially useful has been revealed. For what conceivable human interaction—and teaching implies first and foremost a human interaction—is not the better if the people involved are friendly, cheerful, sympathetic, and virtuous rather than the opposite?

Much of the problem stems from the difficulty of measuring and defining variables related to attitude and personality, especially in what is essentially a normal (healthy) population. Further, it seems reasonable to assume that teacher classroom behavior and technique are more important than attitude or personality. Of course, dimensions of attitude and personality are reflected in the teacher's classroom behavior (Turner and Denny, 1969), particularly the degree to which the behavior can be modified through training. Whatever the influence of personality and attitude factors, it is the teacher's classroom behavior that the student responds to, and we do not yet understand how this behavior is related to student achievement.

Teacher Characteristics and Student Achievement

In contrast to the bulk of research on teacher characteristics, there are only a few (10 experimental and 50 correlational) recent studies that relate teacher classroom behavior to student achievement. There are two general approaches for studying the effects of teacher behavior on student achievement. The more powerful is an experimental approach whereby teachers are trained in a specific method; student achievement under this method is compared with student achievement under an alternative method. Studies of this type must meet all the demands of an experimental approach (for example, random assignment of students to teachers) in addition to special demands arising from the situation. Foremost among these special demands is the requirement for measures of actual classroom transactions, since only by observing the teacher can one be assured that the intended method was actually used. Moreover, data on classroom transactions are the only source of information on the content (rather than result) of the student-teacher relationship. Many studies in education lack measures of classroom transactions, and studies of the effectiveness of different teaching methods are rendered useless as a result. For example, training a teacher in a specific method is no assurance that the method will be used in the classroom, and the only way to determine the actual method used is by observation. In an excellent review of research on teaching, Rosenshine and Furst (1971) could find no more than 10 studies that use the experimental method adequately and provide data on classroom transactions.

The more frequently used approach for relating teacher performance to student achievement is to correlate the two as they occur in the normal classroom. That is, no attempt is made to manipulate teacher variables experimentally; various dimensions of teacher behavior are observed and rated, and these ratings are correlated with some measure of student achievement. The danger in this approach is that correlational relationships can suggest false causal connections. For example, a high correlation between clarity of presentation and student achievement does not mean that clarity *causes* high achievement. It is just as likely that both are the result of some other factor, say, teacher verbal ability or general intelligence. Rosenshine and Furst (1971) find approximately 50 studies that use the correlational procedure.

Studies using the experimental and correlational approaches have produced some consistent and significant results. These are summarized by Rosenshine and Furst, and the results are grouped according to 11 kinds of behavior significantly correlated with achievement scores. Five of these are strongly supported by the research, the others not so strongly. The first five variables are: clarity of teacher's presentation, variability of teacher's classroom activities, teacher enthusiasm, degree to which the teacher was task- or achievement-oriented or businesslike, and student opportunity to learn criterion material. The six variables less strongly related to student achievement are: use of student ideas or teacher indirectness, use of criticism, use of structuring comments, use of multiple levels of discourse, probing, and perceived difficulty of the course.

At first glance, the above list of the strongest findings may appear to represent mere educational platitudes. Their value can be appreciated, however, only when they are compared to the behavioral characteristics, equally virtuous and "obvious," which have *not* shown significant or consistent relationships with achievement *to date*. These variables ... are listed below, and the method by which they were assessed follows in parentheses: nonverbal approval (counting), praise (counting), warmth (rating), ratio of all indirect behaviors to all direct teacher behaviors, or the I/D ratio (counting), flexibility (counting), questions or interchanges classified into two types (counting), teacher talk (counting), student talk (counting), student participation (rating), number of teacher-student interactions (counting), student absence, teacher absence, teacher time spent on class participation (rating), teacher experience, and teacher knowledge of subject area.[1]

Rosenshine and Furst offer suggestions for refinements in future correlational studies. However, of greater importance is the need for more experimentally controlled research, with better measures of classroom transactions and broad indicators of student achievement. Classroom studies of the effectiveness of teacher and instructional techniques depend on the refinement and increased use of observational data systems. This need is commented on in many articles, and there have been a number of attempts to develop and refine observational data systems (Bloom *et al.*, 1971; Hanley, 1970; Rosenshine, 1970a). Unfortunately, none is used widely enough or consistently enough to realize its potential fully.

Teacher Skills and Effectiveness

Teachers' skills in the classroom are rarely determined in terms of their effects on student achievement; most investigations simply rely on supervisors' ratings. The only studies we could find that measured teachers' skills directly were by Turner (1968). He investigated differences in skills and characteristics as a function of characteristics of school districts. In this study and in previous ones, he developed instruments for measuring teachers' skills in diagnosing learning difficulties and organizing or sequencing learning material in the subject areas of reading, arithmetic, and science. His 1968 study also included measures of teachers' personal-social factors encompassing warmth-spontaneity, classroom organization, educational viewpoint, emotional stability, and involvement in teaching.

The validity of the various scales was determined by measures of internal consistency—the degree to which teachers score consistently on each scale. Validity was not determined on the basis of a relationship to student achievement.

The results of the study indicate that teachers differ a great deal in the characteristics examined, and that there is a relationship between the attractiveness of school districts and teachers' characteristics (which should come as no surprise). It is of interest to know that attractive school districts (in terms of location, money, and students) obtain teachers who apparently have the more desirable characteristics. However, the important question is whether these characteristics of teachers make a difference in the achievement of students, and, further, for what kinds of students they make a difference (if any).

In a later study, Turner and Denny (1969) relate the above-mentioned characteristics of teachers to student activity, as measured on a scale developed by Denny and others:

> Teacher characteristics are distinctly associated with changes in pupil characteristics, as well as with teachers' behaviors in the classroom, which in turn are associated with changes in pupil characteristics. Specifically, the results reported suggest that teachers characterized as warm and spontaneous and teachers characterized as child-centered tend to obtain the greater positive changes in pupil-creativity. These changes appear to come about through teacher classroom behaviors that involve positive reinforcement of pupil responses, through adaptation of activities to pupils, through attention to individuals, and through variation in activities and materials.

Unfortunately, the authors do not present their procedures or data in sufficient detail to allow us to evaluate their study. However, if the results can be replicated, the findings and method used are certainly important. For one thing, a measure of educational outcome other than cognitive achievement was used, although the results would have been stronger if a measure of cognitive achievement had *also* been used.

If teachers vary significantly in teaching skills and classroom behavior, one would expect differences in teacher effectiveness to show up in student achievement. Rosenshine (1970b) provides a critical review of nine studies of teacher effectiveness. Four concern long-term effectiveness; of these, three measured effectiveness over a school year and used grade school teachers. All four studies were based on teaching the same material to different students (in different semesters). The three studies of interest used standardized achievement tests that give subtest scores in various abilities or achievements (Stanford Reading Test, Metropolitan Achievement Tests, and others). The correlations (between the means of groups of students and teachers) obtained in these studies for the various subtests were generally around .35 or much lower, with one study showing a correlation of about .50 for two out of five subtests. The results indicate that teachers are not generally stable in teaching effectiveness when presenting the same material over time.

The studies of short-term effectiveness used teaching sessions of 30 minutes or less. In these studies, teachers taught (1) the same topic to different groups of students (three studies), (2) different topics to the same group of students (four studies), or (3) different topics to different groups of students (four studies). In each case three of the studies were carried out by the same investigator. Students ranged in grade level from Head Start to grade 12. When teachers taught the same topic to different students, the correlations (between student groups and teachers) were moderate (.22 to .70); but in the other two cases the correlations were generally low, and few were statistically significant.

These findings, showing a lack of consistent teacher effectiveness, raise doubts about the findings of Turner and Denny discussed above. Although teachers may vary in skill, their effectiveness does not appear to be generalizable over time or topics. Studies of teacher skills and effectiveness are extremely limited, however, and any conclusion must be tentative. In addition, although it is necessary to relate teacher skills and characteristics to student achievement, there are grounds for questioning the adequacy of the measures of student achievement used in these studies. Teachers may be consistent in their effectiveness on other dimensions of educational outcome, but we have been unable to find studies that report on this possibility. The lack of stability in teacher effectiveness may explain, in part, why studies of teacher characteristics have proved so futile—these characteristics either have no identifiably consistent effect or are not stable. Then, too, the low correlations may result from a student-teacher-subject interaction. Teachers are not equally effective with all students and all topics; correlations will vary with topic and the specific characteristics of the students. In any event, experiments based on 30-minute teaching sessions may not offer very much evidence about anything.

Teacher Expectations

Rosenthal and Jackson (1968) have reported on the importance of teacher expectations as a determinant of student performance. However, this report has been criticized on methodological grounds (Snow,

1969), and few of the results appear to be as substantial as reported. In addition, these studies lack data on the establishment of teacher expectations and on the mechanisms by which teachers communicate their expectations.

Rist (1970) attempted to uncover factors that establish teachers' expectations concerning students and the effect of these expectations on the classroom behavior of both teachers and students. This study followed a single class of ghetto children through kindergarten and first and second grade. Results indicate that in kindergarten the teacher's expectations and identification of "slow" and "fast" learners are based on social class membership. Data on classroom transactions indicate a marked difference in the teacher's attitudes and behavior toward fast and slow learners and a consequent change in the behavior of the slow learners. This study was based on a small sample and needs to be replicated.

Brophy and Good (1970) investigated the process by which teachers communicate their differential expectations to first-grade children. Expectations were determined by teacher ratings of students, but no information is provided as to how the expectations were established. Results indicate that teachers demanded better performance from children they rated high in their expectations and that they praised the children when it was forthcoming. Teachers demanded less from children they expected less from and tended to withhold praise for good performance.

A few other studies have attempted to verify the effect of teacher expectations. In general, it appears that expectations probably influence teacher and student behavior and may influence measured student achievement. More research is needed to follow up on the hypothesis of the "self-fulfilling prophecy."

Student-Teacher Interactions

Throughout this chapter we have occasionally discussed indirect evidence that some teachers are better with some students than with others. Thelen (1967) reports direct evidence of this interaction and outlines a method for using it to improve classroom behavior and outcome. The method involves assigning students to teachers according to the kind of student the teacher works with best. The method begins with the teacher identifying students he believes are "getting a lot out of class" versus those "not getting a lot out of class." The teacher does not describe these students in any way but simply points them out. Different teachers do not tend to assign the same students to the two categories. Thelen (1967, p. 189) notes:

> Finally, we found that teachers recognize four kinds of students: good, bad, indifferent, and sick. But the problem is that each teacher places different students in these categories, so that whatever is being judged is certainly *not* primarily some characteristic of the student.

The method then establishes the characteristics of students placed in the two categories by the various teachers.

Two criteria can be used to assign students to teachers: (1) teachers are given students they work most effectively with (ones chosen by the teacher), or (2) students are assigned to teachers they can learn from most effectively (on the basis of tests). This latter procedure requires determining the kinds of students that have higher achievement than their usual performance with a teacher, and then assigning teachers students of these types. Thelen's study indicates that the same student-teacher grouping would not necessarily result from the application of these two criteria, although there would be considerable overlap. In any case, however, Thelen claims that the students are better off being assigned by either criterion.

It follows not only that some teachers do better with some students but also that there is no single "best" or "right" way to teach. Future research on teaching must account for the different preferences and abilities of the teacher. It makes little sense to talk about teacher skills without also considering the population of students best suited for these skills. Studies of long-term trends in teacher effectiveness must designate which kinds of students the teacher is effective with, as well as how effective he is. There is strong evidence of an effect of teacher expectations on student performance. It may be better to put this characteristic of teachers to use than to oppose it or lament its existence.

THE EFFECTS OF INSTRUCTION

This brief overview of research on instruction is separated into two main parts. In the first, we examine studies of methods of instruction primarily related to learning in the classroom; in the second, we review psychological research, mostly in the field of learning, that has direct relevance for the design of instructional techniques. Studies reviewed in the first part involve classroom learning; those in the second involve learning tasks that are usually unlike normal classroom material, being theoretical rather than applied. These are studies of the laboratory type, although the laboratory may be a classroom.

The distinction between the two kinds of research is based primarily on the learning tasks used rather than on where the study occurs. It is an arbitrary distinction at best and one becoming less clear each year as an increasing number of psychologists are turning their attention to school learning. However, studies in both parts flow directly from the experimental learning tradition in psychology, and as a result there is little reference to individual characteristics of the learner. This tradition attempts to devise general propositions about learning. Studies that do attempt to account for unique learner characteristics are discussed later in this chapter.

Much of the research on instructional design is based on child developmental variations over time, but it rarely considers individual patterns of development; some research that does is reviewed below. In application to instruction, results from both approaches are sometimes combined under the same heading. For example, individualized instruction may, as it implies, be tailored to the unique characteristics of the student. More often, however, it accounts only for individual differences in rate of learning.

Classroom Instruction

Instruction typically refers to the interaction between teacher and student in the use of instructional material. Curriculum refers to the design and organization of the instructional material. An enormous amount has been written about curriculum design and use.

Westbury (1970, p. 239) begins a review with the comment:

> Curriculum evaluation appeared as a topic of a chapter in three of five issues of the 1969 *Review of Educational Research*. The emphasis on this topic is, if nothing else, disconcerting to a reviewer who must plow the same field again; it is also puzzling when compared with the infrequent appearances of evaluations of actual curricula or curricular materials in either the research or the subject journals.

and later:

> Evaluations exist in the files and reports of those who developed curricula. Yet, while these evaluations remain in files, the proposals and prescriptions of developers circulate freely, without any readily available critical scrutiny. There is a literature of curriculum evaluation, but it is neither publicly available in journals nor has it grown out of an

accessible tradition of formal or informal appraisal of curricula. There is no "consensus of public knowledge" on the nature of curriculum evaluation which warrants methodological formalizations about its character or provides the substance of such formalizations.

The curriculum research reviewed here is limited to literature that appears in the professional journals and that attempts to evaluate curricula. This represents only a small part of the total writings on the subject. We have omitted the descriptions of curricula and discussions of theoretical issues. In general, evaluations have not led to many encouraging findings. Because of the complexity of the process they often lack sufficient scope, so that an absence of positive findings is not surprising. Westbury (1970, p. 245) summarizes the problem of matching evaluation schemes to curriculum objectives:

> Two separate though interrelated analytical problems must be faced: curriculum must be conceptualized in such a way that it no longer carries the connotation that it is a unitary notion, often a treatment; evaluation must be seen in ways that permit the development of sets of methods and criteria so reasoned judgments, appropriate to all senses of curriculum, become possible. Curriculum evaluation theorists must attempt to formalize these criteria and methods so they can prescribe rules for the application of criteria to the full range of concrete curricular issues. No current theoretical prescription for curricular evaluation approaches these goals, although parts of the problem have been acknowledged by some writers.

Curriculum development programs in science and mathematics have been evaluated, at least in some aspects. Some of these are reviewed by Rombert (1969), Smith (1969), Welch (1969), and Westbury (1970). Evaluation studies of curricula developed by the Physical Science Study Committee (PSSC), Biological Science Curriculum Study (BSCS), Chemical Education Materials Study (CHEM), and School Mathematics Study Group (SMSG) are inconsistent in their findings. Oftentimes, differences between these curricula and conventional ones are small, and sometimes results favor the conventional method. Some interactions are noted between student ability and measures of learning for different curricula; that is, low ability students may do better in the conventional curriculum in terms of one measure of learning but poorer in a new curriculum. All learning measures do not disclose this interaction, and on some of them the new curriculum is better (Welch, 1969, p. 439).

Westbury (1970, p. 250) summarizes a study by Heron (1969) that showed how a teacher's misunderstanding of a program might affect the program's success or failure. Heron made no attempt to evaluate curricula in terms of output measures. Rather, the study explored three evaluative questions related to CHEM, PSSC, and BSCS curricula:

> (1) To what extent is the "inquiry" objective of these programs actually embodied in the materials produced? (2) How do the teachers through whom the materials filter perceive this objective and do they understand "inquiry" well enough to operationalize any conception of what it might mean in their classrooms? and (3) How does this objective compare to the explicit and implicit goals teachers set in their classrooms?

Westbury summarizes the findings:

> The results of his application were disappointing. Despite the claims of the developers for their materials, they were found to present little more than a "somewhat sophisticated" version of a "less competent" view of method. The teachers who had been attending workshops on the new materials were found to have almost no conception of what might be meant by a claim to teach the "nature of scientific inquiry."

The innovative science curricula such as those discussed above place heavy emphasis on the role of inquiry or learning by discovery, an emphasis that Ausubel (1965, p. 259) has severely criticized:

> Much of this "heuristics of discovery" orientation to the teaching of science is implied by the view that the principal objectives of science instruction are the acquisition of general inquiry skills, appropriate attitudes about science, and training in the operations of discovery. Implicit or explicit in this approach is the belief that the particular choice of subject matter chosen to implement these goals is a matter of indifference (as long as it is suitable for the operations of inquiry), or that somehow in the course of performing a series of unrelated experiments in depth, the learner acquires all of the really important subject matter he needs to know.

Later in this chapter we discuss theories of instructional organization (including Ausubel's). These approaches emphasize the importance of instructional structure in acquiring knowledge. It is not surprising that Ausubel should conclude that incidental learning as a by-product of discovery cannot compare to a graded and systematically organized approach.

The idea of learning by discovery has become popular throughout education, particularly among those calling for reforms in classroom teaching. The complex issues involved in this concept are the topic of an excellent book edited by Shulman and Keisler (1966), in which some authors emphasize that learning by discovery does not mean laissez-faire education. The difference is in the way control is exerted, not the lack of it. In general, learning by discovery has not been proved to have a great advantage over conventional methods. Cronbach (1966) points out that research is needed to determine what advantages learning by discovery offers, and under what conditions its benefits are accrued.

Although curriculum development is far from being on firm ground, and in spite of a general lack of evaluation, some progress is being made. The current status of curriculum development and evaluation in terms of its accomplishment and shortcomings is seen in the following quotations:

> In brief summary, during the past decade significant progress has been made in the precise definition of curricular objectives, in the analysis of ends/means relationships, and in the effective ordering of stimuli for learning. Substantial progress has been made in extending both the understanding of the evaluative process and the use of evaluative data in diagnosing the possible causes of discrepancies between curricular expectancies and curricular accomplishments. In the realm of explaining curricular realities, however, we appear to know little more in 1969 than we knew in 1960. Curricular theory with exploratory and predictive power is virtually nonexistent (Goodlad, 1969, p. 374).

> Research during the period of this review shows a desirable tendency toward a broader spectrum of concern, but still lacking are systematic longitudinal studies showing the impact of varied methods and materials on student attitudes, understanding, performance, and motivation. Current research seems to be mainly discipline-centered rather than pupil- or learning-centered, and the ends of education appear to be too often subordinated to transitory fashions in educational haberdashery (Smith, 1969, p. 409).

> One conclusion seems obvious. Only at centers where there has been a concentrated effort to investigate many facets of a course or teaching method by a group of researchers does one find any discernible evidence of advancement (Welch, 1969, p. 441).

> Theory must inform the deliberation that is evaluation but at the same time it must grow from deliberation. The problem implicit in this assertion is mapped by the requirement that curriculum and evaluation workers find a theoretical structure that permits them to embrace the particular and concrete with seriousness before they attempt theoretical speculation of any kind. We are far from this at the moment (Westbury, 1970, p. 257).

Rosenshine (1970a) indicates that a central problem in evaluation is determining the actual teaching practice that takes place within any given curriculum. Because teachers vary widely in their skills, attitudes, beliefs, and dispositions, they do not all do the same thing given the same curriculum. Simply producing a curriculum does nothing in terms of its implementation, and evaluations of different curricula are generally useless without data on classroom transactions. In summarizing the shortcomings of evaluation of curricula, Rosenshine (1970a, p. 296) states:

> Currently, three major needs are: greater specification of the teaching strategies to be used with instructional materials, improved observational instruments that attend to the context of the interactions and describe classroom interactions in more appropriate units than frequency counts, and more research into the relationship between classroom events and student outcome measures.

Some progress is being made in defining classroom transaction and relating it to student outcome. Some studies that relate specifically to the teacher's mode of presentation were discussed previously; however, as yet there is little demonstrable evidence for accepting any particular curriculum as being better than another. This is a gross generalization and perhaps does not give credit to some programs. Of course, some curricula are undoubtedly better than others and "everyone knows it." Unfortunately, demonstrating curriculum effectiveness is extremely difficult.

Instructional method studies have failed for essentially the same reason as curriculum studies: a lack of classroom transaction data. Reported studies find no consistent indication for the superiority of any instructional method. For example, research on discussion versus lecture has a long history, but as Stephens (1967, p. 81) concludes: "It has been found in summary after summary that no distinction between the two methods can be found."

Studies of instructional method rarely control for student or teacher characteristics, and it is entirely possible that one method may be superior to another for some students and with some teachers. It is unreasonable to assume, for example, that all teachers are equally effective using the discussion method, or that because one is effective using the discussion method, he will also be effective using the lecture approach. Before instructional methods can be evaluated, certain student and teacher characteristics must be defined, and data must be provided on the transactions between them.

We turn now to the topic of teaching machines, programmed instruction, and other technologically oriented aspects of instruction. The research on teaching technology has been much reviewed, and we mention only the major studies. A detailed and lengthy history as well as a critical and summary review of such research is provided by Saettler (1968). A brief overview of history and research including comments on general shortcomings of the field is given by W.H. Allen (1971). A lengthy evaluation and review of research on learning from television is provided by Chu and Schramm (1967).

The early and intense interest in television learning led to a large-scale development with little in the way of controlled research. Many claims were made for the success of these programs. Subsequent research did not support the claims, although as Chu and Schramm (1967, p. 176) point out:

> In a sense, instructional television is more complex than the research that deals with it. Complex behavior has baffled learning theorists for years. A number of variables are clearly at work determining what a given individual learns from the television. In many cases these variables interact, and the total must be a great deal more complex than can be represented by the one-variable experiments that typically make up the research literature, no matter how clean and skillful they are.

After hundreds of studies, it can only be concluded that learning by television is about as effective as conventional classroom learning, and a case cannot be made for the superiority of either. Effective television teaching grows out of the application of sound teaching methods, such as simplicity, organization of material, and practice, and apparently *not* from any special mode of presentation. The advantages of television learning are not evident in any identifiably superior result, but rather in the ability to reach a larger audience and to augment conventional methods. Further research is required to determine under what conditions television learning takes place and what specific factors in television presentation are responsible for learning. However, the same comment holds for conventional teaching. In general, little is known about factors that actually promote learning.

The most direct application of learning principles has been in the area of programmed instruction. This literature is reviewed in many places and is commented on in almost every review of educational research. Interest in programmed instruction, which surged in the early

1960s, has now waned considerably (Corey, 1967). The conditioning approach of Skinner (1968), following his success in conditioning behavior in animals, has been applied to human learning. In spite of the early bloom and rapid spread of programmed instruction based on the Skinnerian method, however, later evaluations of the effectiveness of programmed instruction have not been highly positive.

The behavioristic learning approach of Skinner and his followers was criticized early in its development on the grounds that, because their teaching practices derived from work with animals, programmed instruction was devoid of meaningful structure and concentrated too much on rote material. The Skinnerian approach thus has many critics; some criticisms relating specifically to programmed instruction can be found in Pressey (1963) and Thelen (1963a,b).[2]

Theoretical issues aside, programmed instruction has not proved to be the success in the classroom that it was first thought to be (Allen, 1971; Gotkin and McSweeney, 1967; Saettler, 1968). It is about as effective as conventional work when student achievement is used as the criterion, but its superiority has not been affirmed. The issue of effectiveness of programmed instruction is further clouded by the untested claims made by the manufacturers of teaching machines (Saettler, 1968, p. 269). Few, if any, of the claims made for the high efficiency of teaching machines have in fact proved out. An early such claim held that by properly sequencing material in small steps, dull students would be able to perform better, perhaps even as well as bright students. However, in their review of this research, Cronbach and Snow (1969) could find no evidence to support these claims.

Interest in programmed instruction and teaching machines has had some positive outcomes. Allen (1971), points out that research on programmed instruction has had the important effect of producing interest in the development of individualized instruction. Whereas early research and application focused on group instruction and one-way communication, the current work is shifting to the unique characteristics of the individual student as a central issue in the design of instruction. Interest is turning, however slowly, to the study of interactions among student, task, and material.

Instructional Psychology

Instructional design is mostly based on inferences drawn from theoretically relevant work in experimental and learning psychology but, until recently with little direct activity in the research by psychologists. In the last decade an increasing number of psychologists have turned to the applied aspects of instructional research and classroom learning. In 1967 the *Annual Review of Psychology* for the first time carried a summary of research on instructional psychology. After this first review, by Anderson, were reviews by Gagné and Rohwer in 1969 and Glaser and Resnick in 1972. Each covers broad areas of research. Even over the relatively short time span of these reviews one can note that research is steadily increasing. But there is a long way to go in this respect. Psychologists still tend to study highly constrained, often artificial, and generally more theoretical problems. In this respect Gagné and Rohwer (1969, p. 381) note:

> Remoteness of applicability to instruction, we note with some regret, characterizes many studies of human learning, retention, and transfer, appearing in the most prestigious of psychological journals. The findings of many studies of human learning presently cannot be applied directly to instructional design for two major reasons: (a) the conditions under which the learning is investigated, such as withholding knowledge of learning goals from the subject and the requiring of repetition of responses, are often unrepresentative of conditions under which most human learning occurs; and (b) the tasks set for the learner (e.g., the verbatim reproduction of verbal responses, the guessing of stimulus attributes chosen by the experimenter, among many others) appear to cover a range from the merely peculiar to the downright esoteric. This is not to imply that such studies do not further an understanding of the learning process. However, it would seem that extensive theory development centering upon learning tasks and learning conditions will be required before one will be able to apply such knowledge to the design of instruction for representative human tasks.

In regard to learning from written material Glaser and Resnick (1972) make only a slightly more optimistic comment:

> A nagging impression that one gets in reading the literature as it grows in this area is that it could become another insular activity like the traditional field of verbal learning. If this is to be prevented, researchers must live down their past habits of empiricism untempered by theoretical analysis, the neglect of processes which can account for individual variation, and the retreat to artificial laboratory tasks such as arbitrary verbal associations. So far, however, the increased attention to learning from written materials is an exemplary trend in attempts to close the gaps that exist between our knowledge of learning and the processes of everyday school instruction.

Much of the difference between learning experiments in the laboratory and in the classroom must lie in the direct or indirect influence on psychology of behaviorism, which is based on stimulus-response relationships and control through the manipulation of reinforcement. The inadequacy of this model, even in simple animal learning, has been questioned repeatedly, and its application to human learning (particularly verbal) is considered by many to be grossly inadequate (Deese, 1969; Garrett and Fodor, 1968). Of course, there have always been severe critics of the behavioristic tradition in general; and recently, some psycholinguists, led by Chomsky (1959), have leveled devastating criticisms. Although there are other theoretical formulations, behaviorism dominates in learning and experimental psychology; the methods used in learning studies are almost exclusively behavioristic. Some examples of widely used methods are summarized below.

Studies of human association learning typically present pairs of stimuli (words, symbols, pictures) to the subject during the learning phase, and test for his recall of the second stimulus by presenting him with the first. A recognition measure of retention (or learning) may be used in which the subject selects the correct stimulus out of several presented to him. An even more primitive form (serial learning) simply presents stimuli in lists; learning is measured by the degree of recall (or recognition) of the list. In the study of human learning, hundreds of laboratory studies involving serial and association learning occur each year, but the value of studies of paired-associate learning for the classroom has been repeatedly questioned, and it is generally concluded that their value is minimal. However, Rohwer *et al.* (1971) caution against this conclusion, because substantial relationships have been reported between paired-associate and school learning. What this means is certainly not clear.

Another frequently used method for studies of human learning is discrimination learning. In this method, the subject learns to make a differential response to different stimuli through the application of a reinforcer. Usually there are two stimuli and two responses. For example, the subject may be reinforced (with a reward or with feedback concerning the correctness of his response) for responding to one stimulus, and not reinforced for responding to another. Learning is measured in terms of the time or number of responses necessary for the subject to "learn" to respond only to the "correct" (the reinforced) stimulus. This method may make use of an irrelevant stimulus (one present but not necessarily attended to by the subject); the subject is then tested for how well he "correctly" responds to this incidental stimulus (incidental learning).

There are other methods, and the reader interested in pursuing the topic can refer to any basic text on experimental psychology. The examples cited above suffice to make clear that although laboratory methods may be important for theoretical issues, they are extremely limited for investigating classroom learning.

The review that follows is based largely on the reviews of Anderson (1967), Gagné and Rohwer (1969), and Glaser and Resnick (1972). These reviews are based on an enormous number of reports, and we do not attempt to give primary references.

Transfer of Learning

A central issue in learning theory and a critical one in classroom learning is that of transfer or generalization of learning. A disappointment of preschool and compensatory education programs has been the fading of achievement gains over time. This has led to an interest in the question of how achievement in basic skills such as reading and mathematics might be generalized to future achievement and to concurrent achievement in other school subjects. However, there appear to be no direct attempts to measure this generalization in the classroom.

Although we lack studies in the classroom, the psychological research on generalization (referred to as transfer) is large. Gagné (1962) distinguishes two kinds of transfer. In one case, there is transfer from the learning of a specific task to performance on the same general class of tasks. He terms this *lateral transfer.* It is equivalent to generalization. In other words, generalization operates whenever two learning problems require common rules for solution or depend on some common stimulus or response sequence.

Vertical transfer operates when the learning of a specific task facilitates the learning of another. For example, training in stimulus coding—that is, a translation of meaningless symbols into meaningful ones via mnemonic devices—transfers to paired-associate learning. Subjects trained in coding learn faster. In this case, stimulus coding is a subordinate skill to paired-associate learning; however, it is not necessary to, or a part of, the learning task. This is the kind of transfer that Gagné and others consider in studies of "hierarchical organization," where learning a task lower in the hierarchy facilitates the learning of higher-order tasks.

Lateral transfer is a less popular research topic than it once was, and results of recent studies hold no surprises (Gagné and Rohwer, 1969). Much of the research on lateral transfer has centered on learning general rules. Research shows that verbalizing the rule is better than not, and using a wide variety of examples of the rule in the learning phase helps to promote transfer.

Studies of vertical transfer are on the increase, and results carry a number of important implications for the design of instruction. The notion of hierarchical organization was first outlined in detail by Gagné (1962). He asserts that knowledge of a subject can be arranged in a hierarchy such that knowledge at any one level of complexity depends upon the attainment of knowledge lower in the hierarchy. Theory predicts that in learning a subject students cannot "pass" a post-test unless they also have "passed" tests for skills lower in the hierarchy of knowledge. It is important to note that the learning hierarchy is made up of what the student can do, or his demonstrated intellectual skills. Glaser and Resnick note (p. 211):

> Certain failures of instructional sequences based on learning hierarchy analysis to show evidence of positive transfer from one level of the hierarchy to the next have occurred; these failures are attributed to the fact that the hierarchy component described what the learner needed to know rather than the intellectual operations that he could perform. Thus, Gagné explicitly excludes verbalizable knowledge from consideration and makes little contact in his present formulation with the large amount of work going on in meaningful verbal learning and the organization of memory.

A number of studies designed to test for hierarchical theory report results supporting the theory. In a recent review, the originator of the theory comments that:

> Studies of transfer of prior learning are frequently consistent with this hypothesis, although few are confirming in a crucial sense (Gagné and Rohwer, 1969).

Ausubel (1963) has developed a theory of hierarchical organization of meaningful verbal material. The hierarchy begins with detailed and specific bits of knowledge and builds to a level containing the most abstract and general concepts. The learning of new prose material can be facilitated by the use of "advanced organizers," which help the learner integrate new material into his existing knowledge. Advance organizers are highly generalized statements or questions that the subject reads prior to studying new material. Their purpose is to prepare the reader for new material in terms of what he already knows; or the advance organizers may outline and brief the material. In addition to experimental support cited by Ausubel, several other studies (Allen, 1970; Merrill, Barton, and Wood, 1970) also find supportive evidence for the theory. Glaser and Resnick (1972) summarize this research around the theoretical issues involved.[3]

A topic closely related to transfer involves a technique that has come to be called "fading" or "vanishing." In this technique one stimulus is faded out and slowly replaced by a new one. Anderson (1967) reports on research in this area and concludes that it may have practical value for teaching children who cannot understand or hear verbal instructions. In this technique, students are able to learn correct responses to new stimuli without trial-and-error behavior. A recent study by Karraker and Duke (1970) found the fading technique to be superior for the errorless learning of the letters b and d by kindergarten children. However, Samuels (1970) summarizes reading research using the fading technique and finds contradictory results. In these studies, a picture and word are shown together, and the picture is gradually faded out. It appears that the desired attention shift from the picture to the word does not always take place. In view of the contradictory evidence, this technique appears to have limited usefulness in the classroom at this time.

Reinforcement and Feedback

Reinforcement is a central concept in almost all learning formulations, and many learning theorists and experimentalists insist that learning cannot occur without reinforcement. Without a clearly defined external reinforcer, these theorists assume that reinforcement is provided by the subject and is internal. For example, a subject may be reinforced with some tangible reward for reading, or he may read because he finds it personally rewarding. The latter is considered to be a case of intrinsic reinforcement. Other learning is said to take place as a result of the operation of social reinforcers (that is, broadly generalized extrinsic ones). The importance of reinforcers to learning has been realized in the laboratory through the strict use of an operational definition (for example, if a stimulus presented immediately after a response leads to an increase in the response rate, it is a reinforcer). It is frequently argued that using this operationally defined reinforcer concept in complex learning is at best unproductive. The stimulus properties of the reinforcer are not known, nor is the response that is to be reinforced well-defined. There is, moreover, no generally held theory of reinforcement, and it does not have the status of a basic psychological process (Carroll, 1971). The reinforcement concept, when carried to its limits, becomes tautological and therefore of little practical value in educational research.

Psychologists have, however, tried to address complex learning. For example, the term "feedback" has been used by some psychologists to indicate an information-processing and volitional aspect of complex learning. It is a general term that may be used to denote the reinforcing event, the subject's interest in and use of the event, or both. Obtaining a reward for the correct response in a discrimination learning task may be thought of as providing feedback about the correctness of response and defining how the subject can obtain further reward. Providing knowledge of results to the learner (feedback) is considered by many theorists to be a reinforcer for wanting to learn, and the reinforcing event is primarily intrinsic, although partly under control of the external event.

Although studies of various factors of reinforcement have dominated much of the psychological study of learning, it appears to us that few of the results have any real value in determining classroom learning. The application of a term like feedback does not solve issues, because it is difficult to find consistent rules of feedback. Gagné and Rohwer (1969, p. 401) note:

> A characteristic of recent research is that it reveals clearly the highly variable nature of feedback effects. Moreover, the research indicates that the sources of this variance are to be found in learner characteristics, type of feedback, timing of feedback, direction of feedback, and type of task.

In spite of the controversy over reinforcement in theories of human learning, the term has come into vogue in a number of quasi-theoretical contexts. Behavior modification is perhaps the best known; less well known but more critical is the application of "reinforcement theory" to classroom learning. These applications are loose extrapolations from laboratory studies and cannot in fact be supported by the learning theories that originally spawned the concept.

A frequent controversy that arises in the application of reinforcement theory to instruction is the relative importance and function of "external" versus "intrinsic" reinforcers. A related issue centers on the question of tangible versus social reinforcers. For example, it has been found that culturally deprived children learn best with tangible reinforcers (candy, money, etc.), but middle-class children learn best with social reinforcers. Some argue that reinforcement should be "intrinsic" (that is, the child learns what is self-rewarding); others argue that external rewards internalize over time and become intrinsic. There is no experimental support for this notion, however. Glaser and Resnick (1972) comment on the lack of crucial research on these issues, and make recommendations for a future course of action (p. 229):

> As we have noted for some other issues, this debate is characterized by more talk than experimentation. Small-scale, tightly controlled empirical studies usually demonstrate the effectiveness of one or another kind of reinforcer in controlling behavior and ignore other motivational variables that might be operating concurrently. Intervention studies are often more eclectic, claiming to employ both intrinsic and extrinsic forms of reinforcement, but the research reports on these programs do not attempt to separate the effects of the different forms. Current theories of reinforcement suggest that the distinction between intrinsic and extrinsic reinforcement is an artificial one, and that reinforcement from both sources controls behavior in similar ways. This new view suggests that debates concerning internal versus external reinforcement may be fruitless and that a more profitable line of research for instructional psychology will be the interaction of self-produced and externally provided reinforcers in learning.

Attention Factors in Learning

Factors in attention have played a central role in learning experiments. A well-established body of research indicates that stimulus novelty promotes learning and helps to maintain attention. In human learning, guessing and delayed feedback lead to better learning than no guessing and immediate feedback. In general, factors that increase the uncertainty of a stimulus complex lead to heightened curiosity or increased attention. In reading material, it has been found that retention is improved when questions are inserted throughout the text. These results are generally interpreted as indicating increased attention and inspection time. Bull (1973) presents a brief review and summary of the major empirical findings and theoretical thinking in this area.

One of the more easily manipulated factors in instruction is the mode of presentation of the learning material. In summarizing research on stimulus presentation, Gagné and Rohwer (1969) state:

> Considerable evidence has now been amassed indicating that when there is a choice of method for presenting equivalent information, the following results prevail: pictorial materials are superior to verbal; concrete verbal materials are preferable to abstract verbal; and grammatically structured are better than unstructured materials. In contrast, the conditions that might dictate choices among various available modes of presenting stimuli are almost entirely undetermined thus far. Finally, stimulus context appears to be one of the most potent of the variables determining the effects of materials presented, although tasks other than traditional laboratory ones remain to be investigated.

Research that finds pictures superior to words is mostly based on the paired-associate method. These studies typically require the subject to learn lists of paired words, paired pictures, or a word paired with a picture. Although results favor the picture presentation, the relative effectiveness of each mode appears to depend on a number of factors, including student characteristics and age and task characteristics. However, on the basis of studies of classroom learning, Samuels (1970) finds that pictures have a negative effect on learning to read, especially for the poorer students. Pictures are interpreted by Samuels as distracting stimuli that produce attention shifts. This is consistent with other findings about the effect of distracting stimuli on learning by poor students. The studies reported by Samuels involved young children learning to read, while most of the studies using the paired-associate method used older subjects. Thus, age differences may account for the disparate results obtained by the different methods.

Retention of Learned Material

Studies of retention and forgetting are as old as the study of learning, and one of the principal measures of learning has always been amount of retention. Gagné and Rohwer (1969, p. 401) give an excellent review of the research, the principal findings, and the basic issues involved. Unfortunately, like much of the other research reviewed in this chapter, work on retention depends on the paired-associate method, which makes generalization to the classroom hazardous.

Earlier studies that seemed to demonstrate better retention for free recall than for recognition learning have since been shown to depend on the degree of original learning rather than the method of learning. A number of studies have confirmed that when control is introduced for the degree of original learning, retention is approximately the same for all methods of learning (within the limitations of paired-associate learning). Even the degree of meaningfulness of the material does not affect retention when the degree of learning is controlled for. Of course, "meaningfulness" here is used strictly in the framework of paired-associate learning, where it refers to the use of words instead of nonsense syllables, or the use of grammatically correct sentences instead of random orders of words. This does not seem to be too closely related to what educators generally mean when they talk about meaningful material.

Other factors affecting retention have been isolated. Retroactive inhibition, for example, occurs when a learning task inserted between the learning of an original task and the measure of retention causes the original material to be forgotten. It has also been found that elaborating on (talking about) the stimuli in the learning phase promotes retention.

STUDENT CHARACTERISTICS

In this subsection, we discuss evidence showing that a general failure to match student characteristics with specific educational programs may be a major reason for the lack of positive findings in educational research and for the consequent lack of success in defining factors that substantially affect educational outcomes. Little attention has been paid in the literature to identifying pertinent student characteristics or to developing specific educational programs to fit individual characteristics. A priori, it seems reasonable to believe that students respond differently to different kinds of classroom and instructional methods and to different types of teachers. As reasonable as this hypothesis may sound, there is little research to support it, although some exceptions are pointed out below.

Although there are undoubtedly many social reasons why individual student differences have not been a major part of research, it is worth noting psychological reasons. Cronbach (1957) has pointed out that psychology is split into two disciplines. Some psychologists (mostly psychometricians and, to some extent, personality theorists) have been greatly concerned with individual differences and have mostly ignored the development of a general theory of behavior. Others (notably learning theorists and experimental psychologists) have attempted to develop theories of behavior while ignoring individual differences. This split has been particularly damaging to education, because learning theorists have little to say that bears directly on learning in the classroom. Gagné (1967, p.13) notes:

> First the widespread inattention to individual differences seems to indicate that psychologists have been uniquely optimistic in their expectations for the generality of behavioral laws. In the pursuit of these laws, the assessment of ranges of generalization and of limiting conditions has been by-passed. If we recognize learning as a process of transition from an initial state to an arbitrary terminal state, then with respect to the individual differences problem, we should take a lesson from other natural sciences. We must recognize limitations in the applicability of a scientific law. It is through the specification of limiting conditions that our hypothesized or theoretically derived relationships obtain concreteness.

Below we discuss evidence for the importance of individual characteristics in determining educational outcomes. Some evidence reviewed is directly associated with classroom learning; however, most of it is less direct, originating in studies of personality, developmental psychology, and differential psychology. Studies in these categories seldom use conventional classroom learning as an outcome measure.

Abilities and General Intelligence

The study of human abilities has long been an area of psychological research concerned with individual characteristics. Alternative theories and the experimental literature generated by this effort have been discussed in a number of places (Cronbach and Snow, 1969; Guilford, 1967; Snow, 1971). The most widely accepted theories identify some kind of general ability (general intelligence) and a number of special abilities.

The relative influence of heredity and environment on the development of ability is a topic of continued interest and debate. Some theories hold that abilities are genetically determined, unfolding in the process of development. Others maintain in varying degrees that abilities are learned and that heredity places only loosely defined boundaries on their development. Snow (1971) comments that "The bulk of the evidence seems to be against the unfolding hypothesis, but the alternative learning hypothesis remains largely untested."

The most recent upsurge of interest in genetic determinants of intellectual ability was prompted by the work of Jensen (1969), who reports on the interaction of two broad categories of ability (Levels I and II, to use his terminology) and types of learning (associative and conceptual). His findings and his interpretation in terms of heredity are a matter of much controversy; more research is needed before any firm conclusion can be made. In particular, the effect of "tuning"[4] on students low on tests of Level II ability must be investigated, since there are subjects who have had little exposure to, or use for, conceptual thinking.

In a well-designed study by Rohwer et al. (1971), several hypotheses deriving from the Jensen model are investigated. Some results support the model and some conflict with it. The authors present an alternative explanation, one independent of an assumption of differences in innate ability between populations. The study makes clear that part of the problem in verifying Jensen's model lies in the fact that Level I and Level II tasks are not readily defined.

Although the relative contributions of heredity and environment are not known,[5] there is confirmatory evidence of ethnic differences in general cognitive abilities. Stodolsky and Lesser (1967) review the evidence for this conclusion and report on their own carefully controlled study. They find highly significant differences in patterns of achievement across four mental abilities (verbal, reasoning, number, and space) for various ethnic groups (Chinese, Jews, blacks, Puerto Ricans). That is, the level of attainment in each of the four abilities varied within an ethnic group, but ethnic groups differed in terms of which ability they attained best. Within an ethnic group, differences were also found for lower- and middle-class children, and although the patterns were very different for different ethnic groups, they were nearly identical for the two classes within an ethnic group. Thus, whatever factors produce differences in ethnic patterns of mental performance operate in both lower and middle classes. The authors point out that more research is necessary to determine the specific antecedents of the differential patterns of mental ability.

Some recent successful attempts to improve the IQ scores of black ghetto children argue against a genetic explanation of the children's generally lower scores. Through work with parents, some recent attempts to modify IQ in preschool children show promise, as do some programs that focus on language learning (see Elkind and Sameroff, 1970, for a review of these studies). Two recent programs beginning with preschool children show promise: one at the University of Illinois

(Engelmann, 1970) and the Ypsilanti-Carnegie Project (Lambie and Weikart, 1970). The Illinois programs, especially, demonstrated substantial gains in IQ scores and school achievement. However, past studies have shown a decline over time of IQ gains resulting from special programs, so that one needs to know longitudinal effects before making a final evaluation on these programs.[6]

Aptitude-Treatment Interaction:
Special Abilities

The above studies are examples of success in identifying special abilities. The important question for this report, however, is how these abilities affect educational outcome. The aptitude-treatment hypothesis holds that students need different educational treatments (instructional design, teachers, and so on) depending on their individual characteristics. Studies that investigate the effect of special abilities on learning have been summarized and evaluated in a number of places (Ferguson, 1965; Fleishman and Bartlett, 1969). However, Cronbach and Snow (1969) and Bracht (1970) find serious methodological flaws in much of the research and conclude that there is little clear evidence for the assumption of an interaction between special abilities and learning. Bracht concludes (p. 639):

> In experiments on ATI, the experimenters usually identified alternative treatments and then through trial-and-error tried to find personological variables to interact with the treatments. The analysis of an interaction effect was often an afterthought rather than a carefully planned part of the experiment, i.e., the alternative treatments were not developed with the ATI concept in mind. This approach has not been successful for finding meaningful disordinal interactions.

Cronbach and Snow (1969) and Bracht (1970) point out that in order to study ATI adequately the psychological processes used by students to acquire specific skills under alternative treatments need careful study before being related to specific and unique student abilities. In this regard Bracht concludes (p. 640):

> The real test for the concept of ATI will come as more experimenters use process analysis for developing alternative treatments. One of the most significant contributions to the topic is the excellent project report by Cronbach and Snow (1969). If aptitude-treatment interactions exist, experimentation and a continuing dialogue among educational psychologists should soon help to identify the salient treatment differences and personological variables which are relevant to the occurrence of ATI.

Perhaps the most important result of ATI research is that it is causing psychologists to reexamine definitions of aptitude. Glaser (1972) provides a brief but thought-provoking treatise on the implication of the lack of positive ATI effects. The problem stems from aptitude definitions based on psychometric studies (concerned with prediction from test items) rather than from studies of psychological processes. This was pointed out by Cronbach in 1957, who called for new definitions of aptitude. Glaser attributes much of the future of research in individualization and adaptive education to an inadequate understanding and formulation of human abilities.

Aptitude-Treatment Interaction:
General Ability

Whether general intelligence (or general ability) as opposed to special abilities is related to learning is a matter of some controversy. Evidence from factor analytic studies indicating that intelligence is not a unitary ability, and low correlations from studies of IQ and learning and among several learning tasks, led Fleishman and Bartlett (1969) to favor an interpretation that does not define intelligence as the ability to learn. Cronbach and Snow (1969) take issue with this point of view; after reviewing research and reanalyzing some of the existing data, they conclude that general intelligence is consistently and substantially correlated with learning. Much of the confusion, according to these authors, arises because many studies of the relationship between intelligence and learning use laboratory tasks that do not allow general intelligence much effect. In addition, most of the support for special abilities comes from the factor analytic approach that dominated American research on abilities for several decades. This approach tends to overdifferentiate, because even slight correlations sometimes produce new factors; in the process, a general intelligence factor tends to be submerged. British researchers have used a hierarchical model of abilities (Vernon, 1965). The views of Cronbach and Snow (1969) are more consistent with the British approach.

Along with the finding that general intelligence is correlated with degree of learning, Cronbach and Snow (1969) report evidence of significant interactions between intelligence and instructional method (aptitude-treatment interaction). In other words, instructional methods and learning tasks can be found that are differentially effective on the basis of level of student general ability. For example, under instructional methods A and B, an interaction effect means that if high-ability students do relatively well under treatment A, they do relatively poorly under B. Conversely, low-ability students do relatively well under B and poorly under A. If groups of students given methods A and B are equally mixed in regard to ability, no difference will be found in average performance between the two methods. This is believed to explain much of the failure in educational research to find positive effects due to instructional innovation. The kinds of educational treatments that will produce an interaction with general ability are not well understood, but some suggestive possibilities can be brought out in the following pages.

If we grant an interaction between educational method and student intelligence, then to maximize achievement students should receive differential instructional treatment (at least in some topics) on the basis of intelligence. However, classroom grouping (by intelligence or any other ability) has a long history of failure in promoting any difference in achievement outcome. Thelen (1967) reviews the extensive research on grouping and summarizes the findings of the international conference on grouping at the UNESCO Institute of Education in Hamburg in 1964. Results clearly indicate that heterogeneous groups do about as well as homogeneous groups. The reason for this seems obvious. Grouping on any basis, by itself, cannot be expected to produce improvement. What is needed is differential instruction treatment of the separate groups (Thelen, 1967, p. 188):

> In other words, special grouping makes sense only when the teacher has a clear and accurate idea of what to do with the special group. From this standpoint, the chief difficulty with homogeneous ability grouping is that the guesses about how to deal with the group are often wrong. Thus, we find teachers who think "bright" children "ought" to be more self-directing, more interested in the subject, more creative, or more eager to have a continuous, heavy load of work. By and large, however accurate these guesses may be with regard to impressions of bright adults who are successful in the adult world, the guesses are mostly not true—and certainly not necessarily true—as applied to most bright children under usual school conditions.

Some tentative evidence suggests that differential treatments can be based on general ability. Studies supporting the interaction hypothesis are touched on in the following summary of research on student characteristics.

Student Characteristics and Programmed Instruction

In the past decade, there has been much interest in programmed instruction and the application of what are sometimes referred to as principles of learning theory. The interest in programmed instruction derived almost entirely from the psychological field of learning; as mentioned earlier, this discipline was not oriented toward accounting for individual differences. For that reason, most of the research on instructional methods, especially programmed instruction,[7] has not even considered individual characteristics. Most of the research on instructional methods has been reviewed above. Here we will summarize the findings of studies that have attempted to investigate response to programmed instruction as a function of student characteristics.

Cronbach and Snow (1969) point out one study in this area that is exceptional in its sophistication and that leads to an interesting hypothesis in need of further investigation. The details of this study, by Burton and Goldberg (1962), are too complex to present here. The essential finding was an interaction between treatment (type of feedback) and student aptitude (verbal reasoning), but the interaction reversed according to the difficulty of the learning task. This is particularly important because it points out the presence of higher-order interactions as well as an interaction between ability and task difficulty.

Another excellent study (according to Cronbach and Snow) indicating higher-order as well as simple interactions is that of Maier and Jacobs (1966). In this study, some classes in Spanish had programmed instruction (PI) only, some had PI plus live instruction, and others had live instruction only. In addition, students were tested for general intelligence, Spanish language ability, and attitudes about Spanish. Results indicate that a favorable attitude toward Spanish was associated with PI plus live instruction for high-intelligence students. Second, there were indications that low-ability students tended to favor PI and high-ability students tended to favor live instruction. Perhaps the most significant finding was that some teachers got better results under one set of techniques and student characteristics than under others. It appears that high-IQ students do better under PI plus teacher when the teacher favors the innovative method. We shall return later to this topic of student-teacher-method interaction.

Although far from conclusive, some slight evidence supports the notion that low-aptitude (general intelligence) students may respond differently to some programmed features than high-aptitude students. Well-structured programs may be more effective for duller individuals, and perhaps brighter students respond better than dull ones to a scrambled presentation. In general, however, support for an interaction between programmed instruction and student aptitude is meager.

Student Characteristics and Meaningfulness

The issue of meaningful versus rote learning has a long tradition; introductory psychology texts usually say that meaningful material is more easily learned. Rote learning is generally considered to require less ability, and one is led to expect an interaction between meaningfulness and ability.

Research on meaningfulness of instruction and its interaction with student aptitude is surveyed by Cronbach and Snow (1969). Some evidence of an interaction is noted, but it is not clear what factors actually allow one type of student to gain more from meaningful instruction than others. Tuning is seldom used, so that students who have little or no experience with meaningful material are not on a par with students who have. Cronbach and Snow (1969) comment on a large-scale, well-designed study by Brownell and Moses (1949) that investigated meaningful versus mechanical instruction in subtraction:

> In half the schools, subtraction was rationalized for the children; a major effort was made to explain why certain steps were performed in (e.g.) borrowing. But third graders in some of the schools seemed unable to profit from these explanations. The authors tell us that where instruction had been rote in the two preceding grades the whole concept of explanation in arithmetic was strange to these pupils, and they could not incorporate the meanings offered. The children, then, had developed a positive inaptitude for meaningful instruction, whereas other children had been led to the point where they could profit from explanation. Now this is important first in undermining the concept that aptitude or readiness is simply a matter of intellectual maturity. Secondly, it sharply challenges such a concept as Jensen's regarding a native incapacity. Third, it destroys any lingering attempt to define "one best way" of instruction. Fourth, it urges us in the direction of trying to help the pupil who does not use meaningful instruction effectively by *combining* techniques that will move his skills forward without relying on comprehension, with techniques that will advance his ability to

comprehend. We are in no position to write off these third graders as noncomprehenders—but we do not anticipate that simply tuning will bring them to the level of mathematical reasoning.

A series of articles on the use of advance organizers in the learning of meaningful verbal materials (reviewed above) culminated in a study by D.I. Allen (1970), which reports evidence of aptitude-treatment interaction. As noted earlier, advance organizers are highly generalized statements read prior to the learning of new material for the purpose of facilitating learning by allowing the student to relate the new material to his existing cognitive structure. Results indicate that the advance organizers facilitate learning (measured by delayed retention) in higher-ability students but not in lower-ability ones. This may indicate that students of lower ability do not have the cognitive structure necessary to make use of the advance organizers. This study raises a number of interesting questions that need further exploration.

Concept Attainment

Theories of concept attainment and cognitive development have led to studies that attempt to determine the sequence in which an individual grasps concepts or relates them to each other. Several different theoretical explanation and experimental approaches to the study of concept learning have been taken, and Gagné (1968) presents them in capsule form.

Learning theorists who belong to the associationistic school consider concept attainment as mostly a matter of learning. Others believe concept attainment depends on maturation and biological readiness. The most popular theory currently is that of Piaget, who focuses on the organism's existing cognitive structure in terms of its adaptation to its environment. Changes in adaptation are related to modifications in the cognitive structure. Gagné (1968) proposed a model based on cumulative learning effects (of which association is a small part) within limitations imposed by maturation. These and other models differ markedly in terms of the importance assigned to learning.

Concept development theories and studies define the factors upon which levels of learning depend. If concept attainment is largely a matter of maturation and readiness, or level of cognitive structure, then the student should not be exposed to a task for which he has not developed adequate concepts. If concept attainment depends upon prior cumulative learning, then instruction must build on prior learning and sequence tasks in a hierarchy according to their contribution to other learning tasks. Gagné's theory of hierarchical organization rivals Piaget's ideas, although confirmatory evidence is still mostly lacking.

There are many psychological studies of concept attainment, although most of them look only at modal behavior for age groups, and studies of the interaction of individual concept attainment with learning—especially school learning—are indeed few. In reviewing research on concept attainment Elkind and Sameroff (1970, p. 212) note:

> These various studies reflect the growing acceptance of the role of cognitive processes in a variety of learning situations where they were previously, if not denied, then at least neglected. A caution is in order, however, since there is a danger of cognizing every task. It would be heartening if some investigators reported the deviant as well as the model solution processes used by children in their investigations. The fact that the same problem can be solved by several different kinds of processes cannot be reiterated too often. What we need to know is what processes are used by which children on what tasks under what circumstances. A blind devotion to cognitive processes can produce as narrow an outlook as an equally narrow devotion to processes of association.

Research based on Piaget's theory of intelligence and concept development is steadily increasing.[8] This theory proposes two major steps of cognitive development. The first, beginning at about age seven, is the development of "concrete operations," the most widely studied operations being conservation[9] and classification.[10] The second stage is the development of "formal operations" (logic and so on) beginning in adolescence. Although most studies focus on the developmental aspects of Piagetian concepts, recent research has begun to investigate the possibilities of improving learning through training on these concepts. Glaser and Resnick (1972) provide an excellent summary and discussion on this research. Modest evidence supports the belief that training improves the generalizable learning of these tasks. Some educational innovations are attempting to improve school learning through training in Piagetian concept tasks, although results are not conclusive at this time.

A number of studies attempt to relate various concept learning tasks in elementary school children to socioeconomic status and IQ (for example, Adams, 1970; Guthrie *et al.*, 1971; Wei, 1969). There are also some studies of the relationship of concept attainment and school learning, mostly in reading (Keiser, 1971). This research, however, is still too limited to allow one to make broad generalizations, and among the criticisms one can level at it is that many concept learning tasks are irrelevant to school learning. In spite of the difficulties and complexities of this research there is growing evidence of a relationship between concept attainment (based either on past learning, maturation, or a combination of the two) and school learning. These results have wide implications for instruction design and the timing of specific instruction to specific student.

Personality Differences

No field within psychology is more concerned with individual differences than the study of personality. There is also no other discipline in which controversy is so great, empirical findings less definite, or theory more prolific. Reviews of this very complex area, which are found each year in the *Annual Review of Psychology*, come from several perspectives, including the behavioristic approach (Sarason and Smith, 1971), the psychometric (Wiggins, 1968), the clinical (Klein, Barr, and Wolitzky, 1967). Yet there is little that one can apply directly to education at this time, and methods for assessing personality traits are far from perfected, as noted by Sarason and Smith, 1971, p. 397):

> The pitfalls involved in attempting to assess significant personality attributes are many and varied, and the "true score" of an individual's standing on a given dimension is as elusive as the Holy Grail.

In spite of these pessimistic comments, there are some general results from personality studies with implications in some indirect way for education.

There is a growing conviction and body of supporting evidence that personality differences exist between the high achiever and the low achiever. In reviewing the subject, Klein, Barr, and Wolitzky (1967, p. 534) summarize:

> High achievers show strong internalization of values, indicated by responsibility and socialization. They also have high achievement motivation, in regard to both independent and conforming spheres. They are, however, low on social desirability (need to make a good impression on its own sake) and lack flexibility, apparently preferring order and stability.... As Gough and Fink (1964, p. 380) point out, the pattern of the achiever "is not a pattern of creativity or innovation, but rather that of constructive adaptation to a world in which one's circumstances are modest and one's destiny limited."

Cronbach and Snow (1969) discuss a study that shows an interaction between degree of meaningfulness of instruction and "overachievers" versus "underachievers." The overachievers showed better performance on the less meaningful material, and vice versa for the underachievers.

The concept of anxiety is one of the cornerstones of personality theory, and has also become a major factor in studies of learning. Adelson (1969, p. 231) began a review with, "Anxiety was the most popular single topic in personality this year." And later (p. 233):

After all these years, and after literally hundreds of studies of anxiety, there is still no general agreement as to what the commonly used scales are in fact measuring, whether it is drive level, maladjustment, effect, degree of defensiveness, or several of these in some interaction.

Sarason and Smith (1971) quote suggestions that much of the confusion results from a failure to distinguish between anxiety as a stable personality trait and anxiety as a temporary emotional state.

In spite of the confusion and ambiguity of the entire area of anxiety research, a few suggestions are promising. Across many studies there are indications of an interaction between anxiety and intelligence on cognitive performance; anxiety appears to enhance the performance of low-ability students and decrease the performance of high-ability ones. Cronbach and Snow (1969) report an apparent interaction between personality and instruction. It appears that structured instruction was better for high-anxious, high-compulsive children. For the child who was neither anxious nor compulsive, both structured and unstructured methods were about the same. Cronbach and Snow point out that flaws in the design of the experiment make it dangerous to generalize. It is possible that in some schools and for some students the unstructured method would achieve better results.

Student attitude and motivation are undoubtedly major determinants of achievement level. In applied research, much of the work along these lines has attempted to change the student's attitude about education or to increase his motivation. Another line of research, mostly in the laboratory, has attempted to measure attitude and motivation and to relate them to outcome. Some studies have investigated the relation of motivation level to teaching technique and classroom structure.

A particular aspect of motivation that has received much attention is achievement motivation, referred to as need-achievement. Achievement motivation appears to be a particularly persistent personality characteristic (Ryder, 1967) and one that is more related to cognitive maturation and innate ability than to early experience or child rearing practices (Heckhausen, 1967). Other findings (reviewed in Dahlstrom, 1970; Flavell and Hill, 1969; Hartup and Yonas, 1971) indicate that achievement motivation has different causes in young children than in adolescents. Adolescent and later achievement motivation seems to be related to parental and social rewards and punishments, whereas at a younger age it seems to be related to an assertion of autonomy.

Cronbach and Snow (1969) review the literature on motivation that is related to aptitude-treatment interaction. Theory predicts interaction between need-achievement and educational treatment, but attempts to demonstrate it experimentally have not been successful. Interactions are sometimes reported, but they are small. The tasks used in most studies are difficult to extrapolate to classroom learning. In addition, studies made with college students may have little meaning for students of other ages.

The increased national interest in academic achievement (particularly reading and mathematics in the early grades) has caused a certain amount of alarm concerning possible neglect of other factors in student growth. The focus on achievement and the implementation of accountability systems to monitor and enhance certain cognitive skills introduce the risk of stifling noncognitive growth. Emphasis on rote learning (and it is generally agreed that most compensatory and achievement-oriented programs emphasize rote learning) occurs at the expense of creative development. It is a popular lament among individuals who are identified as creative that formal education is in many respects a liability to creativity. These self-reports may not be particularly reliable, but they should not be ignored. Research on creativity tends to support these notions, although studies of creativity are not highly definitive. In reviewing the research on creativity, Klein, Barr, and Wolitzky (1967) note:

> Psychologists use widely differing criteria in studies purporting to deal with creativity, ranging from the careers of eminent people (which are obviously worthy of consideration), to the idea of creativity in interpersonal relations (which makes one wonder whether this is really "creativity"), down to measures of sales productivity and customer service (which can cheerfully be ignored). Furthermore, even when outstanding achievement is the criterion, it usually does not include what most informed nonpsychologists consider to be creativity, that is, humanistic and artistic creativity.

Reporting on a study of creativity in children, Hartup and Yonas (1971) suggest that there is "no clear support for the use of either test or gamelike contexts in assessing creativity. Scores depend on the task, the measure of creativity, the anxiety level of the subject, and sex."

In summarizing recent studies of creativity, Dahlstrom (1970) states:

> At the present time, therefore, available evidence suggests that the creativity process involves a variety of enhancing variables: interest, involvement, sensitivity, and self-confidence; and a variety of inhibiting variables: fears, self-doubts, and disabling sets and misperceptions acting jointly to determine the degree of expression of whatever the level of skill and proficiency of the individual for that situational demand will permit.

Dellas and Gaier (1970) provide an extensive review and penetrating analysis of the problems, issues, and results in studies aimed at identifying creativity. Research on creativity is marked by a glaring deficit of replicative and follow-up studies; nevertheless the authors are able to conclude (p. 67):

> Despite differences in age, cultural background, area of operation or eminence, a particular constellation of psychological traits emerges consistently in the creative individual, and forms a recognizable schema of the creative personality. This schema indicates that creative persons are distinguished more by interests, attitudes, and drives than by intellectual abilities. Whether these characteristics are consequences or determinants of creativity or whether some are peripheral and of no value is moot. These questions remain insufficiently approached and elucidated.

It is evident that no one is in a position to write a formula that defines creativity. However, it is equally apparent that, in spite of many problems with the research, a great deal is known about the characteristics of creativity. Among other things, the creative person appears to be independent in attitudes and social behavior and not much concerned about his impression on others. An educational program mainly interested in behavioral conformity and standardized achievement has little of positive value to offer the creative person. Accountability systems that at present focus only on achievement in rote learning may well have the effect of further alienating the creative student, especially in the early school years.

Early Development and Learning

Psychologists, especially psychoanalysts, have for a long time stressed the importance of the very early years in the development of patterns of behavior that become persistent. By the time a child reaches school, these patterns cannot be modified by the school. The time to affect cognitive and noncognitive factors in development is during the preschool years. Kagan (1970, p. 9) writes:

> The idea of this suggestion rests on the assumption that a child's experience with his adult caretaker during the first 24 months of life are major determinants of the quality of life motivation, expectancy of success, and cognitive abilities during the school years.

He then reviews data that support this suggestion.

Support for the importance of early development comes from a wide variety of research reviewed every year in the *Annual Review of Psychology* under the heading of Development Psychology. Other support comes from the recent and growing interest in "critical periods" of development during infancy, which determine life patterns. Most of this research has been conducted with animals, although there is supporting evidence from research and observations on humans.

The importance of early experience for education is the topic of a book edited by Denenberg (1970), which is somewhat slanted toward the growing interest at the federal level in day-care centers and the conviction that any really meaningful change in the educability of the culturally deprived will come through modifying and directing very early development of motivation, learning sets, attitudes, and values.

The Ypsilanti Carnegie Infant Education Project is one attempt to modify the educability of culturally deprived children by working with the mother and child. At the last report (Lambie and Weikart, 1970), the project had been in operation for only one year, but interim results show the program to be effective. The authors state (p. 403):

> Perhaps the most important observation is that the process of a teacher, a mother, and an infant getting ready to learn together is even more critical than what is actually done. To be sure, the teacher must have ideas and "expertise" to assist the mother and infant in learning, but that is a long way from simply providing a family with a series of exercises.

There is little doubt that major determinants of learning style and ability are fixed in the early life of the individual and that environment plays a dominant role. A thoughtful discussion of the effects of environmental deprivation on learning is provided by Mason (1970). Perhaps the most dramatic demonstration in the literature is Skeels' study of the effect of maternal care on institutionalized children (1966). Many people concerned with education express the belief that, if successful, preschool education and training will allow for the development of students with better dispositions and abilities for learning. Many of the characteristics of students that appear as given at school age—such as learning set and style, motivation, attitude, and concept attainment—may be open to modification in preschool years.

However, it has been pointed out in an extensive review of the literature (Stearns, 1971b) that organized preschool interventions through day care, Head Start, and other programs aimed at children between ages two and six have shown quite ambiguous and contradictory results. It is not possible at this stage to offer convincing evidence that early childhood interventions are more likely to improve educational effectiveness, by standard measures, than are the regular school programs, beginning at age five or six.

SUMMARY

In this chapter we reviewed research on the educational process, including studies of teaching and learning in the classroom and the laboratory and more remotely related psychological studies of learning and personality. Research was organized in terms of the effects of teachers, instruction, and student characteristics on educational outcome.

Research on the effects of teachers has generally been extremely uninformative, largely because until recently there have been few attempts to use student achievement as a criterion. Studies of teacher personality and attitudes have produced little, and in view of test instruments for these factors, their future prospects are also poor. Teacher skills and classroom behaviors are measurable, and some behavior of teachers in the classroom appears to be consistently associated with better student achievement. Studies of teacher effectiveness over time or across subject areas indicate little stability in teacher effectiveness. This could result from the transitory nature of teacher skills and other characteristics, or it could result from uncontrolled differences in comparative groups of student-teacher interaction. The teacher's expectation about the student has been found to affect student achievement, although these findings are not as firm as some authors would have us believe. Teachers are differentially effective with students, and it appears possible to improve classroom performance by assigning students to teachers on the basis of their ability to work together.

Studies of instructional method in the classroom and of curriculum design have produced no clear and consistent results. The problem, again, is basically one of evaluation and a lack of adequate data. Television learning, teaching machines, and programmed instruction appear to have no general superiority over conventional methods, although they can reach more students. Psychological studies of the factors affecting instruction use tasks generally different from classroom learning tasks, and as a result they tend to have limited value for determining the efficacy of instructional methods. A promising area of research concerns transfer of learning, especially organizing instructional material. Apparently, instructional material can be organized in a hierarchy, although the rationale and basis for the organization is not clear. More research is needed on almost every factor being studied. In addition, data are badly needed to bridge the gap between laboratory and classroom. There is some discussion and some evidence about the importance of interaction among the individual student, the instructional method, and the type of learning task, but this area has hardly been touched.

Research on the effects of student characteristics in classroom learning are few, although there is a vast amount of research on the topic in psychology. The study of ability structure is complex and lengthy, and there is no general agreement about the level of specificity necessary to describe the structure nor is there agreement about the degree of genetic influence on abilities. Moreover, there is no conclusive evidence for an interaction between any special ability and educational factors, although there are some indications that these interactions exist. However, general intelligence is substantially correlated with ability to learn, especially for abstract and complex material; and in addition, there is preliminary evidence of an interaction between intelligence and educational treatment. Such findings imply that for programs to be effective, educators must develop methods tailored for individual ability. Previous attempts to do this through ability-grouping failed because educational programs were not developed that specifically fitted the needs of the separate groups.

Other scattered research findings indicate that many factors differentiate students and their responses to specific educational programs. For example, creativity is not highly dependent on intelligence (using the terms to define broad categories rather than unitary abilities), nor does high intelligence guarantee creativity; but there are indications that the creative person requires a different educational approach than the less creative individual. More generally, differences in level of concept attainment exist at school age and thus carry important implications for instructional design.

A number of personality variables (autonomy, anxiety, and need for achievement, among others) appear to influence school achievement and to interact with educational factors, but the evidence is not highly conclusive. The apparent importance of noncognitive factors for school achievement has led to a growing interest in the effect preschool years have on educational outcomes. Findings from a number of experimental studies and preschool educational programs support the assumption that major determinants of achievement are established in these years.

NOTES TO CHAPTER IV

1. See Rosenshine and Furst (1971). "Counting" refers to the number of times a specified behavior occurred. "Rating" refers to subjective estimates by a judge (teacher, student, observer) of how the teacher performs with respect to some behavior. The behavior is rated into a number of categories in terms of desirability.
2. Of course, the Skinnerian stimulus-response approach drew instant fire from the gestalt psychologists, who insisted on a field approach with emphasis on meaningful units instead of fragmented, serially presented (and rote-learned) programs.
3. Vertical transfer has been studied under a number of other theories and experimental approaches, including rule learning, concept learning and attainment (see discussion of the work by Piaget), verbal learning, and problem solving. The results of the many studies on transfer clearly indicate the importance of the sequence of tasks for instruction effectiveness. These results appear to have more direct bearing on classroom learning than any others we have reviewed, although much more needs to be known.
4. Some students have little or no practice in the use of mediation, or the search for general principles in problem solving. Thus, they do poorly in abstract or conceptual problem solving compared with children who come from an environment that encourages the use

of mediation. From this it is concluded that the poor performers are unable to do conceptual thinking. Tuning is a pre-training in which subjects are taught the use of mediation. Differences between groups often disappear after tuning is used.
5. See the discussion of General Intelligence Tests in Chapter II.
6. See Stearns (1971b) for a detailed review of the literature on the effects of preschool programs in raising children's IQs.
7. Programmed instruction refers to the detailed sequencing of instructional tasks. It is planned to procure continuous activity on the part of the learner, with immediate feedback concerning the correctness of his response. (See Corey, 1967.)
8. For example, see Elkind (1969); Gollin and Moody (1973); Inhelder and Piaget (1958).
9. These studies determine the child's ability to recognize certain features of an object such as number, length, weight, volume, and so on. For example, a child might be required to estimate how large a container is necessary to hold the contents of another container of different shape; that is, conservation of volume.
10. Classification refers to the child's ability to place objects in categories based on some feature or dimension of the object.

V. THE ORGANIZATIONAL APPROACH

INTRODUCTION

As noted in Chapter I, the point of view of the organizational approach is quite different from that of the input-output and process approaches. In this approach, better educational outcomes for individuals are supposed to result from improving the functioning of the organizations that deliver the education. The school is seen as having to adapt to the needs of a changing set of students and to a changing set of pressures from the outside. Consequently, focus on the output side is on determinants of innovation and responsiveness; and focus on the input side is on rules, incentives, procedures, leverage, and so forth.

Although there is a very large body of literature in educational administration and organization, the studies are concerned primarily with how schools are administered, and their aim is to provide rules and techniques for efficient management. Few studies are quantitative, and they rarely address the same issues. It is rare to find two works that define outcomes in the same way and especially rare to find any studies that establish differences in outcomes, however defined, as a function of organizational or bureaucratic behavior. Nevertheless, educational policies, particularly those concerned with finance, seem to exert greater leverage on organization than on resources or processes. Attempts to tie overall policies to the internal use of resources or processes would create severe administrative problems. It is possible, however, that educational policies could make educational organizations and institutions more receptive to more effective resource allocation or processes.

We have found no review articles that try to evaluate the organizational studies. Our own attempt at evaluation was hampered by the lack of agreed-upon tests of validity, either internal or external, for the analysis of case studies.

After a general survey of the work on educational organizations, we selected eight organizational case studies for review here. We also chose to deal with two recent evaluations of experimental attempts to change school organization, the performance contracting experiments. We selected the eight case studies on the basis of the following criteria:

(1) The studies were done with an intent to compare and generalize—to draw "lessons" rather than to be descriptive.
(2) There was some attempt to discern differences in outcomes, however defined, as a function of organizational rules, incentives, or behavior.
(3) The studies concerned important policy issues.

The case studies selected encompass within-system studies and cross-system studies.[1] Only four are quantitatively oriented (Anderson; Crain; Gross and Herriott; James, Kelly, and Garms) and really seek to test hypotheses in a rigorous way. Table 1 indicates where an explicit identification by city can be made of the school systems studied. Where the studies address approximately the same issue and report enough data, we can directly compare study findings.

The evaluations of performance contracting were also selected on the same grounds.[2] Table 2 indicates the cities where performance contracting was evaluated.

RESEARCH PROBLEM AND METHODS

The research problem in the organizational approach is finding the determinants of innovation and responsiveness. Students' educational outcomes—cognitive achievement measures and the like—are seldom explained in detail. These traditional foci are considered irrelevant, not because the researchers are unconcerned with students' outcomes but because improving such outcomes is only a part (albeit a very important part) of what educational organizations attempt to accomplish. The educational organization is seen as playing a central role among many conflicting groups and individuals—taxpayers, parents, state and local governments. These groups have goals and values that they believe schools should take into account. The problem facing the schools is that the various goals and demands pressed upon them are inconsistent

Table 1

GEOGRAPHICAL COVERAGE OF SCHOOL SYSTEMS—EIGHT CASE STUDIES

	Anderson	Crain	Gittell and Hollander	Gross and Herriott	Havighurst	Leggett	James, Kelly, and Garms	Rogers
Atlanta		x						
Baltimore		x	x				x	
Baton Rouge		x						
Bay City[a]		x						
Boston							x	
Buffalo		x					x	
Chicago			x			x		
Cleveland							x	
Columbus, Ga.		x						
Detroit			x		x		x	
Houston								
Jacksonville, Fla.		x						
Laundale[a]		x						
Miami		x						
Milwaukee							x	
Montgomery		x						
Newark		x						
New Orleans		x						
New York			x					x
Philadelphia			x					
Pittsburgh		x				x		
St. Louis		x	x				x	
San Francisco								
Washington						x	x	
Unidentified	x			x				

and often conflicting. Accordingly, good research in organizational terms finds ways to satisfy a broad range of interests and means for reasonable compromises among goals.

Organizational studies generally use the case study as a research strategy. The researcher examines a school system and attempts to understand why it behaves the way it does. The range of activities involved in the examination is unlimited. Interviews with "key" persons—those who make or influence important decisions—are almost always a part of a case study. The formal decisionmaking apparatus of the organization—the rules and regulations, the procedures, the lines of authority, and so on—is generally the focus of careful investigation. In some cases the researcher is able to "sit in" on decisions, to attend the conferences and meetings where decisions are made. Occasionally the study will include formal empirical analyses.

Case studies are, in essence, *ad hoc.* The researcher may (and should) begin his study with carefully specified objectives and a clear idea of what he must do to achieve those objectives. But there is no way he can anticipate the issues he will encounter once the study begins. Accordingly, case studies normally require considerable flexibility. The researcher constantly has to revise his plans and questions as he accumulates knowledge and understanding of the system he is investigating.

The implication of all this is that the case study approach is neither well defined nor clearly specified. No formal criteria permit an outsider to judge whether any particular case study was done well. Rather, the validity of a case study depends upon the industry, insight, and intellectual integrity of the researcher. By industry we refer to whether the researcher worked hard at his study. How many stones did he leave unturned? Are there likely to have been important data left uncovered? In general one measure of the worth of a case study is the amount of information the researcher was able to obtain. But case studies cannot be judged solely on quantity of data the researcher provides. Beyond this is the question of whether he has been able to combine his data so as to cast light on the issues he addressed. There is a close relationship between the researcher's insight and the "quality" of the data he provides. It would be foolish to assume that any researchers, no matter how diligent, could amass all the information available. Consequently, the researcher must be selective in his examination. And his understanding of the system under investigation guides his selection.

Table 2

GEOGRAPHICAL COVERAGE OF PERFORMANCE CONTRACTING EVALUATIONS

	OEO	Rand
Anchorage	x	
Athens	x	
Bronx	x	
Dallas	x	
Fresno	x	
Gary		x
Gilroy		x
Grand Rapids	x	x
Hammond	x	
Hartford	x	
Jacksonville	x	
Las Vegas	x	
Liberty-Eylau		x
McComb	x	
Norfolk		x
Philadelphia	x	
Portland	x	
Rockland	x	
Seattle	x	
Selmer	x	
Taft	x	
Texarkana		x
Wichita	x	

Finally, there is probably no completely unbiased observer. The researcher filters the information through his preconceptions and beliefs. What he expects to observe has a strong influence on what he actually observes. Accordingly, whether the investigator was open-minded when he conducted his study becomes an issue. In case studies where the data tend to be soft, almost impressionistic, without repeating the case it is impossible to judge whether a researcher wore blinders.

What confidence can we have in these studies? We define "confidence," as before, in terms of the condition that the studies meet criteria for distinguishing good ones from bad ones. Presumably, a good case study should provide an extensive description of behavior so the reader is persuaded that this is "the way it really is." Presumably, too, a good case study should present hypotheses for testing in other contexts, since the hypotheses presented in a given study are drawn from the case. The presentation of hypotheses will have to be conditional, since the analyst will not be able to "control" important variables. In fact, since the case is approached without a particular model in mind, it is an open question which variables to study. This is an important choice not often faced explicitly, for the resources available for case work are limited.[3]

The problem of external validity is as vexing as that of internal validity. A fundamental unresolved dilemma is that it is hard to generalize from small samples, but large samples are costly. Furthermore, as the number of sample points increases, one is forced to aggregate, to trade the rich descriptions for variables that vary across all the samples.

Measuring or defining innovation or flexibility or responsiveness is a major problem. Often it rests on the subjective assessment of the analyst. Other observers may have different definitions.

RESULTS FROM THE CASE STUDIES

The following statements summarize the most important propositions from the eight studies.

Statement 1: There is a positive correlation between size of system and degree of centralization.

Statement 2: Large educational bureaucracies and large numbers of rules *decrease* innovation and adaptation.

Gittell and Hollander (1967, p. 1), for example, argue that extreme school district size is counterproductive in terms of the adequacy of educational programs and the returns to educational expenditures. They feel that sheer physical size introduces such complexities that "staff communication, public expectancy, and unit variability are seriously hampered." Note the lack of emphasis on student achievement. The authors go on to say (p. 2) that achievement tests have little usefulness in comparing fiscal and administrative matters: "Further, the heavily weighted influence of socio-economic factors limits the usefulness of this measure in comparing and evaluating fiscal and administrative operations.... We determined to try an alternative approach that would measure output at the margin, in terms of the innovation in a school district."

Gittell and Hollander go on to claim that the results of their study of six school systems support the finding that "large systems appear to have an absolute rigidity that defies the forces which are so important in shaping the operations of small systems."[4] An important consequence of this finding is that the large urban systems facing extreme changes in their communities and clientele tend to be the least adaptive and, for that matter, are often directly resistant to innovation. They found no effective innovation, in the sense that the innovation has widespread and positive influence on the system, in any of the six systems they examined.

Rogers' (1968) study of the New York City school system arrives at similar conclusions. Over time, as the school system grew in size, it has become progressively more centralized. Central headquarters, he argues, has assumed responsibility for even the most trivial decisions involving such matters as light bulbs, door knobs, and erasers. The result of this increased centralization is to seriously complicate administration, making it increasingly difficult to operate the schools, let alone introduce substantive changes.

Some indirect evidence for Statement 2 is also provided by Rogers (p. 212). "It is in such areas as Harlem, Brownsville, and Bedford-Stuyvesant that the pathologies of the centralized board have become most obvious." The point is that the areas where the traditional ways of doing things seem least effective are precisely the areas where one would most expect to find innovation and adaptation.

Evidence for Statement 1 can also be found by putting together empirical findings on budget processes. James, Kelly, and Garms (1966,

The Organizational Approach

p. 91) found that the size and complexity of the operations of large systems tend to generate a centralized budget process. A substantial part of the control that resides in the budget process passes into the hands of the bureaucracy itself. Moreover, the centralized budget process itself imparts tremendous inertia into the system. "The basic structure of the budget decision in big city school systems is to assume that existing programs will continue and to focus budget analysis upon proposed changes in, or additions to, the existing program."

In his cross-sectional study of schools within a large system, Anderson finds: "In general resistance to innovation increases significantly in large schools."[5] "As size increases so does the impersonal treatment of students and in general the resistance to innovation."[6]

Statement 3: Rigidities in a school system can be partly overcome by an appropriate choice of teachers.

Anderson (1968, p. 163) feels that more experienced teachers tend to be less innovative. His study demonstrates, he claims, that "attempts to personalize instruction as well as interest in new teaching techniques and curricula decrease as the teacher gains experience in the schools." The reason for this behavior is that as teachers gain experience they tend to become more and more doctrinaire. Their treatment of students becomes increasingly impersonal and their adherence to traditional instructional practices tends to become more rigid. Anderson's basic point is that the bureaucratic rigidities of the systems are exacerbated by experienced teachers to the point where the value of teaching experience is offset. An implication of this observation is that new, inexperienced teachers are more willing to innovate and adapt; hence, a leavening of "new blood" can partly counterbalance inertia of a centralized system.

Statement 4: Rigidities in a school system can be partly overcome by an appropriate choice of principals.

A widely held assumption is that principals who provide a high degree of leadership will have schools that are more productive and staffs that enjoy higher morale. The case studies we have reviewed provide considerable support for that assumption. Havighurst (1964, p. 173), for example, argues·

In every type of school certain qualities in the principal appear to be essential to making the school operate effectively. In the inner-city and common-man types, the principal seems to make almost the whole difference between a school that holds teachers and gets a fair amount of teaching done on the one hand, and a school where teachers and pupils are demoralized on the other hand.[7]

Some empirical evidence on this point is provided by Gross and Herriott (1965). They define a quantitative measure of "executive professional leadership" (EPL) and examine the relationships between a principal's EPL score and characteristics of his school. Teachers' morale, their professional performance, and pupils' learning[8] are all positively related to the measure. The implication of these findings, according to Gross and Herriott, is that "to confine the principal to routine administrative tasks would be to eliminate a force conducive to improved teaching and learning" (p. 151). They go on to argue that the findings justify a view of the principal as affecting the learning process through his influence on the staff. Their policy proposal is to identify and implement strategies to enhance the principal's leadership role.

These results argue for the importance of the principal as a leader. Consequently, principals who are "poor" leaders are not likely to provide the sort of environment where innovative ideas will flourish. Conversely, "good" leaders are relatively likely to introduce innovation, even in the face of rigid bureaucracies and teachers who are set in their ways. The "good" principal can overcome the inertia of his staff through his influence on their morale, their outlook, and in general the "style" of the school—the way it goes about its business.

We have enclosed the words "good" and "poor" in quotation marks to indicate that we simply do not have a very clear idea of what makes a "good" (or "poor") administrator. Some of the definitions found in case studies are tautological. Principals are identified as being "good" if they are effective leaders (their staffs have high morale, they successfully innovate, and so on). Obviously, if this is how one defines a "good" principal, it is no surprise to find that "good" principals are effective leaders.

Ideally, we should like to have a set of measures of the "qualities" of principals that could then be correlated with parameters of their performance. Qualities that had a high positive correlation with desirable performance parameters could then be used as indicators of "good" principals. Unfortunately, no such set of qualities exists.[9] As a consequence we cannot legitimately claim that good principals can affect student performance. All we can say is that some principals seem to be able to provide effective leadership, which, *it is assumed but not proven*, will affect student performance. We can say that these are good principals; but that is only applying a label to them.

The point we want to make here is that it is possible for the principal to influence the rate of innovation and adaptation in his school. Consequently, a system can, by an appropriate choice of principals, help to offset the rigidities of the large, centralized bureaucracy.

The principal is not, of course, an independent entity. Just as the principal provides leadership to his staff, the higher administrative levels provide leadership to the principals. The central authorities can support and guide the principals, permitting the "good" principals relatively free rein and helping the relatively "poor" principals overcome their deficiencies. But the centralizing tendency suggested in Statements 1 and 2 more often results in the imposition of constraints and rigid guidelines on the principals. Some principals are able to resist this influence, but the majority become timid and unenterprising. Havighurst (1964, p. 175) describes one such principal: "He operates everything by the book, without realizing that you have to adapt the book to the situation. He's afraid to operate on his own because he's afraid of how it will look downtown if someone questions him." These observations lead to the following:

Corollary to Statement 4: A principal's effectiveness in carrying out change is positively related to the amount of support from higher administrative levels.

Empirical support for this corollary is provided by Gross and Herriott (1965, p. 118) who note: "The stronger the higher administration's approval of a principal's introducing educational change, the greater his EPL."

The observations provided above have a common theme. School systems tend to grow larger over time, and, as a result of this growth, the administration of the system becomes increasingly complex. The growth in complexity, in turn, gives rise to an increasingly powerful central administration. Finally, as the central bureaucracy grows in size and power, the system becomes more and more rigid, increasingly resistant to change, less and less responsive to new ideas and new ways of doing things. How, then, does innovation ever take place?

Statement 5: Innovation in a school system depends upon exogenous shocks to the system.

In reviewing the data, however, it is clear that federal aid has in its short history influenced innovation in all of the cities . . . for political as well as economic reasons, federal funding has pushed school people to innovation (Gittell and Hollander, 1967, p. 22).

Federal funding for the introduction of nonprofessionals and for the expansion of existing programs is clearly of prime importance (Leggett, 1969, p. 181).

It is evident from the survey of community participation that the six city school systems display different degrees of openness and receptivity to such groups. In Detroit the system appears to encourage outside participation and involvement which is not necessarily supportive of the establishment. . . . It is not surprising therefore that Detroit proved to be the most innovative of the school systems studied (Gittell and Hollander, 1967, p. 116).

The implication is clear: As the system becomes increasingly bound up in itself, strong pressures from the outside are required to introduce innovation.

RESULTS FROM PERFORMANCE CONTRACTING STUDIES

The performance contracting experiments were an attempt to relate organizational change and innovation directly to increases in the achievement of disadvantaged students. In one case there was a complete substitution of the traditional organizational forms by a set of new ones.[10] Controlled organizational experimentation is one way around the difficulties we have noted in conducting organizational case studies. Treatment populations, grade levels, and instructional techniques can be combined in such a way that a proper causal inference can be made. As OEO put it in discussing its 18-city experiment:

The OEO's experiment in performance contracting, then, represents the first attempt to submit an educational fad to any sort of controlled scientific evaluation that would have nationwide relevance. The goals of the experiment were straightforward: It would test the capabilities of educational technology firms to improve the reading and math capabilities of underachieving youngsters, in the context of a performance or incentive-based contract.[11]

The Rand approach to the analysis of performance contracting was to consider a "reasonable" set of cases[12] to assess outcomes on a

The Organizational Approach

wider number of dimensions than had OEO. Although student achievement was the main focus, in the Rand studies we find discussion of student and parent responses toward performance contracting as well as those of administrators.

In a social experiment we can pursue only one or two questions at best without raising cost, managerial, or design difficulties, and OEO chose to focus on student achievement. Thus the published OEO reports do not discuss organizational outcomes. Rand looked for changed organizational behavior: "Performance contracting fostered a healthy emphasis on the student and his learning as a measure of the success of programs. But OEO from its experimental viewpoint is properly interested in whether or not students scored better."[13]

The following statement is drawn from both the OEO study and the Rand studies:

Statement 6: Cognitive achievement is not significantly increased by the organizational changes represented by performance contracting.

OEO finds no differences in mean gains between control students and experimental students across all sites.[14] "The single most important question for all concerned with the experiment is: Was performance contracting more successful than traditional classroom methods in improving the reading and math skills of poor children? The answer . . . is: No."[15]

Rand puts this finding somewhat less emphatically: "The performance contracts did not produce dramatic gains on standardized achievement tests, but in most instances gains were respectable."[16]

The mean gain scores Rand reports are larger than those OEO reports, but Rand also states, "Evaluation designs were often haphazard or non-existent." The OEO finding is the more persuasive one, since there is wider variation and more control. Rand does not state the criterion of respectability. Presumably Rand means that since performance contracting modes cost about the same as other remedial programs, performance contracting is at least no worse in inducing cognitive achievement. In any case, respectability is not enough, for Rand concludes that unless future performance contracting programs produce more than respectable gains, they will have to be justified on external benefits, such as curriculum development.

In its analysis of the organizational effects of performance contracting, Rand finds that performance contracting served as a change agent. This provides further support for Statement 5, that innovation comes from exogenous shock. Similarly, Rand finds that people not a permanent part of the school system are freer to implement radical changes in the classroom than are regular school personnel.

EVALUATION PROBLEMS IN PERFORMANCE CONTRACTING

The performance contracting experiments increased the debate over the use of standardized tests in measuring achievement. In this case large amounts of money depended on their validity and reliability.[17] We have already discussed testing problems in Chapter II.

Besides the technical issues, a whole host of issues arose in the organization and administration of the experiments. What is actually done in response to organizational constraints may diverge markedly from *a priori* design. In fact, Rand reviews its performance contracting cases as examples of learning by doing.

> In most districts the need for extensive program changes had not been anticipated nor had the contract provisions and program administration been designed to accommodate such changes.... The developmental nature of performance contracting programs implies that both LEA's (Local Educational Agencies) and LSC's (Learning Systems Contractors) should build flexibility into programs and contracts. It also means that programs that last a single year or less labor under a great handicap because most of the time must be spent on tailoring the system to the school district and its students.[18]

The OEO experiment was designed as a one-year experiment. So the question remains as to what the actual programs were that OEO evaluated. The published OEO documentation gives very little sense of what the early operations were and how well they were implemented.[19]

SUMMARY

Research using the organizational approach has not provided any clear guidance on the structure and organization of school systems that would help schools achieve the multiple goals ascribed to them. In terms of responsiveness to a changing clientele and willingness to innovate, the evidence suggests that many of our school systems may be too large, and willing to change only through external pressures. In cases where there has been organizational change, such as performance contracting demonstrations and experiments, as yet there has been no clear improvement in outcomes, suggesting that the organizational alternatives tried so far may not be drastic enough to create differences in outcomes. Study designs in the organizational approach need to become more rigorous, and questions should be stated more precisely. Research in the organizational approach has perhaps the closest relation to educational finance. Although the choice of processes and resources within the schools is hard to control through financial means, the gross organization of our schools can be. But at the moment we have no clearly superior systems on which to use dollar leverage.

NOTES TO CHAPTER V

1. Anderson (1968); Crain (1968); Gittell and Hollander (1967); Gross and Herriott (1965); Havighurst (1964); James, Kelly, and Garms (1966); Leggett (1969); and Rogers (1968).
2. The performance contracting studies are OEO (1972a and b) and six Rand Corporation studies: Carpenter (1971); Carpenter, Chalfant, and Hall (1971); Carpenter and Hall (1971); Hall and Rapp (1971); Rapp (1971); and Sumner (1971). Carpenter and Hall (1971) is the Summary volume.
3. In this connection, the Rand performance contracting case studies are instructive. They are case studies of nominally controlled organizational experiments. As we examine the particular case, each seems to be evaluated on different criteria, and the derivation of the summary findings is unclear. Because of the flexibility requirement for going into a system, there does not seem to have been an *a priori* evaluation design.
4. They attribute this statement to Austin Swanson.
5. Anderson (1968, p. 146). His word "significantly" means statistically significantly, using a chi-square test on two-way contingency tables.
6. Anderson (1968, p. 157). Note that the criteria concern not achievement but treatment of students and resistance to innovation.

7. Havighurst goes on to note that successful schools have principals who are willing to make independent decisions about their schools. But see Statement 1 on trends toward centralization.
8. This is the only case among our eight that seeks to connect organizational issues directly to student achievement. However, the student achievement measures are based on teacher-observer ratings, not standardized tests.
9. See Chapter IV, under *The Effects of Teachers,* for a discussion of the similar problems involved in trying to identify what makes a "good" teacher.
10. In Gary's Banneker School, Behavioral Research Laboratories had a contract giving them responsibility for the entire curriculum over a three-year period. The contract was canceled six months before its scheduled expiration because of disagreement between the school district and the contractor.
11. OEO (1972a).
12. The Rand selection principle is not entirely clear, but presumably maximum variation was sought. The selection principle does not clearly lead to the particular case chosen. "The sample was chosen to provide a diverse group of school districts and programs. Four geographic regions are represented: Southeast, North Central, South Central, and Far West. . . . The cities also vary widely in size of the total population and of the enrollment in public schools. Both urban and rural areas are represented as are black and Spanish-surname minority groups as well as whites. . . . Each of the programs except for the one in Gilroy involved a relatively large number of students. . . . Half the contracts were let by competitive bid and half by sole source, no solicitation. (Carpenter and Hall, 1971, p. 2.)
13. Carpenter and Hall (1971).
14. See OEO (1972a), Table III, p. 18 and the following discussion.
15. OEO (1972a), p. 17.
16. Carpenter and Hall (1971).
17. For a discussion of the OEO position, see J.S. Schiller and E.P. Murdoch, "Implementations of Using Standardized Tests in Performance Contracting," in OEO (1972b).
18. Carpenter and Hall (1971), p. 3.
19. Standards of documentation for social experiments need more attention. The OEO reports do not represent a coherent system-

atic account of the experiment. If experiments provide lessons learned to be transmitted to others, then the reporting designs deserve more attention and resources than they apparently get. The Rand reports are more comprehensive and better designed, but the processes by which conclusions are reached are ill-defined.

VI. EVALUATION OF BROAD EDUCATIONAL INTERVENTIONS

In Chapters III and IV we discussed the effectiveness of well-specified educational treatments and experiments that were for the most part designed to measure the influence of specific program characteristics such as teaching strategies and curricula. In this chapter we attempt to analyze the effectiveness of broader educational interventions much more directly related to large issues of social policy. These are programs in which treatments are devoted to "groups of children as a whole in diverse programs taken as a whole" (Stearns, 1971a, p. 6). Although there is no reason why such interventions need to be limited to specific types of children, almost all broad intervention programs have been directed toward overcoming the effects of the environment of poverty. The most obvious examples are Head Start and Title I of the Elementary and Secondary Education Act (ESEA) of 1965. There have been a number of smaller, more experimental studies of broad educational intervention programs as well.

In such interventions the resources devoted to each child are normally increased substantially. This can take the form of smaller class sizes, additional instructional personnel (often specialists or paraprofessionals), more individualized instruction, or more intensive use of audio-visual equipment. Usually, the emphasis has been on achieving program goals and not upon the needs of careful research and evaluation. Because of this, research designs are often much less precise than those discussed in the chapter on the process approach. Since any number of educational inputs are changed at the same time, it is

Evaluation of Broad Educational Interventions 117

difficult to tell precisely which program features are responsible even when there is demonstrated success. Control group perfection has naturally been sacrificed to the more pragmatic goal of educating the children who need it most. The research materials available concerning such broad programs of educational intervention are therefore considerably inferior to those used in the process discussion above. Consequently, these evaluations, discussed in the first two sections, are subject to a number of analytical problems. Interventions designed basically for research are treated in the third section. These studies are much more analytically solid, but they suffer sample size problems in that few individuals are included in the typical study. The fourth section deals with attempts to identify the components of "successful" interventions. We conclude with a discussion of the costs of compensatory education.

FINDINGS FROM LARGE-SCALE EVALUATIONS

Several large surveys have been made of federally funded national intervention programs and one large project conducted by the New York City School System. These programs are so well known that they do not require extensive description. The largest program, funded at more than one billion dollars annually, is ESEA Title I. Congress did not stipulate how the funds were to be spent beyond stating that they were to be used for compensatory education of children from culturally disadvantaged environments and that projects must be approved by an appropriate state education agency. Most Title I instruction has been in the elementary grades; a few high school and preschool programs have been conducted.

The other national program, Head Start, is completely a preschool compensatory education program. It has emphasized general child development and not the teaching of skills per se. Most Head Start Programs have been "permissive-enrichment" programs, characterized by their "whole-child-orientation, their strategy of watching and waiting, and the resultant low degree of structure" (Bissell, 1970, p.13). The Head Start program is also large; an average of more than 12,000 centers annually have been in operation over the past five years.

Since early in 1968 there has been a second phase of the Head Start program, termed "Follow Through." In this program Head Start children are given additional instruction in kindergarten and first grade.

The New York City Schools' Higher Horizons program was the first major effort toward compensatory education, beginning in the 1959 school year. Each of 52 elementary and 13 high schools was assigned an additional allotment of teachers who helped to train other teachers, improve student performance in reading and arithmetic, or perform other tasks at the discretion of the building principal. The funding level was about $60 per pupil. During the first three years the program structure was left primarily to the option of individual principals, after which management was centralized with most schools having an allotment of three teachers, two for academic improvement and one for cultural enrichment.

The findings from numerous surveys of these programs (a majority of which are for Title I) are that, with the possible exception of the Follow Through program, there is very little convincing evidence leading one to believe that the resources invested have made much difference in the progress of children from disadvantaged environments.

Another type of broad educational intervention, children's educational television, often bypasses the formal schooling system. In at least one instance, namely *Sesame Street,* produced by Children's Television Workshop, the audience of preschool children registered significant cognitive gains, varying in amount according to the frequency of viewing and socioeconomic status of families. Another Children's Television Workshop program, introduced in late 1971, *The Electric Company,* is aimed more specifically at slow readers of school age (7-10), and includes school-based as well as media-based materials. Evaluation evidence of *The Electric Company* and *Sesame Street* effectiveness is summarized by Yin (1973).

ESEA Title I

The most pessimistic findings come from the Title I surveys. We have carefully examined the reports commissioned by the U.S. Office of Education for the last three fiscal years (including a draft report by Gordon for 1971) and in addition have read several papers written by independent scholars. We do not attempt to summarize the results of each of these studies separately because they are all quite consistent in their findings. The following quotations are representative:

> An analysis of the reading achievement scores of 155,000 participants of 189 Title I projects during the school year ending in June 1967 indicates that a child who participated in a Title I project had only a 19 percent

Evaluation of Broad Educational Interventions 119

chance of a significant achievement gain, a 13 percent chance of a significant achievement loss, and a 68 percent chance of no change at all. This sample of observations is unrepresentative of Title I projects. It is, more likely, representative of projects in which there was a higher than average investment in resources. Therefore, more significant achievement gains should be found here than in the more representative sample of Title I projects (Piccariello, no date, p. 1).

For participating and non-participating pupils, the rate of progress in reading skills kept pace with their historical rate of progress. . . . Compensatory reading programs did not seem to overcome the reading deficiencies that stem from poverty (U.S. Office of Education, 1970, pp. 126 and 127).

It will be noted in the following reports of analyses that all outcome data indicated a distinctly higher than average reading gain for non-participants than for participants (Glass *et al., Report for Fiscal Year 1969*, 1970, p. 6.3).

Participants in the compensatory programs continued to show declines in average yearly achievement in comparison to non-participants who included advantaged and non-advantaged pupils. . . . It was not possible from these data to determine whether participants in compensatory programs showed a reduced decline in average yearly achievement (Gordon, 1971, p. 23).

These findings are all qualified heavily in subsequent discussion by the study authors, who cite problems we discuss below. Nevertheless, the fact remains, qualified or not, all the findings themselves are consistently negative.

Head Start

There have been two national surveys of Head Start and a third is in progress. The first was an inquiry early in the program (Wolff and Stein, 1967). It showed some positive effects of the Head Start program which, however, disappeared in the first grade. The report indicated that Head Start children who went on to kindergarten or first grades composed mostly of other Head Start children did better than those who had fewer Head Start children in their classes.

The other survey of Head Start is much better known. It is the study commissioned by the Office of Economic Opportunity in 1968 and known as the Westinghouse/Ohio University Report (Cicirelli *et al.*, 1969) Since the Westinghouse Report was more recent and had a much more comprehensive research design, we will discuss its findings in somewhat more detail. They are slightly more optimistic than those just quoted for title I, although the overall prognosis is still rather bleak.

The Westinghouse project picked some 104 Head Start centers (out of more than 12,000 centers throughout the nation) at random, and all children eligible to enter each center were identified. From these children were chosen groups of eight who attended Head Start and a carefully matched comparison group of children who did not. The children in both groups were extensively tested during the 1968-69 school year. Since the program began in the 1965 school year, it was possible to compare program and non-program children in grades one, two, and three.

The study found that there were small but significant differences in favor of full-year (but not summer) Head Start children at the beginning of grade one on the Metropolitan Readiness Test (a generalized measure of learning readiness). But Head Start children at the beginning of grade two from either summer or full-year programs did not score significantly higher than the controls on the Stanford Achievement Test. There were no differences found in children's self-concept or teacher ratings of classroom behavior between the Head Start children and the control children. When children from full-year programs were stratified by region and race it was found that the centers in the Southeastern region, in poorer cities, and of mainly black composition were more successful than the others.[1]

A third broad evaluation of Head Start, conducted by the Huron Institute, analyzes a planned variation program similar to that for Follow Through discussed below. Eight variations of instructional strategies were employed and the performance of experimental and control children in each compared. Results from the first and pilot year of the study showed statistically significant gains for Head Start children over controls. Thus the preliminary results look hopeful, although fairly serious evaluation design problems preclude our placing great faith in them at the present stage of the analysis.[2]

Follow Through

Follow Through is a program for disadvantaged children from kindergarten through third grade who had previously been enrolled in Head Start or similar programs. Programs were developed by a group of sponsors who had been active in compensatory education. Although

Evaluation of Broad Educational Interventions 121

there is some built-in variation among sponsors, all programs were intended to develop the academic abilities of the children through reduced class size, small group and individualized instruction, parent involvement, use of teacher aides and classroom volunteers, and so on. All programs also sought to increase the self-esteem and motivation of the project children.

The Follow Through program was evaluated by the Stanford Research Institute (1971a). Four groups of Follow Through and non-Follow Through children were compared where degree of poverty was stratified. One group was at the kindergarten level, two in first grade (one had been to kindergarten and one had not), and one in grade two. All four Follow Through groups gained more than their counterparts not in Follow Through, although in only two (kindergarten, and first grade with no kindergarten) were the differences significant. The Follow Through children entering in grade one began the year substantially behind their counterparts, which means that the additional gain involved may have been in part due to the "regression to the mean" phenomenon.[3] There is no indication in the report that an adjustment was made for this.

Higher Horizons

Finally, there is some slight evidence of favorable results in the Higher Horizons program. There were favorable outcomes for program children on one sixth grade IQ test, on a sixth grade arithmetic test, and for grade six reading for below norm pupils. A majority of the Higher Horizons findings were "no difference," however (Wrightstone *et al.*, 1964).

Evaluation of the Evaluations

If we were to base our total assessment of the value of compensatory education programs upon the findings of the surveys just discussed, we could undoubtedly summarize it by the first line in Jensen's now famous paper on the heritability of native ability: "Compensatory education has been tried and it has apparently failed" (Jensen, 1969). But before so concluding, we should have first been assured that the survey evaluations used in arriving at such a verdict were themselves an accurate description of the real world, and no such assurance is possible, even with a considerable stretch of the imagination. Some of the more important reasons follow. It should be emphasized that these are in addition to the problems associated with evaluating educational outcomes with standardized cognitive tests discussed in Chapter II.

The analyses on which these evaluations are based did not assign treatment and non-treatment children on a random basis. Perhaps the only foolproof evaluation strategy involves comparing two groups of children who are identically matched and randomly assigned. But these programs were meant by their originators to be applied to the *most* disadvantaged children. Both political pressures and the decisions of conscientious educators have almost without exception combined to insure that the children who are placed in treatment groups are the most disadvantaged. This being so, the children left to be placed in comparison groups are most likely of greater ability and from better environments than the treatment children.[4]

The problem would appear to be somewhat less serious in the Westinghouse evaluation of Head Start, in which all children who were eligible for the program were identified and then those who had been in the program were carefully "matched" with those who had not. But the matching was done *ex post* and on the basis of race, sex, and socioeconomic background (the last necessarily somewhat crudely) and *not* on the basis of ability. Also, as Stearns points out, the Westinghouse Study tested different cohorts of children in grades one, two, and three, and an equally appropriate interpretation of what was revealed was that "during the years 1965 and 1966, when Head Start was just getting organized, the programs were not as effective in changing children's performance as in the 1967 and 1968 programs" (Stearns, 1971a, p. 92).

In the Title I surveys the selection of the projects was quite obviously not representative of the country as a whole. The bias in project selection is heavily in favor of large and urban core-city school districts because larger districts normally have somewhat more sophisticated evaluation staffs. Many of these large districts are just the ones where the problems are most intractable. None of these surveys is reasonably representative of national experience with Title I.

On the other hand, we must remember Piccariello's point, cited above, that projects in which there were higher than average investments in resources are more likely to be included. Since these are the projects in which the greatest gains are to be expected, there is also some built-in positive bias to these national surveys.

Evaluation of Broad Educational Interventions 123

Even when treatment and control groups are selected reasonably well, spill-over or "radiation" effects going from project to non-project children may contaminate the evaluation. It is seldom possible for program children to be completely quarantined from non-program children. The fact that something new and novel is being done in the school building can be infectious or it may prompt the regular classroom teachers to work harder to keep their children from being shown up.

In addition to the evaluation difficulties previously mentioned, the analysis of compensatory education programs leaves something to be desired. As pointed out by Gordon (1971, p. 4):

> One often finds a low level of expertise and inadequately developed methods. The best educational research scientists often choose to work with basic problems in child development, learning, linguistics, etc., rather than evaluative research.

After carefully analyzing over three hundred evaluation reports for his study of successful projects, Wargo (1971, p. 27) concludes:

> One begins to wonder whether the instructional components associated with compensatory education programs are inadequate or whether the fault lies in the evaluation procedures used to determine their effectiveness.

Despite the evaluation difficulties just discussed, we hesitate to dismiss the findings of the studies altogether. At the very least they have a certain face validity demonstrating that most broadly funded compensatory education programs in the schools are not accomplishing large gains in the performance of target children—at least on the average. This is enough of a conclusion to cause concern even if it were true that compensatory education did offer some beneficial effect.

Sesame Street

In the spring of 1968, Children's Television Workshop, a non-profit agency funded by private foundations and government agencies, began planning daily educational television programs aimed at preschool children (ages 3-5), in particular at disadvantaged children. (Detailed discussions of how the program was developed can be found in Ball and Bogatz, 1970; and Bretz, 1972.) The program, *Sesame Street*, began broadcasting in November 1969. It is nationally distributed mostly through local educational stations and attracts an average annual audience in the "tens of millions" (Ball and Bogatz, 1971, p. 1). Comprehensive evaluations of the program's first two years

(1969-70 and 1970-71) were conducted by Educational Testing Service (Ball and Bogatz, 1970, 1971) and have been discussed by Yin (1973). The testing systems used by Ball and Bogatz included items that *Sesame Street* attempted to teach—recognition of body parts and function; knowledge of letters and sounds; recognition of forms; recognition and use of numbers; understanding of relationships of size, amount, and position; sorting ability; and ability to classify.

The first year's evaluation included pre- and post-testing of 943 children at five locations—Boston, suburban Philadelphia, Durham, Phoenix, and northeastern rural California. The findings were that *Sesame Street* viewers made significant gains in most of the goal areas listed above, compared with non-viewers. The amount of gain was closely correlated with frequency of viewing, which was the major explanatory factor in gain scores. Three-year-old children made the largest relative gains in the 203-item test, with four- and five-year-olds showing progressively smaller gains.

Middle-class children as a whole made larger gains than children from low-income families as a whole, apparently because middle-class children tended to watch the show more. Disadvantaged children who were frequent viewers made as good gain scores as middle-class children who watched frequently.

The second year's evaluation (1970-71) analyzed program effectiveness for three groups: (a) a new study of 283 children from disadvantaged backgrounds in Winston-Salem and Los Angeles who had not viewed *Sesame Street* in 1969-70, including (b) 66 Spanish-background children from Los Angeles; and (c) a follow-up study of 283 disadvantaged children in Boston, Durham, and Phoenix who *had* been sampled in the first year's evaluation.

The new study, with 29 goal areas, indicated significant gains for viewers in 13 areas, equivocal results in 10 areas, and no significant effect in six areas. In general, gains were most impressive in basic knowledge and skills and less impressive in more complex cognitive areas. The study shows, as in the first-year evaluation, that frequency of viewing was an important determinant of gains, as was encouragement of viewing in the home. In the new study, there was some evidence that children with more disadvantaged backgrounds tend to make relatively greater gains.

A subgroup of the new study addressed by the 1971 Educational Testing Service (ETS) study was Spanish-background children. The

1970 study indicated that Spanish-background viewers made the largest gains, but the 1971 evidence, based on a small sample of Los Angeles children, failed to confirm the 1970 results.

The third group included 283 disadvantaged children from the 1970 sample who were watching *Sesame Street* at home for the second year. The study showed that children who watched for a second year performed better on new and complex goals than children of the same age cohort who watched for only one year. For old and simple goals, there was little difference between those who viewed for one year and those who viewed both years, presumably because these goals were easy enough to learn well at the end of one year.

The second-year study also investigated the effect of *Sesame Street* viewing on children's attitude toward school, in light of suggestions that children who viewed *Sesame Street* during preschool might be bored by school. No evidence was found to support this hypothesis, and there was some evidence of positive correlation between previous viewing and teachers' impressions of children's attitude toward school.

The generally favorable results reported in the *Sesame Street* evaluation do *not* indicate that television is a better teacher than the schools. The tests devised by ETS were criterion-referenced, designed specifically to find out whether children made progress toward specified instructional goals. These results cannot legitimately be compared to the norm-referenced tests used to evaluate Title I and other large-scale compensatory programs; nor, as its critics point out, did *Sesame Street* try to develop a broad educational program, comparable to a good nursery school. On the positive side, the results do indicate that television is an effective instructional medium for preschool children, within the limits of the medium. It is not yet clear how much these positive results carry over into the viewers' school performance—the most that can be said is that the influence of *Sesame Street* to date on school performance is clearly not negative. On the other hand, a major original aim of *Sesame Street*, to decrease the relative disadvantage of poor children at preschool age, has not so far been met. On the average, the middle-class audience for *Sesame Street*, whose viewing habits are more regular, clearly maintains its relative cognitive advantage over disadvantaged viewers, if only for that reason.

FINDINGS FROM SMALL-SCALE EVALUATIONS

There are three smaller studies of the overall effects of Title I projects. One is a study by Kiesling (1971a) of a sample of 42 California projects that used the Stanford Reading Test. He found average gain in grade-equivalent scores to be about halfway between the national norm and the rate of progress many educators feel is "normal" for Title I children.[5] Kiesling's sample was picked randomly but was subject to the restriction that the district used the Stanford Test. It is uncertain what bias this restriction may have caused in the findings.

Another careful study was done by TEMPO (General Electric Company) of compensatory education programs for 132 schools in 11 school districts (Mosbaek et al., 1968). TEMPO found that all the children who were in the programs for the 1966-67 school year averaged only one-half month's less achievement gain per year than the national average for all children. This represents a higher rate of progress than previous rates of gain for children in the program.

Wargo et al. (1971) identified some clearly successful compensatory education programs after an exhaustive survey. Out of more than 1,200 evaluation reports for screening, 422 candidate programs were identified and 326 of these answered a written query for additional information. An in-depth analysis was made of these 326 evaluations and in the end only 10 were chosen. The reasons for rejection of the other 316 programs are set forth in detail in Table 3.

Sixty-eight projects were rejected because they did not show results that were statistically or educationally significant. Only 10 projects showed significant gains. This implies, at worst, that there were 6.8 times more failures than successes in well-evaluated programs. Even if we assume that one-quarter of the failures might have been eliminated on other grounds, the failure/success rate would still be five to one. This is far from encouraging, although it should be noted that the restrictions imposed by Wargo and associates were rather stringent with respect to statistical and educational significance. The only projects chosen were those with 30 or more pupils and whose pupils gained at least as fast as the national norm. Hence, many studies showing gains in the neighborhood of those found by Kiesling and TEMPO would have been discarded.

Table 3

FREQUENCY OF PROGRAM REJECTION BY REJECTION REASON, EXEMPLARY COMPENSATORY EDUCATION STUDY BY WARGO et al.

Rejection Reason	Rejection Frequency	Percent
General Information		
1. Unavailable	16	5.1
2. Incomplete	36	11.4
3. Outside scope	15	4.8
	67	21.3
Methodology		
1. Unclear or incomplete	15	4.8
2. Sample	38	12.0
3. Improper comparison or norms	12	3.8
4. Inadequate measures of cognitive benefit	60	19.0
5. Inadequate treatment	8	2.5
	133	42.1
Evaluation		
1. Unclear or incomplete	22	7.0
2. Improper design	20	6.3
3. Pre-treatment reference inadequate	3	1.0
4. Statistics[a]	3	1.0
5. Statistical significance[b]	42	13.3
6. Educational significance[c]	26	8.2
	116	36.8
Total Rejected	316	
Total Reviewed	326	

[a]Improper selection, use, or interpretation of statistical tests.
[b]Gains or differences favoring the program are unreliable; that is, they could occur by chance more than five times in 100 replications.
[c]Achievement test gains that are less than expected in average children during a comparable period of time or, if norms available, gains not significantly greater than those of a comparable control group.
Source: Wargo et al. (1971), pp. 16, 17, 26.

INTERVENTIONS DESIGNED BASICALLY FOR RESEARCH

There are a number of broad educational intervention studies of high quality designed in large part for research purposes. Because of their good evaluation designs their findings are probably quite trustworthy. It would not be possible to describe all of these studies, even only the best ones, in great detail. We briefly outline five examples we consider instructive. They were not picked on the basis of the amount of educational gains exhibited, although we are not sure they are a random representation either.[6] These and many other examples provide an impressive amount of evidence that educational interventions can yield substantial results. It must be remembered, however, that few such programs have been replicated. We therefore have no firm assurance that any of them would be successful if implemented on a large scale. What such interventions show is that an intervention *can* work. It does not mean that any particular intervention will work or is even likely to work.

Stanford University: Computer Assisted Instruction

One of the most interesting sets of experiments in recent years has been the Computer Assisted Instruction (CAI) based at Stanford University. Jamison *et al.* (1971) report on experiments for more than 200 elementary grade children situated in California and rural Mississippi, whose regular classroom instruction was supplemented daily with about 10 minutes of drill in arithmetic and reading skills. The arithmetic curriculum is arranged sequentially in concept blocks composed of a pre-test, five drills, and a post-test. The reading curriculum is based on phonics and is divided into seven content areas. Pupils sit at a console and answer questions that are sequentially more difficult. If the pupil misses an item, the program takes him back for the appropriate review.

The effect of the instruction was quite pronounced in both reading and arithmetic. Differences were significant in all six grades in the Mississippi study. In California the CAI children outperformed the controls in three of six grades; but the overall average gain of the CAI subjects was only slightly more than the controls.

Gordon: Early Child Stimulation Through Parent Education

Gordon (1971) evaluated a home training project for poverty mothers. The object of the program was to accelerate infant learning patterns and to teach disadvantaged mothers how to continue to be effective in teaching their children in the home. The treatment was composed entirely of home visits by paraprofessional "parent educators," averaging about 30 visits per year, in which the instruction was aimed at the mothers rather than directly toward the infants.

The children were all born at one hospital in a six-month period and were randomly assigned to groups before the mothers were contacted. At the end of 12 months, experimental children exceeded the controls in performance of 23 out of 30 tasks in the learning series used. Eight of the differences were statistically significant. Three of the tasks had not yet been reached by the parent educators, which would seem to indicate that mothers were successfully generalizing their instruction into areas not specifically covered. On the Griffiths Mental Development Scale, results in four of six subject areas were significantly in favor of the experimental children, and the effect on the other two subjects was positive as well. At the end of the second study year the children whose mothers had both years of instruction were best, those with one year starting on the first birthday next, those from the third month to the first birthday next, and controls last. All differences were significant except that between the last two groups.

Karnes: Ameliorative Preschool

Karnes (1969b) evaluated a program for economically disadvantaged children in Champaign-Urbana, Illinois. The program concentrated on language development and had class sizes of 15 (five each from low, middle, and high IQ groups with the highest in the low 90s), which met three 20-minute periods daily for instruction in mathematics concepts, language development and reading readiness, and science-social studies. Most teaching took place in small cubicles containing materials appropriate to the three content areas.

Teachers adjusted their teaching according to pupil performance on the Illinois Test of Psycholinguistic Abilities. Language development was continually emphasized, and the teaching strategy centered on verbalization in conjunction with concrete materials. Pupils in the program gained about twice as many points on the Stanford-Binet over the two-year period as a control group. Pupils in all three IQ groups showed gains, unlike those in many studies where only higher IQ disadvantaged children show gains.

DiLorenzo: Pre-Kindergarten Programs in New York State

In this study of pre-kindergarten programs in eight school districts in New York State (DiLorenzo, 1969), project staff assigned experimental and control groups completely at random in all eight participating districts. Goals in all were concentrated on language development, self-concept, and physical growth. All children were from families of lower socioeconomic status according to the Warner Scale. Each district had one 150-minute class daily (with one exception—a four- rather than five-day week). Teams of observers working in pairs made extensive observations concerning the teachers in each district. The districts had programs with differing amounts of structure, but a majority of the districts organized the children's activities externally to at least a moderate degree.

The overall effect of all programs was to make a slight but significant difference on the Stanford-Binet. Language development on both the Peabody Picture Vocabulary Test and the Illinois Test of Psychological Abilities was significantly better in favor of experimental groups. Despite these gains, however, the disadvantaged children narrowed the gap between themselves and higher-SES control children by only a small (though statistically significant) amount on the Binet and Peabody tests.

Project Conquest, East St. Louis, Illinois

In the Project Conquest reading remediation programs, children who have the potential to read at their grade level but who are more than one year behind the norm are selected to receive four 15-minute periods of instruction in reading rooms or two 45-minute periods in reading clinics weekly. The instruction is individualized, with considerable problem diagnosis. Teachers are trained specialists and teacher-pupil ratio is usually one to six. There is also a program of extensive in-service training for classroom teachers in techniques of remedial reading training.

During the 1969-70 school year, 87 elementary school pupils in the reading rooms gained about 1.3 months per month of instruction on the Gates Primary Reading Test and 268 children of the clinics gained about 1.4 months per month of instruction (Wargo, 1971).

LONGITUDINAL ANALYSIS

The programs described just above are all interventions in which there was at least some treatment during the same year as the testing. Such outcomes, even though impressive, do not answer the most important questions concerning broad educational interventions, which are concerned with longer term effects. Does a year or two of educational intervention, even if highly successful, have effects that are still visible three or four or more years later? In general, if program children do not have their intervention education constantly reinforced, will it last?

We might be justified in considering the results of the Westinghouse study as being longitudinal, since it considered Head Start children one, two, and three years after they were in the program. As there were no significant differences between Head Start and non-Head Start children in first and second grades, it would appear that any gains had faded out. However, as Stearns (1971a) points out, since the same children were not retested, the result could be explained by earlier cohorts having poorer programs.

Intelligence Test Findings

One of the most interesting longitudinal studies is that by Gray and Klaus (1970) of a group of 88 black children born in 1958 living in the Upper South. The children were divided into two experimental groups and one control group, all of whom lived in the same ghetto-like community of 25,000; a second control group, 27 children, was drawn from residents of a similar community 65 miles away. The first experimental group (T^1) attended a 10-week preschool program during each of three summers beginning in the summer of 1962 and received weekly visits from a specifically trained home visitor for three years. The second group (T^2) had the same treatment except that it began a year later and lasted only two years. The local (T^3) and distal (T^4) control groups received all of the tests but no intervention treatment.

After the program ended, all four groups were retested each year through the seventh year of the program, which was 3-1/2 years after the last home visitor contacts. The pupil populations were extremely stable over the whole time period, which meant that attrition was a minor problem. Over the treatment period the T^1 group gained 10.5 points in the Stanford-Binet and the T^2 group (two-year treatment period) 4.9 points. The control groups gained 6.0 points and 2.1 points respectively, and their gains are completely explained by the effect of beginning school in the first grade. After treatment ended the gains began to fade away, and the two treatment groups averaged a one-point loss on the Stanford-Binet for the entire six-year period. The local control group also lost about one point, but the distal control group lost nine points over the period. The difference between the two control groups has been widely interpreted as showing that diffusion effects were important between the experimental groups and the local control group. If the nine-point loss for the distal control group is taken as the benchmark for children with no treatment, then the overall effect of the intervention is +8 points on the Stanford-Binet over the six-year period.

The project tested for diffusion effects further by testing younger siblings of the four groups of children. Treatment siblings were found to be superior to control siblings; T^1 siblings to T^2 siblings, and T^3 siblings superior to T^4 siblings. Most of the variance in the results was found to be due to the younger siblings closer in age to the target children.

Stearns (1971a) examined the four longitudinal studies in which IQ changes were greatest in the preschool period. These include the Gray and Klaus and Karnes studies described above, the highly structured Ypsilanti Perry Preschool Project (Weikart, 1971a), and a study of a diagnostic curriculum (structured-cognitive) for a group of Appalachian children (Hodges, McCandless, and Spicker, 1971). Stearns has added the results of unpublished material to both the Karnes and the Hodges *et al.* results. Stearns' results are presented graphically in Figure 7. They represent the best findings we have on the longitudinal results of educational interventions.[7]

The results for all four studies are quite consistent. After large initial gains there is slow fading. The one exception consists of the experimental children in Weikart's study, who began to pick up again in the third grade. In all four studies control groups are closing the distance between themselves and the treatment groups one to three years after the end of treatment.

Figure 7

Longitudinal results of experimental preschool intervention on Stanford-Binet intelligence scale

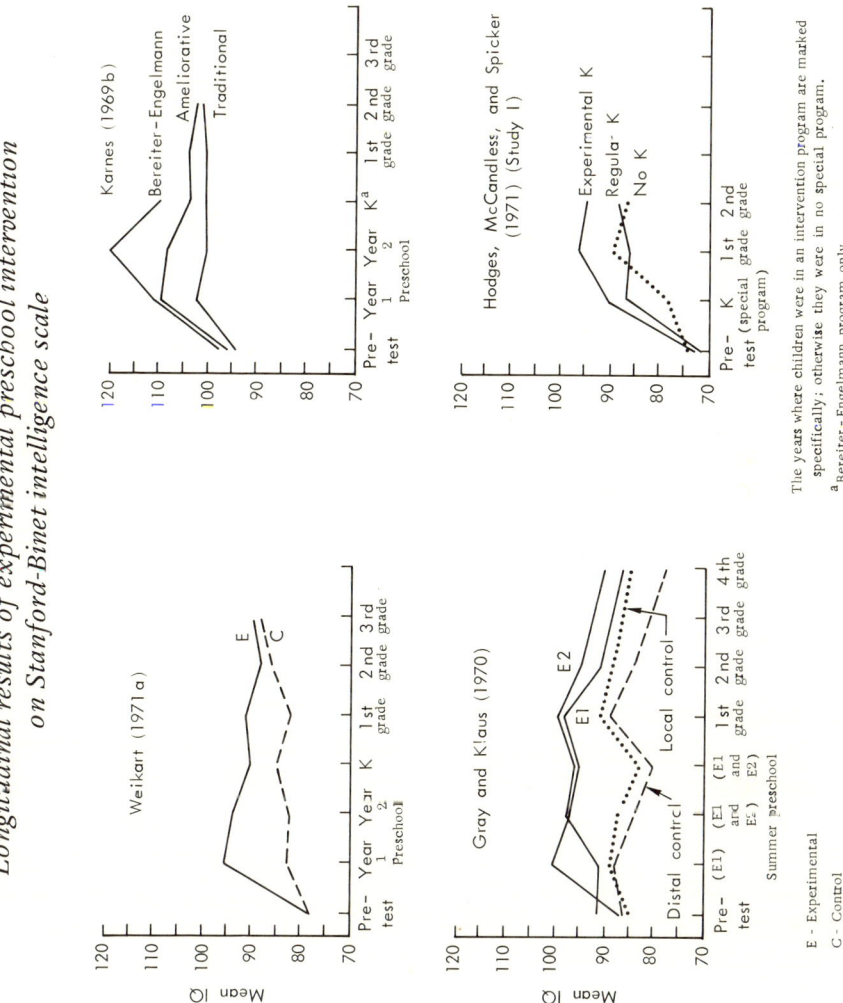

Although children in experimental groups tend to lose their initial gains over time, it is important to note that in none of these four studies do the non-program children *completely* close the gap between themselves and the program children. In addition, if the Gray-Klaus findings with respect to diffusion effects are correct (if the proper benchmark for "no treatment" in the Gray-Klaus results shown in Figure 7 is the distal control group result), then the positive effects of the educational interventions would be even greater. The important point to remember in interpreting these findings is that, even though the children lost their original gains in IQ score over a two- or three-year period after treatment, if they had not had treatment they might have slipped to a level *below* their starting point. The evidence shows that educational interventions can work and still make some difference some three or four years after treatment ends. The amount of difference we can conclude remains after that period of time depends on the extent of the diffusion effects. If they are as great as suggested by the Gray and Klaus work, then the effects are reasonably large; otherwise they are quite small. Until the Gray and Klaus findings are replicated we probably ought not accept them too literally, but there are at least some grounds here for optimism concerning the effect of educational interventions. This is more likely because the evaluation work in the Gray and Karnes study seems to have been of very high quality.

Achievement Test Findings

According to Stearns (1971a, b), for disadvantaged children the maintenance of gains is less pronounced in achievement tests than in intelligence tests. DiLorenzo presented achievement results on the Upper Primary Reading battery for one group of children who had scored much higher at the end of preschool than had their controls. The difference still existed in first grade but was not large, and by the end of second grade the difference had vanished.

Gray and Klaus found that their experimental children's large first-grade superiority over the controls on the Peabody Picture Vocabulary Test had mostly vanished by the end of fourth grade, although the distal control group at that time was doing significantly poorer. In the Hodges, McCandless, Spicker study original better performance mostly faded away in first and second grades.

Evaluation of Broad Educational Interventions 135

There were more stable gains in both the Perry Preschool and the Karnes Ameliorative Preschool projects. In the Perry Preschool project there was a highly significant difference in favor of program children after three years (at the end of third grade) on the California Achievement Test; but this result depended on exceptionally good performances of five children with the other experimental children doing little better than the controls. However, Weikart's most recent report (Weikart, 1971b) also showed significant differences for children in grade three. Karnes' Ameliorative Preschoolers were performing very close to the norm on the California Reading Test at the end of the third grade. Karnes' subjects had somewhat higher beginning IQ scores (mid-90s) than most of the groups we have been discussing.

Summary of Longitudinal Findings

For those who may have entertained high hopes about the effects of educational interventions the findings evaluated here are disappointing. After intervention ends, program children do not continue gaining nor do they maintain much of the gain that they accomplished in the treatment period. The preschool effects in IQ seem to hold up better than those for achievement tests.

The Gray and Klaus study is especially interesting. Treatment levels were not massive (cost levels per child were only slightly above $300, see below). As Gary and Klaus (1970, p. 920) state:

> Perhaps the remarkable thing is that with the relatively small amount of impact over time differences should still be significant. After all, the child experienced only five mornings of school a week for 10 weeks for two or three summers, plus weekly home visits during the other 9 months for 2 or 3 years. This suggests that the impact was not lost. It was not sufficient, however, to offset the massive effects of a low-income home in which the child had lived since birth onward.

PROGRAM CHARACTERISTICS ASSOCIATED WITH SUCCESS

This section is concerned primarily with broad educational interventions, which restricts our efforts to analyze the effects of specific treatment characteristics in detail. Even this broad survey allows us to identify interesting differences in types of interventions.

Bissell has constructed a very useful typology of educational ...d primarily on the amount of program "structure," or ...of external organization and sequencing of children's experiences" (Bissell, 1970, p. 11). Her concept of structure also includes the degree to which objectives are organized hierarchically and the degree to which the role of the teachers is directive or non-directive. Programs that are not structured are designated as "permissive." Using the structure concept and also the degree to which interventions are devoted to purely cognitive goals, Bissell constructed a five-fold typology as follows (Bissell, 1970, pp. 11-13):

- *Permissive Enrichment* programs, which have "multiple objectives oriented toward the development of the 'whole child' and, among specific objectives, having heaviest emphasis on promoting psycho-social growth. The relatively unplanned strategy of these programs involves letting children's needs determine the activities of the pre-school—a strategy which provides only minimum structure to children's experiences." *Example:* Most Head Start Programs.

- *Structured Enrichment* programs, which also have a "heavy specific emphasis on language development. The strategy of these programs centers around the teacher's capitalizing on informal experiences for learning, thereby providing a moderate degree of structure to children's experiences." *Example:* "Traditional" preschool programs for disadvantaged children.

- *Structured Cognitive* programs, which have "objectives oriented towards the development of learning processes and relatively heavy specific emphasis on language growth. The strategies of these programs revolve around the teacher's directing activities in which the children participate, sometimes in prescribed ways and sometimes flexibly. The programs in this category range from those providing a moderate degree of structure to those providing a high degree of structure to children's experiences." *Example:* Karnes' Ameliorative Preschool.

- *Structured Informational* programs, which have "objectives oriented towards teaching specific information—in particular, language patterns. The strategy of these programs involves the teacher's directing activities and children participating in

Evaluation of Broad Educational Interventions 137

them in prescribed ways. The resultant structure in the children's experience is extremely high." *Example:* Bereiter-Engelmann Programs.

- *Structured Environment* programs, which have "objectives oriented towards the development of learning processes. Some of these programs have a heavy specific emphasis on language development, while others—traditional Montessori programs—do not. The strategy in these programs is in the form of self-instructing with classroom materials and the teacher's mediation of child-material interaction. This strategy provides a moderate degree of structure for children's experiences." *Example:* The Montessori Method.

Bissell also outlines a "quality" attribute of interventive programs, by which is meant the nature and amount of program supervision and personnel training: The degree of coordination and cooperation of program staff would probably also be included in her idea of quality, since it is presumably highly related to the nature of program management and supervision.

Several sets of research results can be analyzed using the criteria just developed, and most of the findings from these seem to assume a similar pattern, at least for short-run effects. The pattern is that program success is positively related to both program structure and program quality.

A number of writers have found the structure result. Gordon (1971, p. 24), after surveying all the research on Title I projects nationwide, concludes,

The tightly structured programmed approach including frequent and immediate feedback to the pupil, combined with a tutorial relationship, individual pacing and somewhat individualized programming are positively associated with accelerated pupil achievement. (Emphasis in original.)

The painstaking work by Hawkridge, Wargo, and their associates at the American Institutes of Research, already mentioned, is difficult to summarize briefly because it is composed of descriptive material concerning the successful programs identified. The same is also true of Kiesling's study of successful California Title I and Senate Bill 28 (a California demonstration program) projects. Their results strongly support Bissell's notion of the importance of good program supervision and personnel training ("quality"). Careful planning and good teacher training are mentioned both by Hawkridge at the preschool level and by Kiesling. Hawkridge mentions the careful specification of objectives as being important at all three educational levels. Perhaps this can be interpreted both as a quality and as a structure characteristic.

Another study that carefully traced differences in the effectiveness of program types that can be related to the structure criterion is that by Miller and Dyer (1970) for two kinds of kindergarten after four types of Head Start. The four types of Head Start (exclusive of controls) were: Bereiter-Engelmann (Structured Informational), DARCEE (Structured Cognitive), Montessori (Structured Environment), and Traditional (Structured Enrichment). The Follow Through Kindergarten was a highly academic program structured as a token economy where the school day was divided into earn and spend periods. Children not in Follow Through kindergarten were placed in regular kindergartens of the Louisville, Kentucky city schools.

The evaluation design in the Miller study was carefully drawn and the findings are quite rich and complex. However, the best single summary of the findings is probably the results for the Metropolitan Readiness test at the end of kindergarten. The most striking results are the unambiguous superiority in the performance of Follow Through children. Otherwise, the findings with respect to type of Head Start are more ambiguous. The two groups that did best had Follow Through (relatively structured) along with relatively unstructured Head Start programs. The most highly structured program—Bereiter-Engelmann—yielded good performance for Follow Through children but was a "disaster" for non-Follow Through children who scored seven points lower than the regular kindergarteners who had had no preschool at all. Montessori children did worst of the Follow Through groups and best of the traditional groups.

On the Stanford-Binet, the Bereiter-Engelmann children started highest at the beginning of kindergarten (thus they did best in preschool) and the Follow Through group ended four points higher than any other group, while the non-Follow Through Bereiter-Engelmann children fell five points. The traditional Head Start plus Follow Through combination was next best followed by the regular kindergarten DARCEE and Montessori children. On the Dog-and-Bone Inventiveness Test, comparing all kindergarten children by Head Start program, the Montessori children did best, followed by DARCEE, controls, traditional, and Bereiter-Engelmann, in that order.

Although the Miller-Dyer findings appear confusing, there are some generalizations that can be drawn. Short-term cognitive performance is better in the more structured programs; children in traditional and Montessori programs do better with such skills as curiosity and inventiveness. Also the more structured programs—especially Bereiter-Engelmann—seem to create more dependence on the part of the children toward the treatment, and therefore these children, when thrown into a regular "sink-or-swim" school situation where there is much less individual attention, seem to lose their former high gains rapidly.

The last set of studies we will discuss with respect to features of successful programs are those, also more broadly discussed above, of Karnes, DiLorenzo, and Weikart, as reanalyzed by Bissell. The methodology used by Bissell, in which she co-varied for beginning score level (which was not done by the original authors) is what we consider to be the best approach for controlling for the "regression to the mean" phenomenon.[8]

Bissell's reanalysis found similar results for each of the three programs, with the more structured programs achieving the better results.[9] In some further analysis according to degree of disadvantaged pupil environment, Bissell concludes that the more highly structured programs make the largest difference for the most disadvantaged children; less structured approaches are more effective with less disadvantaged children. Bissell concludes that the most disadvantaged children probably have difficulty in being self-directing and require constant supervision and guidance much more than the relatively more advanced children.

COST OF COMPENSATORY EDUCATION[10]

Evaluations seldom provide the data required for an accurate computation of the costs of educational programs that are built into a superstructure of an existing educational program. However, for the purposes of broad policy analysis, calculations to the last dollar are not particularly necessary; broad estimates can be illuminating.

The original funding for Title I equalled a sum half the average state expenditure per pupil for each disadvantaged child, the implication being that this much (which fell in the $250-$300 range in 1966) was to be spent on each child. Subsequently Title I has been underfunded from the standpoint of this rather rich objective and the current average appropriation for each child officially designed as poor is less than $200. Head Start was not funded as broadly as Title I, but per-pupil expenditures in most Head Start centers range roughly around the $300 mark. These expenditures include both instructional expense and such related services as health care, hot meals, and parent education.

The New York Higher Horizons program provided, in effect, three extra full-time teachers, plus some equipment, materials, and so on, devoted to schools with enrollments in the neighborhood of 1000 to 1200. This amounts to an expenditure level of around $60 per pupil.

At the other end of the spending spectrum are any number of the projects described in the literature that have been exceptionally successful. For example, the Karnes Ameliorative Preschool program, discussed in several places above, takes, as nearly as we can tell, the equivalent of three special teachers one hour a day for 15 children. If we assign an additional hour a day for preparation time, this amounts to one full-time teacher for 15 children, or about $800 per year per child for instructional costs alone. The Bereiter-Engelmann program used in the Karnes-Teska-Hodgins study would require a similar pattern of resource use. The Gordon experiments with home training of mothers by carefully trained paraprofessional peers is also surprisingly expensive. As in many of these program descriptions, we found it difficult from this one to ascertain the exact (or even near exact) pattern of resource use. Our best guess is that, with an average of 30 home visits a year (as stated in the report), with salary for the parent educators placed at $5500 per year (including fringes), and figuring necessary transportation and supervision costs, the program would cost in the range of $500 to $600 per child per year.

The 1971 publication by Wargo *et al.* listed ten exemplary projects, which is all they could find out of 326 they reviewed carefully. Of these, three were in an expenditure range far above current levels, even if we allow for reasonable one-time research and development expenses. These were the Fernald School at UCLA, which gave highly individualized instruction to disadvantaged children at a *total* cost of $1200 per child (or $400 to $500 more than most public schools cost); the Lafayette Bilingual Center in Chicago, which offered English and Spanish instruction to disadvantaged Spanish-speaking children, costing in total $1500 per pupil; and Project Breakthrough, also in Chicago, a preschool project that used "Talking Typewriters," at a total cost of $3600 per pupil. The other seven "successful" projects cost between $100 and $367 per pupil, above normal per-pupil expenditures.

Kiesling (1971b) has provided a set of cost estimates constructed on the basis of his observations of successful Title I and Senate Bill 28 projects. Twelve program prototypes were defined based on the configurations seen in the actual programs and cost estimates generated with the use of a standardized list of resource costs. The actual per-pupil cost varies from one program prototype to another; and, within each program prototype, per-pupil costs vary with the scale and intensity of the program. The minimum estimate is $153 per pupil in a program that relies heavily on volunteer aides. The maximum estimate is $445 per pupil for a program in which pupils leave the regular classroom to see a specialist in a resource facility.

The Gray and Klaus preschool program had 10-week summer programs and weekly home visits by a trained teacher. Assuming a summer employment of the teacher at one-fifth her yearly salary, $4000 for four aides, and other miscellaneous expenses, we estimate a figure of about $140 per child per 10-week summer program. The teachers' weekly visits probably cost at least $200 per child per year, which places the yearly cost in the $350-$400 per pupil range. It should be remembered that there were some diffusion effects and so the benefits cannot strictly be limited to the program children.

Barbrack and Horton (1970) reported a somewhat similar preschool experiment to that of Gray and Klaus. There were three experimental treatments: home visits by a professional teacher, home visits by paraprofessional peer mothers well supervised by a professional teacher, and home visits by paraprofessional peer mothers supervised by more experienced mothers who were in turn supervised by a professional teacher. Per-pupil costs were calculated by Barbrack and Horton for these three treatments to be $440, $300, and $275, respectively.

The schools in the New York project discussed by DiLorenzo (1969) had daily instructional sessions of 2-1/2 hours with an average class size of about 15. If we assume one teacher saw two cohorts per day and add costs of room, materials, and supervision, the cost of these programs is in the $400-$500 per-pupil range.

The Higher Horizons 100 Project in Hartford, Connecticut gives remedial language and intensive counseling to 100 disadvantaged ninth grade students annually. The program has small classes and considerable counseling and individualized instruction, with emphasis on remedial language instruction. Program *total* per-pupil costs are $900, which is perhaps $100 to $300 more than the per-pupil costs in most northern school districts (Wargo, 1971).

Wargo (1971) discussed one preschool home instruction program similar to the Gray and Klaus, and Barbrack and Horton studies discussed just above. A trained "Toy Demonstrator" visited each mother-child combination twice weekly. The cost was $387 per pupil, not unlike the professionally staffed programs of Gray and Klaus, and Barbrack and Horton.

Another remedial reading program discussed above was Project Conquest in East St. Louis. Project children received remedial reading instruction in 45-minute sessions four days a week in reading rooms or twice weekly in reading clinics. Per-pupil cost was $263. Another was Project MARS in Leominster, Massachusetts, where pupils spent 45 minutes daily in special reading classrooms at a cost of $300 per pupil. Another was the Remedial Reading Laboratories in El Paso, Texas, where pupils were taught in small groups of about eight pupils for 50 to 60 minutes each day. The cost of this program was $210 per pupil.

Finally, the PS 115 Alpha One reading program in New York City used the commercially available Alpha One language arts program in which children play reading and writing games and participate in creative and dramatic play, and so on. The average cost over three years appears to have been about $200 per pupil.

SUMMARY OF FINDINGS

This discussion of intervention programs leads us to the following conclusions:

• Without exception, all of the large surveys of the large national compensatory education programs have shown no beneficial results on average, as measured by achievement tests or IQ scores. However, the evaluation reports on which the surveys are based are often poor and the research designs suspect. This generalization does not apply to the preschool television program, *Sesame Street,* which showed positive results using criterion-based tests, over a two-year period.

Evaluation of Broad Educational Interventions 143

- Two or three smaller surveys tend to show modest and positive effects of compensatory education programs in the short run.
- A number of intervention programs have been designed quite carefully and display gains in pupil cognitive performance, again in the short run. In particular, pupils from the more disadvantaged socioeconomic backgrounds tend to show greater progress in more highly structured programs. (Programs that are highly structured are those in which the sequencing of the children's experiences is heavily organized externally.)
- There is considerable evidence that much of the short-run gain from intervention programs fades away after two or three years if not reinforced. This "fade-out" is greater for gains on achievement tests than for gains on intelligence tests, and it is also greater for the more highly structured programs, which are most unlike regular public school practice. However, there is some evidence that all of the gain from intervention is not lost in the three- to four-year period. If some bits of evidence we have that program effects spill over to the performance of control-group children correctly describe the real world, the amount of gain retained after three or four years may be fairly substantial. As yet, such evidence is scanty, however.
- It would appear that incremental per-pupil costs of successful educational intervention vary anywhere from $200 on up, with the "feasible range" for such programs falling between $250 and $350. However, numerous interventions funded at these levels have failed. Clearly the level of funding is not itself a sufficient condition for success.

NOTES TO
CHAPTER VI

1. The Westinghouse study was controversial and has been widely criticized on methodological grounds. However, in a detailed and balanced review of the controversy Stearns (1971b, pp. 117-134) concludes, "Head Start has been only 'marginally effective' on the average."
2. Some of the more serious evaluation design problems included: 1. The failure to adequately control for socioeconomic differences by family and community. Families and communities quick to

take advantage of the program could be expected to be more highly motivated than the average. 2. Additional support services were given to some of the more disadvantaged children in the program but not to the comparison children. 3. Kindergarten and first grade cohorts were confounded by region, with the former mostly in the North and the latter in the South.
3. Since gain scores are calculated by subtracting initial test scores from later test scores, any error in the initial test scores will result in a spurious negative bias in the measured correlations between initial scores and gain scores. If the initial score is overstated, for example, the difference between the initial score and a later score will be understated, and conversely.
4. Those of us who have interviewed compensatory education personnel extensively have found that it is widely accepted among managers of compensatory education programs (Title I in particular) that the most disadvantaged pupils are picked for treatment. Evaluation designs where experimental and control children are assigned and evaluated in a completely random manner with large enough group sizes to insure meaningful outcomes are almost non-existent. Only one comes easily to mind, the DiLorenzo New York Study discussed below. This comment applies to "on line" projects only, and not to the more research-oriented projects that will be discussed later.
5. This so-called "normal" rate of gain for such children is .7 months of gain per month of instruction. The average figure found by Kiesling was .87 months gain per month of instruction. The comparable figure for the TEMPO study discussed below is .95.
6. Our choice of projects to discuss and much of the substance of the discussion that follows is heavily dependent upon the excellent studies of this literature by Stearns (1971a) and Bissell (1970).
7. In a later report on the progress of five cohorts of Perry Preschool children, Weikart found that 34 experimental children were only slightly and insignificantly ahead of 39 control children in grades two and three (Weikart, 1971b).
8. See Note 3 above.
9. Weikart also reemphasized the importance of structure, concluding that well-organized programs with definite goals will succeed within a wide range of possible curricula (Weikart, 1971b).

Evaluation of Broad Interventions 145

10. In this section, unless otherwise noted, we refer to costs of compensatory programs—those that are in addition to the incremental "normal" or customary expenditure level.

VII. THE EXPERIENTIAL APPROACH

INTRODUCTION: THE APPROACH DEFINED

The experiential approach arises from recent renewed interest in school reform. For the past decade a number of writers—notably Dennison (1969), Friedenberg (1963), Goodman (1965 and 1970), Henry (1963), Herndon (1968 and 1971), Holt (1967), Illich (1971), Kohl (1967), Kozol (1968 and 1972), Postman and Weingartner (1969), Silberman (1970)—have assailed America's existing educational system on a variety of grounds. Despite the diversity among these and other reform writers' views, common elements emerge, which we call *the experiential approach.* It states in effect that the *most important thing about schooling is the way in which school experiences affect students' lives and self-concepts, both while they are students and for the rest of their lives.* Therefore, to these authors, the other approaches discussed in this report—input-output, process, organizational, evaluation—are all irrelevant, unless they affect: (1) the student's concept about himself as an individual and as a member of the society (classroom, school, community, and so on) that impinges on him; (2) the style that the student develops to deal with school experiences (notably teacher-student and student-student transactions); (3) the attitudes toward social institutions that students develop as a consequence of their first major experience with one such institution—in this case, the school system.

This doesn't mean that the reform writers believe that cognitive skills are unimportant. What they generally do believe is that the nature of the school experience is a dominant factor that determines not only how well cognitive skills are acquired, but also how effectively they can be used after school. Many of them also raise serious questions about whether the cognitive skills that the schools actually do transmit are helpful or hurtful to individual development (for example, Henry, 1963, pp. 287-288; Silberman, 1970, Part II). In Chapter II we pointed out that a number of research studies have come to similar conclusions concerning the value of cognitive skills, especially Gintis (1971).

More generally, it must be emphasized that there is a wide diversity of views among those who pursue the experiential approach. They range from voices of moderate reformism (Silberman, 1970) to those who would abolish the schools entirely (Illich, 1971), to those who would completely change school governance as a way of changing the nature of experience (Levin, 1970a).

This is not an exhaustive review of the experiential literature. We have chosen what we considered to be a representative selection of the most important and influential books and articles, and we believe that our selection fairly represents the current range of views.

OBJECTIVES AND METHODS

The objective of the work under this approach is to describe how children's experiences in school affect their lives and to prescribe changes necessary to improve their lives. The literature is therefore one of reform and severely criticizes the current system (both social and educational). It is in this respect that the reform writers markedly differ from classical researchers; both are involved in diagnosis of problems, although in quite different ways, but the reform writer also presents his views of the nature of desirable reforms. The researcher rarely gets involved this way except in the very limited sense of offering hypotheses to be tested, generally about very specific issues. Proposals for reform are based on the authors' impressions of problems existing in current classrooms and frequently on examples of more successful educational experiences (for example, Ashton-Warner, 1963; Featherstone, 1969 and 1971; Holt, 1967; Kohl, 1967; Silberman, 1970; U.K. Ministry of Education, 1969).

The basic method used is that of observation; sometimes within the general context of research (for example, Henry, 1963; Silberman, 1970), in which the observer is outside the system, and sometimes in a more personally involved framework wherein the observer is part of the system (for example, Herndon, 1971; Holt, 1967; Kohl, 1967). Authors are forced to analyze not only observational data but also their own values in interpreting the data. In the second case they must also attempt to account for their interactions with the system being observed.

None of these authors test hypotheses with standard kinds of data, and in most cases "data" are difficult to identify. In addition, there is an individual choice in the selection of what is observed and interpreted. One can select schools, teachers, classrooms, students, and so on to fit whatever conclusions one wishes to draw. One can select and interpret experiences to suit one's bias. Although writers are not necessarily biased, they do present evidence that is consistent with their point of view. The important question is whether the point of view or the evidence came first. Finally, these authors are not presenting "proof" in any scientific sense of the word, but rather they are presenting ideas for consideration, backed up with arguments for why the idea or suggestion is important. Henry (1963, p. 3) explains the approach:

> Most of this book is based on studies in which I have participated either as director or researcher or both, and much of the research has been by direct observation. However, I do not *use research as proof* in any rigorous sense; rather I write about the research from an interpretive, value-laden point of view. Since I have an attitude toward culture, I *discuss data as illustrative of a viewpoint and as a take-off for expressing a conviction.* So I do not consider statistical frequency or regional differences, but have rather settled for the attitude that the materials reflect feelings, ideas, and conditions that seem to occur often enough in the United States to merit deepest consideration.

VARIABLES

The reform writers attempt to deal at various levels of detail with a number of common variables or issues. A child's experiences are shaped by parents, the community, teachers, and the school. In addition, teachers are affected by the organization of the educational system and this in turn affects the student. Underlying everything, and affecting all the players who participate in the education scene, are social values. Thus, we find the reform writers discussing such variables as: (1) student-teacher relations and their effect on student-student relations; (2) student-school (system) relations; (3) teacher-organization relations; and (4) school-society, student-society relations. This list by no means exhausts the combinations of interrelationships that may be examined.

These kinds of variables are also studied in the other approaches we have reviewed. In those cases, however, experimental (or statistical) controls were introduced to eliminate confounding influences and high-order interactions between variables that confuse data interpretation. The success of this venture was discussed in previous chapters, but we note in passing that researchers have not been overly successful in applying valid experimental designs to social situations. The reform authors observe these variables in a completely unconstrained environment, which allows more meaningful behavior to occur but makes data interpretation more difficult. The variables interact in complex and unknown ways, and even worse, variables change as a result of interaction with other variables. For example, teachers generally behave in a way that they perceive the system expects them to. This in turn fortifies the system's bias in that direction.

The difference in viewpoint between conventional educational researchers and the reform writers is shown when one considers the kinds of outcome measures endorsed by each. In Chapter II we point out that educational research almost exclusively uses standardized tests to measure educational achievement. We further point out that these tests measure only a fraction of possible educational outcomes. Of course, the extensive use of standardized tests for measuring the retention of bits and pieces of material, largely learned by rote, in part reflects the objectives of the school. The reform writers attribute little importance to performance on standardized tests and associated curriculum material. As noted above, they generally feel that it is important for children to acquire reading and math skills and so on, but they view this as almost an incidental accomplishment within the broader objective of student achievement.

Students can acquire skills in the pursuit of more meaningful goals. Illich points out one way that learning of skills might occur (1971, p. 13):

> The strongly motivated student who is faced with the task of acquiring a new and complex skill may benefit greatly from the discipline now associated with the old-fashioned schoolmaster who taught reading, Hebrew, catechism, or multiplication by rote. School has now made this kind of drill teaching rare and disreputable, yet there are many skills which a motivated student with normal aptitude can master in a matter of a few months if taught in this traditional way. This is as true of codes as of their encipherment; of second and third languages as of reading and writing; and equally of special languages such as algebra, computer

programming, chemical analysis, or of manual skills like typing, watchmaking, plumbing, wiring, TV repair; or for that matter dancing, driving, and diving.

Instead, according to these writers, children are required to learn irrelevant "facts" and "skills," which they know are unimportant and which bore them and turn them off to meaningful learning. Postman and Weingartner (1969, p. 49) call this process the school game of "Let's Pretend":

> The game is called "Let's Pretend," and if its name were chiseled into the front of every school building in America we would at least have an honest announcement of what takes place there. The game is based on a series of pretenses which include: Let's pretend that you are not what you are and that this sort of work makes a difference to your lives; let's pretend that what bores you is important, and that the more you are bored, the more important it is; let's pretend that there are certain things *everyone* must know, and that both the questions and answers about them have been fixed for all time; let's pretend that your intellectual competence can be judged on the basis of how well you can play Let's Pretend.

Standardized tests are viewed as relatively unimportant for a number of reasons. To begin with, achievement on standardized tests is to a high degree a matter of sophistication about test taking and one's attitude about it. Research reviewed earlier on the effect of teachers' expectations indicate test achievement is not always an indication of the amount learned (for example, Rist, 1970). Kohl (1967) also cites evidence that achievement test performance is only incidentally related to learning. At the very least, for achievement testing to be a valid and important measure of learning, the test must accurately assess how much a student learns about some specific subject. As Holt (1967, p. 135) notes:

> It begins to look as if the test-examination-marks business is a gigantic racket, the purpose of which is to enable students, teachers, and schools to take part in a joint pretense that the students know everything they are supposed to know, when in fact they know only a small part of it—if any at all. Why do we always announce exams in advance, if not to give students a chance to cram for them? Why do teachers, even in graduate schools, always say quite specifically what the exam will be about, even telling the type of questions that will be given. Because otherwise too many students would flunk. What would happen at Harvard or Yale if a prof gave a surprise test in March on work covered in October? Everyone knows what would happen; that's why they don't do it.

Even if one could realistically measure how much a student knows about a specific subject, there are still grounds on which to question the relevance of what is learned. To quote Holt again (p. 177):

> We must ask how much of the sum of human knowledge anyone can know at the end of his schooling. Perhaps a millionth. Are we then to believe that one of the millionths is so much more important than another? Or that our social and national problems will be solved if we can just figure out a way to turn children out of schools knowing two millionths of the total, instead of one?

Holt and others believe that it is more important for students to learn how to learn, to solve problems, and to be curious than to acquire specific and mostly irrelevant bits of information. The reform writers focus on those outcomes that involve higher cognitive processes (abstract reasoning, creativity, problem solving, and so on) and affective factors (self-concept, happiness, interest, attitudes, and the like). Within the framework of these goals they feel that the basic skills can be developed.

LIMITATIONS OF RESEARCH

The material reviewed in this chapter is descriptive research rather than analytical research, and our comments on "limitations" are based on broader considerations than they were in previous chapters. The social scientists, and especially social reform writers, attempt to cope with variables that defy precise and operational definition and generally are impossible to measure with an acceptable degree of reliability. In general the social scientist is always faced with a choice of alternatives in examining policy issues. On one hand he may be experimentally and methodologically rigorous, but he is then limited to studying only simple or highly constricted problems. These, even if solved, may have little relevance to "real life" problems. If one elects to study the "real life" problems, there is little or no methodology that adequately applies. As a result "solutions" cannot be convincingly demonstrated or generalized on the basis of the evidence presented. Experimental research is therefore often criticized on the grounds that it defines a problem too narrowly; conversely, experiential literature is often criticized on the grounds that it is not methodologically sound.

The most serious limitation of the "research" of the reform writers lies in the necessarily inconclusive character of the obtained results and the elusive nature of "proof." The influence of their findings depends upon their ability to convince. Even if the results are convincing to the reader, it is difficult to implement the policies suggested, because the reform writers rarely present a detailed prescription for moving to the better learning environment they envision.

RESULTS

The results presented in this chapter are in terms of the opinions of the authors, with a focus on issues where they show a general consensus. Some writers are relatively conservative and limit their criticism and plan for reform to something that they believe to be feasible within the current social-political structure (for example, Silberman, Herndon). Others are more radical and call for broad and extensive social as well as educational reform (for example, Friedenberg, Illich). However, differences among authors are mostly of degree—there is consistency in their attitudes about educational reform.

The results will be organized under three headings: social values and educational objectives, the learning environment, and reformation. This differentiation is not clear-cut, and issues and evidence overlap the categories. In the first two sections the diagnostic impressions of the writers are summarized, and in the third we consider their prescriptive recommendations. It is impossible in this brief summary to give more than a rough indication of the findings reported by these authors.

Social Values and Educational Objectives

Before we discuss the authors' views on educational objectives, we note that their comments are based on objectives inferred from classroom activities and, therefore, there is little relationship to the idealistic jargon and lofty platitudes often found in curriculum philosophy regarding school objectives. For example, creativity is generally found to be one of the major objectives stated in curricula; but these writers would contend that there is little in the actual instruction, classroom activity, or testing that is even remotely connected with creativity.

Each author, in his own way, questions the content and priorities of educational objectives, and they criticize the social values underlying them. Friedenberg, Goodman, and Illich present the most direct assault on the influence of middle-class values—primarily conformity—on education, although more conservative writers, Silberman, for example, also make it clear that educational problems are not restricted to the schools but lie rather in the social and political values that determine educational practice. Although some authors do not make a major thesis of an attack on social values, it is nevertheless implied throughout their books. Holt, for example, frequently points out that the submission and subjugation of children begin in the home and continue in the classroom. He states (1967, p. 167):

> We adults destroy most of the intellectual and creative capacity of children by the things we do to them or make them do. We destroy this capability above all by making them afraid, afraid of not doing what other people want, of not pleasing, or making mistakes, of failing, of being wrong. Thus, we make them afraid to gamble, afraid to experiment, afraid to try the difficult and the unknown. Even when we do not create children's fears, when they come to us with fears ready-made and built-in, we use these fears as handles to manipulate them and get them to do what we want.

Silberman (1970) describes the schools as "mindless," tracing the cause repeatedly to social values and institutions. He states (p. 11):

> This mindlessness—the failure or refusal to think seriously about educational purpose, the reluctance to question established practice—is not the monopoly of the public school; it is diffused remarkably evenly throughout the entire educational system, and indeed the entire society. "The problem of policy-making in our society," Henry A. Kissinger has said, "confronts the difficulty that revolutionary changes have to be encompassed and dealt with by an increasingly rigid administrative structure.... An increasing amount of energy has to be devoted to keeping the existing machine going, and in the nature of things there isn't enough time to inquire into the purpose of these activities. The temptation is great to define success by whether one fulfills certain programs, however accidentally these programs may have been arrived at. The question is whether it is possible in the modern bureaucratic state to develop a sense of long-range purpose and to inquire into the meaning of the activity." Kissinger was talking about the problems of government; he might just as well have been talking about higher education and the mass media.

and later (p. 36):

> Why the failure of the mass media? The answer is at once simple and complex. What is mostly wrong with television, newspapers, magazines, and films is what is mostly wrong with the schools and colleges; mindlessness. At the heart of the problem, that is to say, is the failure to think seriously about purpose or consequence—the failure of people at every level to ask why they are doing what they are doing or to inquire into the consequences.

The basic social value according to these writers is conformity, and the society is geared to produce it, as Friedenberg (1963, p. 11) notes:

> The essence of our era is a kind of infidelity, a disciplined expediency.
>
> This expediency is not a breach of our tradition, but its very core. And it keeps the young from getting much out of the diversity that our heterogeneous culture might otherwise provide them. This kind of expediency is built into the value structure of every technically developed open society; and it becomes most prevalent when the rewards of achievement in that society appear most tempting and the possibilities of decent and expressive survival at a low or intermediate position in it least reliable. Being different, notoriously, does not get you to the top. If individuals must believe that they are on their way there in order to preserve their self-esteem they will be under constant pressure, initially from anxious adults and later from their own aspirations, to repudiate the divergent elements of their character in order to make it under the terms common to mass culture. They choose the path most traveled by, and that makes all the difference.

He notes the high success attained by society in promoting the acceptance of conformity in students (p. 128):

> For the most part, they do firmly and sincerely believe that people should cooperate with their immediate social order, and that people who don't are troublemakers who come to a deservedly bad end. They are genuinely suspicious of, and hostile to, people who insist on their own privacy and dignity against group demands. They are convinced that strong feelings and loyalties are hazardous, and that it is not merely unwise but wrong to allow such commitments to jeopardize one's future chances. These are all moral principles. In fact, they are just the moral principles that good empiricists need.

Schools are social institutions and as such they perpetuate the values of the society. Although this may be understandable, and to some degree necessary, these writers (and many others) point out an alarming similarity among schools; almost none provide an environment for any kind of individual and creative growth. The gloomiest note is the refrain sounded by Henry (1963, p. 286):

> The function of education has never been to free the mind and the spirit of man, but to bind them; and to the end that the mind and spirit of his children should never escape Homo sapiens has employed praise, ridicule, admonition, accusation, mutilation, and even torture to chain them to the culture pattern. Throughout most of his historic course Homo sapiens has wanted from his children acquiescence, not originality. It is natural that this should be so, for where every man is unique there is no society, and where there is no society there can be no man. Contemporary American educators think they want creative children, yet it is an open question as to what they expect these children to create. And certainly the classrooms—from kindergarten to graduate

school—in which they expect it to happen, are not crucibles of creative activity and thought. It stands to reason that were young people truly creative the culture would fall apart, for originality, by definition, is different from what is given, and what is given is the culture itself. From the endless pathetic "creative hours" of kindergarten to the most abstruse problems in sociology and anthropology, the function of education is to prevent the truly creative intellect from getting out of hand. Only in the exact and the biological sciences do we permit unlimited freedom, for we have (but only since the Renaissance, since Galileo and Bruno underwent the Inquisition) found a way—or thought we had found a way—to bind the explosive powers of science in the containing vessel of the social system.

The Learning Environment

Social values and educational objectives are expressed in the structure of schools and classrooms, in what is often termed the learning environment. It is not surprising, therefore, that most of the writing about the ills of education and need for reform centers around the learning environment. There is a long history of criticism (pointed out by Silberman, 1970) of the overly structured, authoritarian, and strictly disciplined classroom, and all of the writers we are reviewing here advocate less formal classrooms. The authors agree in describing schools as boring and prison-like in character; a feature that exists not only in poor ghetto schools but also, usually in more subtle form, in middle-class schools. Thus:

Postman and Weingartner (1969, p. 155):
> City schools as they now exist largely confine students to sitting in boxes with the choice of acquiescing to teacher demands or getting out.

Herndon (1971, p. 97):
> If kids in America do not go to school, they can be put in jail. If they are tardy a certain number of times, they may go to jail. If they cut up enough, they go to jail. If their parents do not see that they go to school the parents may be judged unfit and the kids go to jail.

(p. 98):
> As long as you can threaten people, you can't tell whether or not they really want to do what you are proposing that they do. You can't tell if they are inspired by it, you can't tell if they learn anything from it, you can't tell if they would keep on doing it if you weren't threatening them.
>
> You cannot tell. You cannot tell if the kids want to come to your class or not. You can't tell if they are motivated or not. You can't tell if they

learn anything or not. All you can tell is, they'd rather come to your class than go to jail.

Holt (1970, p. 68):

> Boredom. Almost all children are bored in school. Why shouldn't they be? We would be. The children in the high status and "creative" private elementary schools I taught in were bored stiff most of the day—and with good reason. Very little in school is exciting or meaningful even to an upper middle-class child; why should it be so for slum children? Why, that is, unless we begin where schools hardly ever do begin, by recognizing that the daily lives of these children are the most real and meaningful and indeed the only real and meaningful things they know.

These writers maintain that schools are too highly structured and too much committed to controlling and disciplining students, not only in the classroom, but in the hallways, and on the playground, and around the school. The school tells them where to go, what to do, and how to dress and provides an endless list of rules involving trivial and petty restrictions. The final travesty, according to these writers, is that in this environment teachers tell them about democracy, and individual freedom, and responsibility, and all the other lofty ideals that every day the school flagrantly violates. These restrictions are imposed immediately by teachers, and more remotely by school administrators, but ultimately by parents and society. Teachers and school administrators are themselves severely limited in the freedom they can exercise in teaching strategies and administrative arrangements, although more freedom is available than they use. Kohl describes the feelings of a teacher in the bureaucratic structure (1967, p. 11):

> When I began teaching I felt isolated in a hostile environment. The structure of authority in my school was clear: the principal was at the top and the students were at the bottom. Somewhere in the middle was the teacher, whose role it was to impose orders from textbooks or supervisors upon the students. The teacher's only protection was that if students failed to obey instructions they could legitimately be punished or, if they were defiant, suspended or kicked out of school. There was no way for students to question the teachers' decisions or for teachers to question the decisions of their supervisors or authors of textbooks and teachers' manuals.

Teachers are too busy controlling children, following inappropriate curricula, trying to please parents and get along with school administrators to have much time available for teaching. Although the teacher is generally the focal point for criticism of schools, the teachers are also victims of a system over which they have little control. Kohl describes the position of teachers (1967, p. 89):

The Experiential Approach 157

Supervisors deal with teachers in the same way they expect teachers to deal with students. They are usually more interested in avoiding problems and maintaining control than in matters having to do with teaching. As far as they are concerned the content of the curriculum has been mandated by a Board of Education or a curriculum committee, and it is the teacher's role to follow the curriculum. A good teacher, like a good soldier, is one who obeys orders. An excellent teacher is one who obeys them cheerfully and willingly.

Silberman comments at some length on the dilemma facing the teacher, and at one point states (p. 320):

> Indeed, given the obsession with silence and lack of movement that so many principals, superintendents, and curriculum supervisors show, and the fact that teachers' ability tends to be judged more on their "control" than on any other attribute, it is essential that *someone* be available to relieve teachers' anxiety about what their supervisors may say if they see children talking or moving about in class. Teaching, after all, is a very lonely profession.

The reform writers point out from time to time that teachers are not basically bad or cruel or disinterested in their students. Mostly they do what they are forced to do by the structure of the school, and many times their behavior is simply the result of not knowing, or more often because they are products of the same kind of system in which they are teaching. Whatever their motives, however, teachers serve as a model and as wardens in the education of children, and for the most part the results are not favorable as Goodman notes (1970, p. 78):

> As Gregory Bateson has noticed with dolphins and trainers and as John Holt has noticed in middle class schools, learning to learn usually means picking up the structure of behavior of the teachers and becoming expert in the academic process. In actual practice, young discoverers are bound to discover what will get them past the College Board examinations. Guessers and dreamers are not really free to balk and drop out for a semester to brood and let their theories germinate in the dark, as proper geniuses do. And what if precisely the Big Ideas are not true? Einstein said that it was preferable to have a stupid pedant for a teacher so that a smart child could fight him all the way and develop his own thought.

All teachers of course do not go along with the administrative doctrine, as viewed by the reform writers, and sometimes they attempt in various degrees to deviate from accepted procedure. Successful education programs and teaching approaches are sometimes reported, especially in schools where students are largely "culturally deprived." These are always the result of deviations from standard procedure and involve independent action on the part of the teacher. These deviations, however, are not generally encouraged by the school and often are not even accepted. Illich comments on the fate of inventive teachers (1971, p. 65):

> The "classroom practitioner" who considers himself a liberal teacher is increasingly attacked from all sides. The free-school movement, confusing discipline with indoctrination, has painted him into the role of a destructive authoritarian. The educational technologist consistently demonstrates the teacher's inferiority at measuring and modifying behavior. And the school administration for which he works forces him to bow to both Summerhill and Skinner, making it obvious that compulsory learning cannot be a liberal enterprise. No wonder that the desertion rate of teachers is overtaking that of their students.

Herndon (1968, 1971) is a classroom innovator who has managed to operate an "open classroom" in an otherwise conventional school. Kohl (1971) reviews Herndon's latest book (*How to Survive in Your Native Land*) and makes the following comment concerning his probable fate as an innovator (p. 11):

> There is one problem however. Jim managed to survive in Daly City for nine years. He took six months off last year and when he returned in February he was told that there was no job for him at his old school until September. He was made a roving sub in the district, one of the bureaucratic strategies used to drive good people out of teaching.
>
> Jim is going back this September but it is clear that he is no longer to be tolerated. The new administration of his school wants him out, the limits of toleration having evidently been reached in Daly City. I guess people have finally begun to understand what Jim is doing and decided that it is better to force him out than re-examine their own lives. I don't know how much longer Jim will survive in Daly City. I think the final irony of the book is that maybe not even Jim can survive in our native land.

If teachers are caught in a web of control and little freedom of choice, so are administrators, for no matter what their plans for innovation they must answer to political pressures and the demands of the community. Everyone considers himself an expert on education because he has been there, and notions about necessary and desirable educational practices are projected on the basis of personal experience. So in the end we come full circle and find that it is society that determines the school practice. However, if the schools are persistent, change is possible, and we close with a note of optimism in this regard. Dennison (1969, p. 7) found:

The Experiential Approach 159

It is worth mentioning here that, with two exceptions, the parents of the children at First Street were not libertarians. They thought that they believed in compulsion, and rewards and punishments, and formal discipline, and report cards, and homework, and elaborate school facilities. They looked rather askance at our noisy classrooms and informal relations. If they persisted in sending us their children, it was not because they agreed with our methods, but because they were desperate. As the months went by, however, and the children who had been truants now attended eagerly, and those who had been failing now began to learn, the parents drew their own conclusions. By the end of the first year there was a high morale among them, and great devotion to the school.

Reformation: Prescription for Education

There is a striking similarity in the prescription these writers offer for education; the differences are mostly a matter of degree and political feasibility—a matter we will not attempt to resolve here. The writers agree that at least part of the solution is to have less formally structured classrooms in which the student can develop more or less unhindered by demands for conformity.

The completely "open classroom" is one in which the student is allowed to wander around pretty much at will and to discover for himself the things he wants to learn. The British elementary school open classroom is often incorrectly used as the model for this approach. Silberman (1970) advocates "informal classrooms," the distinction being that some minimal kinds of structure remain. His conclusions are based on interviews with successful teachers in the British (and some American) open classrooms. Successful classrooms, where students learn required skills and appear happy with the learning environment, result from the ability of the teacher to introduce structure in an unobtrusive way. Herndon (1971) describes an experience in an American school in which the open approach was tried, and failed at first. The children did not discover things they wanted to work on, nor did they develop group projects. Mostly they wandered around the halls and complained that there was "nothing to do." Finally, the introduction of a project, with some rather indirect structure, produced some of the student activity and learning that was expected in the open classroom. Herndon points out that the critical factor in making an open classroom work is the ability of the teacher to learn and adopt new approaches.

Kohl (1967) has attempted to provide a guide to teachers for attempting open classroom techniques, a venture that is not easy, as he points out (p. 80):

> The movement to an open classroom is a difficult journey for most of us. The easiest way to undergo it is to share it with one's pupils—to tell them where you hope to be and give them a sense of the difficulty of changing one's styles and habits. Facing uncertainty in oneself, and articulating it to one's pupils, is one way of preventing a superficial bias "against authority" which, if it fails, can lead one to believe that the open classroom just doesn't work. Freedom can be threatening to students at first. Most of them are so used to doing what they are told in school that it takes quite a while for them to discover their own interests. Besides that, their whole school careers have taught them not to trust teachers, so they will naturally believe that the teacher who offers freedom isn't serious. They will have to test the limits of the teacher's offer, see how free they are to refuse to work, move out of the classroom, try the teacher's nerves and patience. All of this testing must be gone through if authoritarian attitudes are to be unlearned.

An article on the open classroom by Barth (1971) summarizes some of the issues associated with conversion to the open classroom:

> In the final analysis, the success of a widespread movement toward open education in the country rests not upon agreement with any philosophical position but with satisfactory answers to several important questions. For what kinds of people—teachers, administrators, parents, and children—is the open classroom appropriate and valuable? What happens to children in open classrooms? How can the resistance from children, teachers, administrators, and parents—inevitable among those not committed to open education's assumptions and practices—be surmounted? And finally, should participation in an open classroom be required of teachers, children, parents and administrators?

The critical issue related to the open classroom concerns the degree of structure that is necessary for each student and how structure is introduced. The same issue exists in the related subject of learning by discovery—a topic pursued at some length in the research literature and reviewed earlier in this study. This research has produced a number of arguments against the traditional classroom, although the emerging consensus (see Shulman, 1966) is that learning by discovery does not mean laissez-faire learning, and that much needs to be known about how to introduce structure in the discovery or free learning situation. The research of Gagné and Ausubel is particularly relevant to this point (see Chapter IV). They present evidence that indicates some kinds of

The Experiential Approach

material are best learned if the subordinate knowledge is arranged in a sequenced hierarchy.

One purpose of the open classroom is to allow students (and sometimes parents) a choice of activity and learning material, although structure is provided so that the goals are not completely left up to the student. Some writers have gone so far as to suggest that one should also be able to decide whether or not one goes to school, and if so, where and when and what one studies. This stand has been made specific by several, including Postman, Friedenberg, and especially Illich. Friedenberg (1963, p. 249) comments:

> Basically, then, I disapprove of compulsory school attendance in itself. I see no valid moral reasons to single out the young for this special legal encumbrance. The economic reasons are compelling enough; but they are likewise contemptible. A people have no right to cling to economic arrangements that can be made halfway workable only by imposing an infantile and unproductive status on adolescents and indoctrinating them with a need for trashy goods and shallow, meretricious relationships that they know to be degrading.

And Goodman (1970, p. 67):

> The present expanded school systems are coercive in their nature. The young have to attend for various well known reasons none of which is necessary for their well-being or the well-being of society.

Illich (1971, p. 9) states:

> Obligatory schooling inevitably polarizes a society; it also grades the nations of the world according to an international caste system. Countries are rated like castes whose educational dignity is determined by the average years of schooling of its citizens, a rating which is closely related to per capita gross national product, and much more painful.

And later (p. 12):

> A second major illusion on which the school system rests is that most learning is the result of teaching. Teaching, it is true, may contribute to certain kinds of learning under certain circumstances. But most people acquire most of their knowledge outside school, and in school only insofar as school, in a few rich countries, has become their place of confinement during an increasing part of their lives.

Although the idea of non-compulsory education is extreme, it is not haphazard and is presented with jolting logic, especially by Illich, who argues that compulsory education is not personally rewarding, socially desirable, or economically feasible. Illich and others have pointed out the escalating costs of education, most of it tied to the futile quest for equal schooling. Equal opportunity for education as a political issue has been distorted to mean everyone is equally educable, at least to the extent that school children all perform "at grade level" on standardized tests of arithmetic and reading. The billions of dollars poured into compensatory programs have not produced any of the sought-for improvements in basic skills for the so-called disadvantaged child, especially when the money is spent in conventional classroom and curriculum-specific programs. In every respect educational costs are increasing and equal schooling has become economically infeasible. Illich notes (pp. 8-9):

> In the United States it would take eighty billion dollars per year to provide what educators regard as equal treatment for all in grammar and high school. This is well over twice the $36 billion now being spent. Independent cost projections prepared at HEW and the University of Florida indicate that by 1974 the comparable figures will be $107 billion as against the $45 billion now projected, and these figures wholly omit the enormous costs of what is called "higher education," for which demand is growing even faster. The United States, which spent nearly eighty billion dollars in 1969 for "defense" including its deployment in Vietnam, is obviously too poor to provide equal schooling. The President's committee for the study of school finance should ask not how to support or how to trim such increasing costs, but how they can be avoided.

Although the economic arguments are compelling, these authors are not primarily concerned about the dollar cost of compulsory schooling. The reform writers are basically concerned with individual happiness and the construction of a society in which each individual can find useful and gratifying activity. In their view, compulsory schooling has produced an emphasis on amount of schooling as a measure of competence rather than on one's skills or knowledge. Those who might find gratification in grades and crafts are required to complete a specified number of years of school even though the skills they acquire (or don't) are not applicable. Schooling dulls intelligence and perpetuates a social caste system based on wealth. Upward mobility in the caste system is discouraged by the schools even though there is a mistaken notion that more schooling will produce a wealthier person and higher quality of life. The evidence, although still not conclusive (see Chapter II), indicates that such expectations are false, and they are certainly false if broad definitions of "quality of life" are employed. Illich (1971, p. 1) notes:

> Many students, especially those who are poor, intuitively know what the schools do for them. They school them to confuse process and substance. Once these become blurred, a new logic is assumed; the more

treatment there is, the better are the results; or, escalation leads to success. The pupil is thereby "schooled" to confuse teaching with learning, grade advancement with education, a diploma with competence, and fluency with the ability to say something new. His imagination is "schooled" to accept service in place of value. Medical treatment is mistaken for health care, social work for the improvement of community life, police protection for safety, military poise for national security, the rat race for productive work. Health, learning, dignity, independence, and creative endeavor are defined as little more than the performance of the institutions which claim to serve these ends, and their improvement is made to depend on allocating more resources to the management of hospitals, schools, and other agencies in question.

All of the reform writers are subject to the one sweeping criticism that they do not provide any sort of blueprint on how to accomplish the school and social reforms they advocate.[1] Their diagnosis of problems in education is sharp, and often quite valuable, but their prescriptions are vague. Certainly reform is difficult to bring about, but to succeed at all, specific and detailed programs for implementation are needed. Etzioni (1971, p. 87) criticizes Silberman on these grounds:

> Over the recent decades our ambition to fashion society in the shape of our values has swollen. We no longer accept society as a given, as a pre-existing state of nature. We view it as an arrangement, one which we can disassemble and then rearrange. We seek not merely to reform but to transform the relations among the races, the classes, the nations; we seek to deeply affect people's smoking, drug use, drinking, and eating habits, as well as to fundamentally change their education. Our economic, political, and intellectual capacity to effect these changes has increased, but much more slowly than our ambitions. We are not learning, as recent discussions of the "peace dividend" indicated, the full measure of this disparity between ambition and resources. Even if the war is finally terminated and the SALT talks do succeed, there apparently will be available only $15 to $20 new billions per annum for domestic reforms, which require at least $60 to $100 billions. As a nation, it seems we are much more inclined to talk reform than to display the political will required to bring it about. In those domestic sectors where the nation does find the will and the resources, it frequently lacks the necessary know-how. The knowledge and skills needed to provide a viable plan for social engineering are still rudimentary. Frequently we are still guided by well-meaning but inadequately conceptualized and poorly-worked-out blueprints, by semi-utopian programs of which Silberman's book is a recent example.

CONCLUSIONS AND POLICY IMPLICATIONS

Educational research has not produced impressive improvements in education, and the results of compensatory programs have been often disillusioning. It was pointed out earlier in this book that there is little probability of significantly improving classroom performance through the development of new instructional techniques, more educational expenditures, or changes in the bureaucratic structure of the schools, given the present limitations of knowledge and current institutional constraints in the school systems. The reform writers provide a range of observations, which in their eyes help to explain the failure of past educational innovation: (1) schools and research focus on unimportant objectives; (2) for many students learning cannot take place in an authoritarian environment because children's needs and abilities differ; (3) the substance of educational practice is largely irrelevant and boring to the child; (4) children do not necessarily benefit more from compulsory schooling than from voluntary attendance or from learning experiences conducted in the absence of formal schooling.

The reform writers are often a part of the classroom, and they are therefore closer to the problems that exist there than is the typical researcher. Of course, these writers are probably not representative of teachers in general, and there are opposing views. In fact, if the reform writers are at all correct there *must* be a large opposing view, namely the widely held and socially reinforced view that supports conformity. However, one rarely finds supportive views expressed for the current system that are based on a diagnosis of what goes on in classrooms. It is in the role of diagnosticians that the reform writers and other observers can play a major role, for research must be based on correct diagnosis if it is to come up with correct prescriptions.

If these writers are correct—and there is sufficient agreement on these issues to give their ideas some credibility—then the kinds of variables that researchers generally manipulate are indeed irrelevant or at least of small importance. It is not surprising in light of all this that the most promising trends in research are related to student-treatment interaction and student-teacher matching in terms of their ability to work together (Thelen, 1967). What is needed now is a marriage of the diverse approaches of scientific research and the observational diagnoses of the reform writers.

It is imperative that sweeping innovations be attempted, at least on an experimental basis. But the steps must be carefully planned, the consequences considered, and the implementation proceed along carefully designed paths. Title I and Project Head Start are probably not the way to implement new programs, which need to be smaller in scale, more comprehensively planned, and constantly monitored to avoid bad results. However, any major social action program is bound to produce highly disturbing transient effects, and these too need to be planned for in the implementation program. Finally, no single innovative system can succeed along all the dimensions of everyone's values. Disappointments are inevitable. But the quest is not for perfection; it is for progress toward a more effective educational system.

NOTE TO CHAPTER VII

1. McCracken (1970) has offered the most comprehensive critique of the reform literature, essentially on these grounds. He upholds the classical educational values and argues that the reformers' prescriptions are nonoperational or positively harmful.

VIII. CONCLUSIONS

SUMMARY AND DISCUSSION OF FINDINGS
The Input-Output Approach

This approach focuses on the relationship between the amounts of various resources that are provided to students and their educational outcomes (defined as cognitive achievement). Overall, the input-output studies provide very little evidence that school resources, in general, greatly influence student outcomes. When we examine the results across studies we find that school resources are not consistently important. The particular resources that seem to be significant in one study do not prove to be significant in other studies that include the same resources in the analysis.

Background factors, on the other hand, are always important. In study after study a student's background has a strong influence on his educational outcomes. Furthermore, the results are consistent across studies. The socioeconomic status of a student's family—his parents' income, education, and occupation—invariably proves to be a significant predictor of his educational outcome.

The role of peer group influences is more complex. There is good reason to believe that these variables are, in reality, measures of a student's background or of his school district's selection and assignment policies. On balance, there is little evidence that a student's classmates exercise a strong, independent influence on his educational outcomes.

The results from the input-output approach do not mean that school resources fail, actually or potentially, to affect student outcomes. We simply observe that so far these studies have failed to show that school resources *do* affect student outcomes. In particular, the studies do not show what would happen if the educational system received a massive increase or decrease in resources.

The Process Approach

The approach of the psychologist focuses on a very different aspect of education. Resources are taken as given or predetermined. What matters here are the processes applied to students and the interactions between teachers and students. For example, research may concentrate on the relation between teaching style and student achievement, or on the effects of grouping on achievement.

We have divided the results into two parts: those derived from studies of operating classrooms and those derived from the laboratory. For each set of results, we indicate the focus, the questions being asked, and the answers to the questions.

Looking first at the classroom studies, we find the following:
- The research on teaching approaches, teacher differences, class size, and the like shows no consistent effect on student achievement, as measured by standardized cognitive tests.
- Work on instructional methods suggests no difference among methods; none currently appears better than conventional methods. That is, in terms of differences in achievement, conventional methods appear as effective as, say, teaching by television, although the latter enables one to reach far greater numbers of students.

We consider the following results from the laboratory studies to be particularly interesting and important:
- Work on the presentation of material suggests that it is not so much the medium of instruction that is important as its sequencing and organization. There seem to be interaction effects; individual methods of presentation appear superior for some tasks and some students, but it is still hard to match student characteristics, tasks, and type of instruction.
- The work on concept attainment, retention, and learning rewards provides a number of positive findings, but the tasks in the laboratory are so unlike classroom learning that there is a difficult problem of translation. For example, the more meaningful the material, the faster it is learned and the more it is retained. But the definition of "meaningful" is a

laboratory one, relating, say, to the difference between nonsense sentences or syllables and those that make sense.
- What are termed interaction effects seem to exist among various types of personality, methods of reward, ability to grasp meaningful material, and so on; but these interactions have not yet been studied in detail.

In sum, the process approach has not identified the very specific student relations involved in learning and education. There seem to be interactions between students and teachers, between students and methods, between teachers and methods, and (most complex of all) among students, teachers, and methods. The complex three-way interactions have not yet been studied carefully.

The Organizational Approach

In the work on educational organizations, schools are seen as institutions that have to satisfy multiple goals and demands from internal bureaucracies, from the community, from parents, and from students. The allocation of resources and the choice of processes in schools are seen not as the result of a rational decisionmaking procedure but as the outcome of history, of interactions with constituents and with government, and of simple trial and error. The question being asked is, How can we make the schools innovative, adaptive, and flexible, particularly as social demands increase and the composition of the student body changes?

Most of the work in this approach consists of case studies, and the rules for internal and external validity are weak at best. Furthermore, there have been few attempts to extract important organizational propositions from the literature. The case studies provide some evidence for the following:
- There is a positive correlation between system size and centralization.
- The larger the educational bureaucracy and the more centralization, the less innovation and adaptation there is likely to be.
- Rigidities in the schools can be overcome partly by choice of teachers and principals. However, teacher qualities that are purchased—say, experience—have little to do with innovative teaching.
- Real innovation depends on the leverage that can be exerted

from outside the system—by the federal government or by citizens.
- Organizational innovations that have so far been tried (decentralization, performance contracting) as yet show no significant improvement in outcomes compared with traditional forms of organization.

The Evaluation Approach

This approach to educational research consists of *ex post* analyses of comprehensive interventions in existing school systems. These studies are characterized by a macro-view of educational interventions in which treatments are devoted to groups of children in "diverse programs taken as a whole." In short, these studies ask *whether* large-scale interventions have had an effect in general, rather than what has been the effect of any particular intervention.

Without exception, all the surveys of large, national compensatory education programs have shown no beneficial results on average. However, the evaluations on which the surveys report are often based upon suspect research designs.

Two or three smaller surveys show modest positive effects of compensatory education programs in the short run. And a number of quite carefully designed interventions display gains in pupil cognitive performance—again, in the short run. In particular, pupils from disadvantaged socioeconomic backgrounds tend to show greater progress in more highly structured programs. However, there is considerable evidence that many of the short-run gains from educational interventions fade away after two or three years if they are not reinforced. Also, this fade-out is much greater for the more highly structured programs, which are most unlike regular public school practice.

The Experiential Approach

The experiential approach is represented by the literature of educational reform. The observer, either as researcher or participant, describes the way that the experience of schooling affects the student in relation to himself, his peers, authority, and social institutions. The measure, for these writers, is not educational outcomes as indicated by standardized tests but rather the effect of the school experience on people's lives, where cognitive testing measures nothing.

Because this literature is one of social reform, it is not subject to the same tests of internal consistency as the approaches discussed above. In effect there are two elements in this literature, description and prescription.[1] The description of the schools as constituted at the present time almost invariably emphasizes a set of common themes:

- Schools are authoritarian toward students.
- Schools make little or no allowance for individual differences in learning styles and needs.
- Schools focus on methods that stress rightness and wrongness in learning, thereby destroying independence and creativity, as well as equipping children poorly for the complexities and ambiguities of the real world.
- Schools impose a certain set of social, cultural, and ethical views on their students, thereby imposing feelings of inadequacy and resentment on those who share neither those views nor the traditions they imply.
- Schools as institutions are mindless in the sense that they fail, in any operationally useful way, to question either the assumption upon which they operate or the relevance of their approach to children's needs.

The prescriptions are far more varied than the descriptive research. They range from recommendations for moderate reform within the system (Silberman) to abolition of the schools (Illich). In some cases the value systems leading to the prescriptions are made explicit; in others, not. In general, however, the experiential literature agrees on the merits of educational systems that are less rigid, more responsive to individual diversity, and more decentralized than the current system.

LIMITATIONS OF AVAILABLE RESEARCH

Each approach is subject to substantive and methodological problems peculiar to itself. These problems were discussed in other sections and will not be reviewed here. However, some research limitations appear throughout educational research and have, we feel, special importance.

First, educational outcomes are almost exclusively measured by cognitive achievement. But the educational system has many functions and many outputs. Cognitive achievement, in particular that part measured by standardized tests, is only one aspect of student learning. Higher cognitive processes (abstract reasoning, problem solving, and creativity, among others) are obviously important educational outcomes as is noncognitive achievement. Thus, of the many and diverse kinds of student learning, almost all the educational research that examines student learning is based on a narrow range of cognitive skills. Therefore, current research cannot lead to conclusive generalizations about educational outcomes, because it cannot measure most of them well.

Second, there is no examination of the cost implications of research results. By and large, educational researchers have concentrated on discovering effective educational practices. No attention has been paid to the notion of cost-effective educational practices. Research results are thus difficult to translate into policy-relevant statements.

Third, few studies maintain adequate controls over what actually goes on in the classroom as it relates to achievement. Data on classroom transactions are the only source of information on the content of the student-teacher relationship. Studies that omit transactions data can hope to identify only broad associations among variables that hold no matter what might be the nature of the relationship between student and teacher. Thus researchers' results may well be affected by circumstances unrecognized in their analyses.

Finally, the data used by researchers are, at best, crude measures of what is really happening. Concepts such as a teacher's ability to teach or a student's ability to learn are easily discussed, but objective measures of these abilities are extraordinarily elusive; and empirical analysis is based upon measurement. There is no way of knowing the extent to which inconclusive results stem from the researcher's inability to make accurate measurements of the variables he includes in his analysis.

CONCLUSIONS AND POLICY IMPLICATIONS

With the limitations of research clearly in mind, we return to the issue of educational effectiveness. The first major implication of the research is:

Research has not identified a variant of the existing system that is consistently related to students' educational outcomes.

The term "a variant of the existing system" is used to describe the broad range of alternative educational practices that have been reviewed above. We specifically include changes in school resources, processes, organizations, and aggregate levels of funding.

We must emphasize that we are not suggesting that nothing makes a difference, or that nothing "works." Rather, we are saying that research has found nothing that *consistently* and *unambiguously* makes a difference in students' outcomes. The literature contains numerous examples of educational practices that seem to have significantly affected students' outcomes.[2] The problem is that there are invariably other studies, similar in approach and method, that find the same educational practice to be ineffective. And we have no clear idea of why a practice that seems to be effective in one case is apparently ineffective in another.

We must also emphasize that we are not saying that school does not affect student outcomes. We have little knowledge of what student outcomes would be were students not to attend school at all. Educational research focuses on variants of the existing system and tells us nothing about where we might be without the system at all.

Furthermore, nothing we have found in the educational research literature proves that our current educational system *cannot* be substantially improved. But the research results we review above provide little reason to be sanguine. Our general conclusion, so far, is that there are few consistent, positive, policy-relevant findings. That is, the research offers little guidance to what educational practices should be implemented. This condition can arise because that is the way the world really is, or because researchers have been asking the wrong questions, or because the research methods used are not sufficiently powerful, or because the data are "bad." For whatever reason, we can only say that the educational practices examined thus far are only weakly connected to student achievement.

Finally, the educational practices for which school systems have traditionally been willing to pay a premium do not appear to make a major difference in student outcomes. Teachers' experience and teachers' advanced degrees, the two basic factors that determine salary, are not clearly related to student achievement. Reduction in class size, a favorite high-priority reform in the eyes of many school systems, seems not to be related to student outcomes. In general, the second major implication of the research (and the most important one for school finance) is:

Conclusions

Increasing expenditures on traditional educational practices is not likely to improve educational outcomes substantially.

The third major policy implication of the research is:

There seem to be opportunities for significant reduction or redirection of educational expenditures without deterioration in educational outcomes.

Researchers have examined many variants of the existing educational system. As we have indicated, none of these variants has been shown to improve educational outcomes consistently. A fact often overlooked is that few have been shown to lead to significantly worse outcomes either. Consequently, educational research has provided a long list of equally effective variants of the existing system. And, if these variants are not all equally expensive, then choosing the least expensive provides opportunities to redirect (or even reduce) costs without also reducing effectiveness.[3]

Educational research consists almost entirely of effectiveness studies. There are very few cost-effectiveness studies. The tremendous volume of "negative" results—negative according to the peculiar bias of educational research, which seeks only improvement on the effectiveness side—must surely contain many "positive" results in the sense of indicating less costly methods of accomplishing as much as is currently attained.

The research contains some evidence supporting a fourth major implication:

Innovation, responsiveness, and adaptation in school systems decrease with size and depend upon exogenous shocks to the system.

In other words, large systems are less likely to be innovative, responsive, or adaptive than are small systems. Further, whatever the size of the system, innovation is not apt to come from within the system. Outside pressures, from the community or from the federal government, are likely to be needed. We note, however, that relatively little research has been directed toward these issues. Hence, this finding must be viewed as tentative.

The implication of this tentative conclusion is clear. There is currently a good deal of interest in federal leverage and in the question of whether federal aid to the schools should be tied or untied. *The literature that we have examined suggests that federal influence is important in getting innovation into urban school systems,* although the hypothesis has not really been tested rigorously.

Our review of educational research supports a fifth major implication:

> *Educational research is seriously deficient in terms of the size, scope, and focus of research efforts and in the integration of research results.*

Beyond these specific limitations, educational research has tended to be small in scale, narrow in scope, diffuse, maldistributed, and lacking in focus. By comparison with other major sectors, the amount of research activity devoted to educational problems is surprisingly small. For example, the amount of resources allocated to agricultural research and development is more than four times as large, and health research is allocated more than 13 times as much. Moreover, educational research is a relatively recent development. Quantitative research on American education goes back to the work of Joseph Meyer Rice in the 1890s; but significant levels of activity did not begin until the late 1950s when first the National Science Foundation, then the Office of Education, began to fund a wide range of research activities. A comparison of R&D communities by instructional affiliation shows that educational research is very unlike other R&D sectors in the economy because colleges and universities perform the majority of R&D in the educational sector. The academic community tends to conduct relatively small studies on a part-time basis and to concentrate on basic research. Furthermore, educational research has tended to be almost exclusively the domain of the psychologist. Only recently has it begun to attract the attention of more than a handful of well-trained researchers in other fields.[4]

The body of educational research now available leaves much to be desired, at least by comparison with the level of understanding that has been achieved in numerous other fields. This does not reflect the quality of the contemporary educational researcher but rather the nature of the research community and its history. The typical education study is not founded on a wealth of previous knowledge and understanding nor is it directed toward the needs of the educational policymaker. There are no research-based, problem-solving units in the typical operating agency. In 1968 there were only 1,300 man-years devoted to research, development, or innovation in the almost 20,000 state and local educational agencies; most of that was devoted to testing and to gathering statistics (Levien, 1971).

Finally, the sixth major implication of our work is:

Research tentatively suggests that improvement in student outcomes, both cognitive and noncognitive, may require sweeping changes in the organization, structure, and conduct of educational experiences.

This inference follows from the first four conclusions cited above, as well as from the testimony of the experiential approach. Even the fifth conclusion, which cites the paucity of educational research, tends to reinforce this point because it implies that marginal changes in research will be inadequate to indicate clearly the directions educational improvement should take. Below we offer hypotheses that are broadly consistent with the "sweeping change" inference.

WHERE DO WE GO FROM HERE? THE SUBSTANTIVE ISSUES

Our review of educational research found little association between various educational practices—resources, processes, organizations, and so on—and students' educational outcomes. We also inferred reasons why this seems to be so: the role of non-school factors, interaction, and inappropriate forms of education. Although they have been recognized in the past by many educational researchers, they have not been carefully investigated to any great extent. They are *potential* explanations of why research has not revealed the expected connections between educational processes and educational outcomes.

Non-School Factors

There is considerable evidence that non-school factors may well be more important determinants of educational outcomes than are school factors (Jencks *et al.*, 1972). The research repeatedly finds high correlations between students' socioeconomic backgrounds and educational outcomes. A variety of hypotheses as to why this relationship seems so powerful have been put forward.

- At one extreme, there are some who argue that genetic differences among children are associated with their racial, cultural, or social backgrounds. According to this view there are differences among children with respect to their learning

ability, and these differences are, in turn, correlated with their environments.
- Others have argued that environment is correlated with educational outcomes because much of the child's learning occurs outside of school. The child raised in an environment of poverty is seldom exposed to museums or libraries, lives in a home where few books are present, and generally is not exposed to the variety of educational experiences available to the advantaged child.
- A third and somewhat related view also argues that much of a child's learning occurs outside school. What children learn outside school, it is argued, depends upon what their environments offer to them by way of experiences. Thus the child raised in an environment of poverty learns "as much" as a child raised in a middle-class family; but precisely what he or she learns is quite different from what the middle-class child learns. However, this argument goes on, the tests or measures of educational outcomes are oriented toward the middle class and, roughly speaking, give full value to what the middle-class child has learned outside school but only partial credit to what the poor child has learned outside school.
- Still others have argued that a child's background influences his educational outcomes by affecting his attitudes. According to this view, the disadvantaged child lacks motivation or does not aspire to educational success. His parents are likely to have attained relatively low educational levels. He faces racial or class discrimination, which reduces his prospects of success (compared with the middle-class child) despite his educational attainment. The general thrust of this argument is that the disadvantaged child is not encouraged, either directly (for example, by parental pressure) or indirectly (for example, by observation of the "payoff" of education to others like himself), to seek success in the schools.

The above are but a few of the many hypotheses as to why educational outcomes seem to be unaffected by variations in educational practices. They are not necessarily the most likely to be true, but they illustrate how a broad range of background factors may be adduced in asserting their domination of educational outcomes.

Conclusions

None of this means that schools do not or cannot affect outcomes, but it does imply that factors outside of the schools have a strong influence on students' educational outcomes, perhaps strong enough to "swamp" the effects of variations in educational practices. This is the important point: Are our educational problems school problems? The most profitable line of attack on these educational problems, under this hypothesis, may not be through the schools at all. But we have very little knowledge how and to what extent educational outcomes are affected by non-school factors. We can only observe that there is considerable evidence that non-school factors are closely associated with students' educational outcomes. The best information we have, regardless of the deficiencies we have noted, is that schools do not now have a tremendous influence on the achievement that does occur. Therefore, it is logical to infer that the whole substantive area of non-school learning deserves much more attention than it has received from past research.

Interaction

There is some (weak) evidence that the effect of an educational practice may be conditional on other aspects of the situation.[5] Simply stated, this hypothesis argues that teacher, student, instructional method, and, perhaps, other aspects of the educational process interact with each other. Thus, a teacher who works well (is effective) with one type of student using one method may accomplish far less when working with a different type of student, even if using the same instructional method. Accordingly, the effectiveness of a teacher, or method, or whatever, may vary from one situation to another.

We have discussed the notion of interaction at length in Chapter IV and will not repeat that discussion here. The important point to be made is that research has not discovered an educational practice that is consistently effective because no educational practice always "works" regardless of other aspects of the educational situation. Interaction may explain why educational research has thus far failed to identify any educational practice that is consistently effective. There may not be any *universally* effective educational practices.

Thus far, teachers (or students) are generally viewed as interchangeable within broad constraints. Educators voice concern if, say, a sixth grade teacher is asked to teach the third grade, or if a science teacher is assigned to an English class. But if a sixth grade teacher is teaching sixth graders, few have asked whether that teacher would be more effective if assigned to teach a different set of students. If interaction in fact exists, it may be possible to assign teachers to students so that each teacher (and student) is working with the particular type of student (and teacher) with whom he or she is particularly effective. Thus, the concept of interaction should be viewed as not only a potential explanation of our inability to identify consistently effective educational practices but also as a prospective path toward improving educational outcomes.

We must emphasize that we now know very little about interactions. There have been few attempts to examine interactions, and there is some controversy among educational psychologists as to whether interactions actually exist. Most of the evidence for the existence of interactions comes from ex post rationalization of research results. That is, some researchers, confronted with unexpected results in their analyses, have reviewed their data to "see what happened" and "discovered" that there was interaction among student, teacher, method, or whatever. The possibility that any given teacher may be more or less effective when working with one group of students than when working with another is too important to overlook and is therefore another priority field for research.

Different Forms of Education

Finally, there is a suggestion that substantial improvement in educational outcomes can be obtained only through a vastly different form of education. Those who argue this hypothesis question whether the educational system, as currently constituted in the United States, can be substantially improved. It is seen, at the extreme, as being a bureaucratic, rigid, unresponsive structure that no amount of marginal change can improve. Both the organizational approach and the experiential approach argue for this hypothesis.

In some cases, critics of the system focus on the organization of the school's basic unit, the classroom. They argue that traditional instructional practices fail to capitalize on children's natural curiosity and interest in learning. Team teaching, the use of audio-visual aids, and other instructional methods make little difference, according to these critics, so long as the child is forced to devote his attention to the teacher's choice of topics. Open schools, schools without walls, and the like are seen as being the solution.

Conclusions

Other critics have found fault with the incentive structure in the schools. They argue that rewards and penalties are distributed among teachers and administrators according to implicit rules that emphasize factors unrelated to educational effectiveness. Those who share this perspective tend to argue for systems in which incentives are directly tied to educational outcomes, such as voucher systems, performance contracting, and so on.

Research tells us little about how effective these vastly different forms of education might be.[6] They are novel systems that have been only sparingly put into practice, if at all. And there is certainly a possibility that they may prove to be much less effective than the current system. Large-scale experiments or demonstrations of these vastly different forms of education should be implemented and carefully observed and evaluated.

WHERE DO WE GO FROM HERE?
THE METHODOLOGICAL ISSUES

The policy results also raise another issue: What kind of research is now possible and worth doing? To begin, we consider this issue for each approach separately; then we raise the question of what is now needed to create real policy analysis for education. First, with respect to the input-output approach, only one of the studies analyzed (Hanushek, 1970) was able to match student achievement with resources—in particular, teachers—to which the students were actually exposed. (Ordinarily, student achievement is matched to *average* school resources.) This study found that teachers make a difference (for ethnic majority students), but it was unable to identify *what qualities* of a teacher make a difference. Thus, some research should be devoted to pushing this enterprise further. But this means that more resources will have to flow into creating new data. None of the currently used and widely analyzed data sets—EEOS, Talent, Plowden—enable the investigator to match individual achievement with individual resources.

For the process approach it is important to pin down the interaction effects. This will require complex experimental designs. We also believe that it is important to work on translating promising research and development results into the operating classroom. This will mean a much closer scrutiny of the R&D experiments themselves and of the means of disseminating and evaluating results.

The organizational approach is one of the least rigorous and robust. The kinds of questions we want answered about educational organizations need to be expressed more clearly, and the sampling procedures need to be improved. A balance must be struck between the in-depth richness provided by small samples and the generalizability provided by large ones. The organizational approach has a close relation to alternative financial structures. It is hard to influence the choice of processes or resources within schools or classrooms from outside without creating massive problems of control. It may be possible to influence educational organizations through new financial schemes, but the organizational approach has as yet not identified effective methods for applying that influence.

The evaluation approach is the most policy oriented of those considered here. Therein lies its greatest strength and also its greatest weakness. In large program evaluations, across many individual projects, the basic question to be answered is, To what extent was the program successful in general? Large-scale evaluations tend to lump together individually successful and unsuccessful projects to arrive at a general conclusion about program effectiveness. This general assessment provides an estimate of what would happen if the program were implemented elsewhere, which is extremely useful to know. On the other hand, large program evaluations are seldom sufficiently detailed to explain why some projects succeeded while others failed. But this is, perhaps, the most important information. Evaluators clearly must pay much more attention to the differences between successful and unsuccessful projects within programs. If these differences can be identified and understood, the successful projects should be used as models for further within-program development.

We feel that the books and articles that make up the reform literature have provided insights rather than answers. These insights must be checked, verified, refined, and extended. We need to develop methods of analysis that will allow us to distinguish the effects of the ways in which schools are organized, the way in which a particular school is organized, and the personalities of a particular set of individuals. If an elementary school teacher tells us that the children in her school are brutalized, we have to be able to determine whether or not this situation stems from the underlying structure of our schools. Does the way in which we go about providing elementary education build in incentives that stimulate such treatment? Or, alternatively, does this situation come about because of the way a particular school or school district is structured? Or, is this behavior a function of the types of people that happen to staff that particular school? In short, the reform literature describes the pathology of the schools. Is this pathology idiosyncratic, or applicable to a wide range of schools? Can the prescriptions of the reformers be translated into operational planning and generalized to a wide range of schools? If they can, would their prescriptions be acceptable to the clientele of the American education system—in other words, to all of us? There is, after all, substantial evidence that most Americans think the schools do pretty well now. If major increases in effectiveness require fundamental restructuring of education, then effective reform might be unacceptable to the public even if costs were thereby reduced.

We believe three things are needed in educational policy analysis. *First,* it will be necessary to merge the various research approaches. If economists want to fit educational "production functions," they will have to revamp the approach completely to include in their models specific processes and organizational factors that affect students, as well as interaction effects. The failures of the input-output approach are, in fact, causing everyone to look more deeply at fundamental assumptions about education. And so the economists find themselves face to face with the psychologists and educators, being forced into a detailed analysis of what goes on in schools and classrooms. *Second,* we simply must measure education in relation to many more outcomes and dimensions (including time) than is currently being done. More resources must be devoted to designing new measures and instruments, and research will have to focus on outcomes over time. Organizationally, this implies some permanent institutional arrangement that will keep the long-run research policy relevant. *Third,* cost considerations must be brought into analyses. We are almost certainly overlooking many opportunities to redirect scarce educational resources effectively and will continue to do so until a firm base of cost-effectiveness research is built.

We have consciously avoided any extended discussion of the aims of education for two reasons: A study of those aims was not part of our charter; furthermore, since such a study would rely ultimately on personal values, the researcher is no more competent than any other citizen to solve these issues. Yet he cannot ignore them, because to conduct measurement in the absence of aims or functions is to abandon the researcher's social responsibility and in some sense his seriousness of purpose.

Yet as James has said (1971):

> We have been notably unsuccessful as a society in this century in stating our aims of education. The prospect of allowing ourselves to be pressured by narrow concerns, driven by casual circumstances—like our rather uncritical embrace of "accountability"—to set trivial goals for our educational institutions is appalling. We desperately need, for the long range, not to preoccupy ourselves with the trivial, but to shape our goals to fit our broadest perception of the needs of human life, and to challenge our model-builders to reach toward them, and to be critical of failures to reach them.

Our review here of what is known about educational effectiveness is a first short step to responding to that challenge, by identifying the limitations of our present knowledge and methods and pointing out possible paths toward improvement. The larger task set forth by James can come only from interdisciplinary efforts of an intensity, breadth, and continuity heretofore unknown, but not by that token unattainable. Chapter I of this book described the social policy setting for research on social effectiveness. It remains for other studies to refine our definitions of the functions of the public schools and to construct and test measures of effectiveness for each function. Finally, research must go beyond telling us how effective schooling is now and continue its efforts to improve performance under more rigorous criteria as to both theory and practice than are generally called for at the present time.

NOTES TO
CHAPTER VIII

1. The writer's triple role as observer, participant, and social critic necessarily places heavy pressure on his objectivity in describing the phenomena he observes. Nonetheless, there seems to be considerable agreement among writers with respect to the phenomenon.
2. See Chapter VI.
3. This conclusion applies only to questions of educational effectiveness as now measured. It cannot be applied to justify situations in

which constant or decreasing expenditures would impair the health or safety of children and staff.
4. See Levien (1971) for a discussion of the current state of educational research.
5. See, for example, Thelen (1967).
6. But see Carpenter and Hall (1971).

Appendix A
INPUT-OUTPUT STUDIES

This appendix lays out in some detail the studies examined in the input-output approach—the first of the five approaches discussed in the text. In addition to reporting the results claimed for particular studies, we have made some effort to explain what each analyst did. For each of the 21 studies discussed here, the reader will find the following:
- Author(s), title, publisher, date
- Unit of analysis: whether analysis was applied to schools or to individual students
- Sample size and description
- Kinds of data
- List of variables (all independent and dependent variables are included)
- Procedure: what the analyst did as well as the techniques used
- Results

The studies are arranged in chronological order.

[1] William G. Mollenkopf and S. Donald Melville, *A Study of Secondary School Characteristics as Related to Test Scores*, Research Bulletin RB-56-6, Educational Testing Service, Princeton, 1956.

UNIT OF ANALYSIS
   School.

SAMPLE
   (a) 100 schools (9,600 ninth graders), (b) 106 schools (8,357 twelfth graders).

DATA
   Independent variables were drawn from a questionnaire filled out by principals. Dependent variables were drawn from special tests administered in the schools at the request of the Educational Testing Service (ETS).

VARIABLES
Independent
   1. Number of school facilities (e.g., auditorium, gymnasium).
   2. Percent full-time teachers five or more years college training.
   3. Percent full-time teachers five or more years experience.
   4. Percent full-time teachers aged 36-60.
   5. Years of experience of principal.
   6. Degree level of principal.
   7. Percent principal's time—supervision.
   8. Percent principal's time—administration.
   9. Number of special staff.
   10. Pupil/teacher ratio.
   11. Drop-out index [(a) 12th graders/10th graders; (b) 9th graders/7th graders].
   12. ADA/number pupils 7th grade or higher.
   13. Average class size.
   14. Public library in region.
   15. PTA members/number pupils 7th grade or higher.
   16. Percent graduates entering college.
   17. Percent support from state aid.
   18. Average teacher salary.
   19. Supplies and library expenditure/number pupils 7th grade or higher.
   20. Percent fathers high school graduates.
   21. Percent fathers employed as professionals.
   22. Percent fathers employed as farmers.

23. Percent fathers employed as craftsmen.
24. Rate of growth of community, 10 years.
25. Size of community (urban/rural).
26. Number of pupils in school, 7th or higher.
27. South or non-South.

Data were collected for seven additional independent variables that were discarded *a priori.*

Dependent
1. Vocabulary test score.
2. Sentence completion test.
3. Arithmetic reasoning test.
4. Arithmetic computation test.
5. English achievement test.
6. Social studies achievement test.
7. Science achievement test.

PROCEDURE

Questionnaires were sent to 1,877 high school principals. Replies were obtained from 844 (560 indicated willingness to administer tests). A stratified sample (by independent variables 3, 16, and 17, selected by factor analysis of independent variables) was chosen from among these.

Mean aptitude test scores (numbers 1-4) were calculated for each school. Independent variables were dichotomized near the median and correlated with mean test scores. Based on these simple correlations, six independent variables (numbers 14, 17, 19, 20, 25, 27) were chosen for further study.

Parts 1 and 2 of the aptitude test were combined to obtain a verbal score. Parts 3 and 4 were combined to obtain a quantitative score. For each four-way combination of the six independent variables, a multiple correlation coefficient for each score was calculated for the 9th and 12th grade samples. Variables number 19 and 27 consistently appeared in the combinations yielding high correlations.

The simple correlation matrix shows that five other variables were sometimes correlated with the achievement test scores (numbers 9, 10, 13, 16, 21). Stepwise regression was used eight times (9th and 12th graders by three achievement scores and total achievement score) to choose from among these 11 independent variables. Regression coefficients are reported, but no significance levels or standard errors are given. R^2 was generally higher in 12th grade equations.

RESULTS

Average class size and percentage of last year's graduates who went on to college occurred most often.

[2]   James Alan Thomas, *Efficiency in Education: A Study of the Relationship Between Selected Inputs and Mean Test Scores in a Sample of Senior High Schools,* unpublished Ph.D. dissertation (microf.), Stanford University Library, 1962.

UNIT OF ANALYSIS
School.

SAMPLE
206 schools in communities between 2,500 and 25,000 population.

DATA
School output and input data were drawn from Project TALENT data bank. Data on socioeconomic characteristics of home and community were drawn from the Census.

VARIABLES
Independent
1. Size of 12th grade class.
2. Median starting salary—male teachers.
3. Expenditure/pupil (Grades 9-12).
4. Type of school (academic versus comprehensive).
5. Grades included in school (10-12, 9-12, etc.).
6. Number of days in school year.
7. Average class size, science and math.
8. Average class size, non-science.
9. Average amount of homework expected.
10. Number of study hall periods/week.
11. Number of books in school library.
12. Age of building.

13. Provision for grouping.
14. Median starting salary—female teachers.
15. Average experience of teachers.
16. Presence of guidance program.
17. Town population.
18. Adult (in town) median years of schooling.
19. Unemployment rate.
20. Percent labor force in manufacturing.
21. Median family income.
22. Miles to nearest city larger than 100,000.
23. Percent rural farms.
24. Percent children in private schools.
25. Percent population born in state.
26. Percent employment white collar.
27. Percent owner-occupied homes.
28. Quality of housing.
29. Average daily percent absent.
30. Delinquency rate.
31. Percent dropouts after entry into 10th grade.
32. Percent males who went on to college last year.

Dependent
1. Information test, 10th grade, boys.
2. Information test, 10th grade, girls.
3. Information test, 12th grade, boys.
4. Information test, 12th grade, girls.
5. English test, 10th graders, all.
6. English test, 12th graders, all.
7. Reading comprehension, 10th graders, all.
8. Reading comprehension, 12th graders, all.
9. Creativity, 12th graders, all.
10. Mechanical reasoning, 10th graders, all.
11. Abstract reasoning, 10th graders, all.
12. Abstract reasoning, 12th graders, all.
13. Mathematics II, 10th graders, all.
14. Mathematics I, 12th graders, all.
15. Mathematics II, 12th graders, all.
16. Mathematics III, 12th graders, all.
17. Physical science, 12th graders, boys.
18. Mechanics, 12th graders, boys.

PROCEDURE

A stepwise, multiple regression was run for each of the 18 dependent variables. All independent variables were considered in every case.

RESULTS

R^2 ranged from .77 to .87. F tests indicated very significant R in every case (minimum F is 8.12; maximum F, 17.40). In one regression equation (dependent variable number 18), all 32 independent variables were significant at the 1 percent level. (Beta coefficients were all at least 10 times their standard error.) Consistently significant positive (negative) variables were 1-4, 6, 11, 12, 14-16, 18, 21, 24, 25, 27, 28, 31, 32 (5, 7-9, 29). Consistently insignificant variables were 10, 13, 17, 19, 20, 22, 23, 26, 30.

[3]   Charles Benson et al., *State and Local Fiscal Relationships in Public Education in California,* Report of the Senate Fact Finding Committee on Revenue and Taxation, Senate of the State of California, Sacramento, March 1965.

UNIT OF ANALYSIS
School District.

SAMPLE
Fifth-grade pupils in 249 California school districts.

DATA

Data on socioeconomic variables for districts' attendance areas were collected from 1960 Census. Data on school resources were obtained from district records.

VARIABLES
Independent
1. District taxes/total income.
2. State aid/total income.
3. Other aid/total income.
4. Total income/ADA.
5. Instructional expense/total expense.

Appendix: Input-Output Studies

6. Instructional expense/total ADA.
7. Total expense/total ADA.
8. Percent teachers in highest salary quartile.
9. Percent teachers in lowest salary quartile.
10. Percent teachers in provisional salary quartile.
11. ADA/teacher.
12. Teachers/administrators.
13. Mean teachers' salary.
14. Mean administrators' salary.
15. Teacher's/administrators' salary.
16. Teachers' salary/ADA.
17. Administrators' salary/ADA.
18. Median household income.
19. Median adults' education.
20. Unemployment rate.
21. Percent persons under 18 living with both parents.
22. ADA.
23. Size of attendance area.
24. Assessed value/ADA.
25. Tax rate.

Dependent
Score on reading achievement test.

PROCEDURE

The sample was divided by size of district (in ADA) into three subsamples. After preliminary inspection of simple correlations, 10 independent variables (numbers 4, 6, 8, 9, 11-14, 18, 22) were included in a stepwise regression for each subsample.

RESULTS

For the smallest size category, independent variables 6, 8, 18, and 22 were significant and positive. Independent variables 9 and 12 were significant and negative.

For the middle-sized districts, independent variables 8, 13, and 18 were both positive and significant. Variables 12 and 22 were negative and significant.

For the largest districts, independent variables 8 (-), 12 (+), and 18 (+) were significant.

[4] James S. Coleman et al., "Pupil Achievement and Motivation," Chapter 3, *Equality of Educational Opportunity*, U.S. Department of Health, Education and Welfare, U.S. Office of Education, OE-38001, Washington, D.C., 1966, pp. 218-333.*

UNIT OF ANALYSIS
Individual/School.

SAMPLE
645,000 students in the 1st, 3rd, 6th, 9th, and 12th grades in about 3,100 schools.

DATA
1,170 high schools were randomly chosen within a stratified sampling scheme. Every elementary school that sent over 90 percent of its graduates to a selected secondary school was included in the sample of elementary schools. The remainder of the elementary school sample was selected from other feeder schools by a stratified, random process. The total elementary school sample contained 3,223 schools. School resources were derived from questionnaires applied to school superintendents, principals, and teachers. Background factors were drawn from questionnaires applied to individual students. Student outcomes were obtained from a battery of tests administered under ETS direction. Both principal and pupil questionnaires were obtained from 689 high schools.

VARIABLES
Independent
1. Reading material in home.
2. Possessions in home.
3. Parents' education.
4. Number of siblings.
5. Parents' educational desires.

---

*The Coleman report is a massive document presenting the results of research into a number of educational problems. We are concerned here only with that segment of the report dealing with the relationship between school resources and background factors and student outcomes.

Appendix: Input-Output Studies

6. Parents' interest.
7. Integrity of home.
8. Changing schools.
9. Foreign language in home.
10. Urbanism of background.
11. Control of environment.
12. Self-concept.
13. Interest in school.
14. Homework.
15. Preschool.
16. Number of students in school in grade.
17. Nonverbal mean score.
18. Verbal mean score.
19. Proportion Negro in grade.
20. Proportion white in grade.
21. Proportion Mexican-American in grade.
22. Proportion Puerto Rican in grade.
23. Proportion Indian in grade.
24. Proportion Oriental in grade.
25. Proportion other in grade.
26. Average white in class last year.
27. Average white throughout school.
28. Proportion definite plans for college.
29. Proportion mother attends college.
30. Proportion mother wishes excellence.
31. Proportion own encyclopedia.
32. Proportion college prep curriculum.
33. Proportion read over 16 books.
34. Proportion member debate club.
35. Average number science courses.
36. Average number language courses.
37. Average number mathematics courses.
38. Average time with counselor.
39. Proportion teachers expect to be best.
40. Proportion no chance for successful life.
41. Proportion want to be best in class.
42. Average hours homework.
43. Teachers' perception of student quality.
44. Teachers' perception of school quality.

45. Teachers' SES level.
46. Teachers' experience.
47. Teachers' localism.
48. Teachers' quality of college attended.
49. Teachers' degree level.
50. Teachers' professionalism.
51. Teachers' attitude toward integration.
52. Teachers' preference for middle-class students.
53. Teachers' preference for white students.
54. Teachers' verbal score.
55. Teachers' variation in proportion of white students taught.
56. Teachers' proportion male.
57. Teachers' proportion white.
58. Teachers' proportion certified.
59. Teachers' average salary.
60. Teachers' number of absences.
61. Teachers' attended institute for disadvantaged.
62. Teachers' attended NSF institute.
63. Pupils/teacher.
64. Percentage makeshift rooms.
65. Specialized rooms and fields.
66. Science lab facilities.
67. Library volumes/student.
68. Extracurricular activities.
69. Separate classes for special cases.
70. Comprehensiveness of curriculum.
71. Number of specialized teachers and correctional personnel.
72. Transfers.
73. Number of types of tests given.
74. Movement between tracks.
75. Accreditation index.
76. Days in session.
77. Age of texts.
78. Part-day attendance.
79. Teacher turnover.
80. Guidance counselors.
81. Attendance.
82. Percent graduates who go on to college.
83. Principal from teachers college.

84. Principal's salary.
85. School location (urban/rural).
86. Length of academic day.
87. Tracking.
88. Accelerated curriculum.
89. Promotion of slow learners.
90. Attitude toward integration.
91. Instructional expenditure/pupil.
92. School board elected.
93. Teachers examined.

Dependent
1. Score on nonverbal test.
2. Score on general information test 1.
3. Score on general information test 2.
4. Score on general information test 3.
5. Score on general information test 4.
6. Score on general information test 5.
7. Score on general information total.
8. Score on verbal test.
9. Score on reading test.
10. Score on mathematics test.

PROCEDURE

Simple correlation matrices were constructed and examined. The 60 independent variables that appeared to be most important were selected and used for all grades. (At lower grades some variables were non-existent, reducing the total at those grades.) Preliminary regressions were then run and further variables deleted. Final analyses were conducted on 6th, 9th, and 12th grade samples stratified, at each grade level, by race and region (North/South).

In each case a sequence of regression runs was made in which blocks of variables were added to a regression and the additional explanatory power of each block of variables was calculated. Regression coefficients and tests of significance were not reported. Background factors are always entered prior to any of the three main categories of variables: student body variables, school facilities and curriculum measures, and teachers' characteristics. Verbal achievement is the only dependent variable for which results are reported.

RESULTS*

Background Factors

Eight background factor variables (numbers 1-7 and 10) explained about 15 percent and 10 percent of the variance in the achievement of Southern and Northern Negroes, respectively. The explanatory power of background factors for Northern and Southern whites was about 20 percent in each case.

School Facilities and Curriculum

In general, measures of school facilities and curriculum accounted for an extremely small amount of variation in student achievement. Eleven variables (numbers 16, 66-68, 70, 74, 80, 85, 87-88, and 91) were used to measure facilities and curriculum. Instructional expenditures per student (91) accounted for less than .3 percent of the variation in achievement after the six "objective" background factors (1-4, 7, 10) were controlled for three of the four major subgroups. For Southern Negroes, this variable accounted for about 3 percent of the variation in achievement after background factors were entered.

The unique contribution of the school facilities and curriculum measures varied among grade levels and race/region subgroups. But the only cases where the additional explanatory power of these 11 variables (entered after the six "objective" background factors) exceeded about 3 percent were, again, Southern Negroes. There, these variables generally added about 8 percent.

Teachers' Characteristics

Seven teacher variables (numbers 45-47, 49, 52, 54, and 57) were selected. Controlling for the six "objective" background variables, teachers' characteristics contributed between 1 and 2-1/2 percent explanatory power for whites, about 3 percent explanatory power for Northern Negroes, and about 8-1/2 percent explanatory power for Southern Negroes.

Student-body Characteristics

Five student-body variables (numbers 28, 31, 42, 72, and 81)

---

*Results are reported for five grade levels by 10 racial/regional subsamples. We will concentrate on the 9th and 12th grade results for Northern and Southern Negroes and whites.

accounted for far more variation in the achievement of minority group children than did any attributes of school facilities and somewhat more than did attributes of staff. Controlling for the six "objective" background factors and 11 school characteristics (facilities and curriculum), student-body characteristics added about 4 percent to the explanatory power of the Negro regressions and about 1-1/2 percent to the explanatory power of the white regressions.

The variable, proportion white students in school, had a negligible effect upon white achievement under all conditions. For Negroes the variable added to the explanatory power of an equation that includes the six "objective" background factors and instructional expenditures per pupil: 1-1/2 to 3 percent if no other variables are controlled, and a negligible amount if student-body characteristics are also controlled.

Total Effect

The six background factors accounted for about 13 (7-1/2, 16, 15) percent of the variance in the achievement of Southern Negroes (Northern Negroes, Southern whites, Northern whites). The seven teacher characteristics added about 8 (3, 2-1/4, 1-1/2) percent to the explanatory power of the equation. Adding the 11 school variables increased the regression's explanatory power by about 3-1/2 (2, 1-1/4, 1). Finally, adding the student-body variables increased explanatory power by about 2 (2, 1, 3/4) percent. Overall then, the production function accounted for about 26 (15, 20, 19) percent of the variance in students' verbal achievement.

[5] Jesse Burkhead, Thomas G. Fox, and John W. Holland, *Input and Output in Large City High Schools*, Syracuse University Press, Syracuse, 1967.

UNIT OF ANALYSIS
    School.

SAMPLE
    (a) 39 Chicago schools, (b) 22 Atlanta schools, (c) 177 Project TALENT schools.

DATA

Chicago and Atlanta data were drawn from school district records. The TALENT sample was drawn from Project TALENT file. Occasional variables were drawn from the Census.

VARIABLES
Independent
1. Median family income in school's attendance area (Census).
2. ADA.
3. Age of building.
4. Textbook expenditures/pupil.
5. Materials and supplies expenditure/pupil.
6. Median teacher experience.
7. Percent teachers with M.A. or higher.
8. Teacher man-years/pupil.
9. Administrator man-years/pupil.
10. Auxiliary man-years/pupil.

Dependent
1. Percent 11th graders in "stanines" 5-9 on IQ test/percent 11th graders in stanines 5-9 in norm group for test. (A stanine is an interval along a nine-point, ten-equal-interval line.)
2. Identical index calculated from a reading test.
3. Percent dropouts, 11th grade.
4. Percent 11th graders expressing college intentions.
5. Residual from simple regression of 11th grade IQ index on similarly defined index for that year's 9th graders in same school.
6. Identical index calculated from a reading test.

Independent
1. Total experience/pupil.
2. Library experience/pupil.
3. Average teacher salary.
4. Enrollment/teacher.
5. Teacher turnover.
6. Registration beginning of year.
7. Median family income in school's attendance area (Census).

Appendix: Input-Output Studies

  8. ADA.
  9. Age of building.

Dependent
  1. School median on verbal test, 10th graders.
  2. Percent male dropouts, all grades.
  3. Percent graduates who went on to college.
  4. Residual from simple regression of 10th grade verbal test median on 8th graders' median score on same test that year.

Independent
  1. Books in library/12th grader.
  2. Mean class size.
  3. Beginning salary, male teachers.
  4. 12th grade enrollment.
  5. Median family income in attendance area (Census).
  6. Age of building.
  7. Median teacher experience.
  8. Total expenditures/pupil.

Dependent
  1. 12th grade reading scores, school mean.
  2. Percent dropout, all grades.
  3. Percent graduates who went on to college.
  4. Residual of mean 12th grade reading score regressed on mean 10th grade reading score, same test, school, year.

PROCEDURE
Stepwise multiple regression for each dependent variable.

RESULTS
(a) Nothing significant showed up in the IQ residual regression. Family income was *significant positive* in reading and IQ index regressions; nothing else was significant. Teacher experience was *significant positive* in residual reading score regression; nothing else was significant. Family income, age of building (counting from oldest), and material and supplies expenditures/pupil were *significant negative* in dropout regression. There was nothing significant for college intentions.

(b) There was nothing significant for post-high-school. Family income, library expenditures/pupil, and average teacher salary were *significant negative,* and total expenditures/pupil and registration were *significant positive,* in dropout regression. Family income was *significant positive* and registration *significant negative* in verbal score regression. Teacher turnover was *significant negative* in residual verbal score regression.

(c) There was nothing significant in either percent dropout or percent college. Books in library/12th grader was *significant and positive* in residual regression. Family income, building age, teacher experience, and salary were *significant* in reading scores regression.

[6] Eric Hanushek, *The Education of Negroes and Whites,* unpublished Ph.D. dissertation (microf.) Massachusetts Institute of Technology, 1968.

UNIT OF ANALYSIS
School.

SAMPLE
471 schools with five or more white 6th grade students and 242 schools with five or more black 6th grade students. All schools were in the Northeast or Great Lakes regions.

DATA
All data were drawn from the Equal Educational Opportunity Survey (EEOS). All variables were school aggregates across all 6th graders in school.

VARIABLES
Independent
  1. Possessions in home.
  2. Father's education.
  3. Family size.
  4. School in central city.
  5. Percent Negro students.
  6. Teacher's experience.
  7. Teacher's verbal ability.
  8. Percent students had non-white teacher previous year.

9. Percent who attended nursery school.
10. Percent student out-migration previous year.
11. Percent students who wish to finish high school.
12. Percent students who feel they have little chance of success.

Dependent
Verbal score.

PROCEDURE
Two regressions were run in log-log form, one each for white schools and black schools.

RESULTS
In the white sample all variables were significant except family size and student out-migration. The nursery school and out-migration variables were omitted from the black regression. All other variables entered and were significant except father's education and percent non-white teachers previous year. Signs were the same in both regressions, with possessions, father's education, nursery school, percent wishing to finish high school, teacher's verbal score, and teacher's experience being positive.

[7] Martin T. Katzman, "Distribution and Production in a Big City Elementary School System," *Yale Economic Essays*, Vol. 8 (Spring 1968), 201-256.

UNIT OF ANALYSIS
School.

SAMPLE
56 Boston schools.

DATA
Obtained from local (Boston) sources.

VARIABLES
Independent
1. Class size.

2. Percent students in classes greater than 35.
3. Students/staff.
4. Size of school area.
5. Percent teachers with permanent status.
6. Percent permanent teachers M.A. or greater.
7. Percent permanent teachers 1-10 years experience.
8. Percent turnover.
9. Percent seating capacity utilized.
10. Index of cultural advantage.

Dependent
1. Attendance rate.
2. ADA percent of initial enrollment.
3. Median score on reading test, 6th grade; ditto, 2nd grade.
4. Percent taking Latin School test.
5. Percent passing Latin School test.
6. Continuation rate (100 dropout rate of alumni).

PROCEDURE
Stepwise, multiple regression for each of the dependent variables.

RESULTS
The index of cultural advantage was significant and positive in all equations except 4 and 5. Also, the size of the school area was significant and positive in 1-3 and 6. Teacher inexperience was significant and negative in 3, significant and positive in 1, 2, and 6. Students/staff was significant and negative in 3. Nothing was significant in 4 and 5.

[8] Elchanan Cohn, "Economies of Scale in Iowa High School Operations," *Journal of Human Resources,* Vol. 3 (Fall 1968), 422-434.

UNIT OF ANALYSIS
School district.

SAMPLE
377 Iowa high school districts, of which 372 are one-school districts.

Appendix: Input-Output Studies

DATA

Provided by the Iowa State Department of Public Instruction.

VARIABLES
Independent
1. Average number college semester hours/teaching assignment.
2. Average number different teaching assignments/teacher.
3. Median high school teacher's salary.
4. Number of credit units offered (1 unit = 1 course 1 year).
5. Building value/pupil.
6. Bonded indebtedness/pupil.
7. Class size (number pupils/number teachers).
8. ADA.

Dependent

Average composite score on the Iowa Tests of Educational Development administered to 12th graders in 1963 less the average composite score on the same battery administered to 10th graders in 1961. No correction for student-body changes.

PROCEDURE

Multiple regression.

RESULTS

Independent variables 1 and 2 (3 and 4) were significant and negative (positive). Transforming all variables into logs and rerunning yielded the same result. When the sample was restricted to 87 districts whose 1960 population exceeded 5,000, only variable 2 was significant (it was still negative).

[9] Richard Raymond, "Determinants of the Quality of Primary and Secondary Public Education in West Virginia," *Journal of Human Resources,* Vol. 3, No. 4 (Fall 1968), pp. 450-469.

UNIT OF ANALYSIS

School district

SAMPLE

Approximately 5000 students entering West Virginia University (WVU) between September 1963 and September 1966 from 49 West Virginia county school districts.

DATA

Outcome data were obtained from the University. Data on school resources were obtained from various state agencies. Background factors were derived from the Census.

VARIABLES
Independent
1. Average teacher's starting salary weighted.
2. Average teacher's salary.
3. Average elementary teacher's salary.
4. Average secondary teacher's salary.
5. Average weighted (by degree level) teacher's salary in contiguous counties.
6. Average teacher's salary in contiguous counties.
7. Percent teachers teaching in two or more fields.
8. Students/teacher.
9. Number of library volumes in excess of standard.
10. Non-teaching expenditure/pupil.
11. Median income of professional, managerial, and kindred occupations in county.
12. Median family income in county.
13. Median years of schooling by adults in county.
14. Urbanization of county.
15. Percent employed in professional level occupations in county.

Dependent
1. Mean grade point average in freshman year at WVU for sampled students in county minus the county quality measure computed from grade point averages (see procedure, below).
2. Mean composite ACT score for sampled students in county who went to WVU minus the county quality measure computed from achievement test (ACT) composite score (see procedure, below).

Appendix: Input-Output Studies

PROCEDURE

The set of students from each county who go on to WVU is not a random sample of all high school graduates from that county. To control for this, two quality measures were defined. A stratified, random 10 percent sample of the students who did go on to WVU was chosen. Their grade point average in freshman year at WVU was regressed on their grade point average in selected high school subjects. (The regression was not forced through the origin.) Then the difference between each student's freshman-year GPA and his selected-high-school-subjects-GPA times the regression coefficient on high-school-GPA was calculated. The value of this calculated variable, averaged over all students in a county, was taken to be the GPA quality index for that county school district.

The ACT quality index was calculated for each county by an identical procedure, using the ACT composite scores of the students in the subsample as the dependent variable in the simple regression.

Four regressions were run for each dependent variable. Independent variables 7 through 15 enter every regression. Independent variables 1 through 4 each enter one regression for each dependent variable. Independent variable 5 enters the two regressions with independent variable 1. Independent variable 6 enters the six regressions with independent variables 2 through 4.

RESULTS

None of the independent variables 4 through 15 was ever significant. Independent variable 1 was significant when the second dependent variable was used, but not when the first dependent variable was used. Independent variables 2 and 3 were each significant in their two (each) regressions.

[10] Samuel Bowles, *Educational Production Function*, Final Report, U.S. Department of Health, Education and Welfare, Office of Education, OEC-1-7-000451-2651, ED 037 590, Harvard University, Cambridge, Massachusetts, February 1969.

UNIT OF ANALYSIS

Individual/school.

SAMPLE

(a) Black male high school seniors in U.S. Office of Education regions 1, 2, and 3 in 1960 who responded to both the initial and 5-year follow-up Project TALENT surveys, (b) EEOS data on black students enrolled in the 5th grade in 1965.

DATA

Drawn from TALENT and EEOS data banks. Background factors on individual level, school resources on school level, in both data banks.

VARIABLES
Independent
1. Father's occupation.
2. Mother's occupation.
3. Father's education.
4. Mother's education.
5. Own room, desk, typewriter.
6. Appliances.
7. TV, telephone, radio, phonograph.
8. With whom living.
9. Average class size, science and math.
10. Senior class size.

PROCEDURE

(a) In order to maximize observations, regression coefficients were estimated from the relationship cov (x_i, x_j) b = cov (x_i, y), where the ijth element or cov (x_i, x_j) is calculated on the basis of all observations for which data on i and j are available, and similarly for cov (x_i, y). Separate "regressions" were run for each dependent variable and beta coefficient calculated. Beta coefficients for class variables were summed, as were those for school variables. The social respective sums were compared in each case to estimate the relative importance of each set of variables with respect to each dependent variable. Bowles apparently (it is never stated one way or the other) "fitted" his equations, deleted insignificant variables, then "refitted" the equations.

(b) Essentially the same steps were repeated using EEOS data.

Bowles then examined the specification bias stemming from the omission of initial endowments.

Appendix: Input-Output Studies

RESULTS

(a) Father's occupation and the measure of consumer durables appeared in all three equations with positive signs. Mother's education and mother's occupation appeared once each; both were positive. The sums of the beta coefficients for social class variables were .62, .46, and .69 in the reading, mathematics, and composite score equations, respectively. Teachers with graduate training/class appeared in all three (positive); class size in science and mathematics appeared twice (negative), but not in the mathematics equation. Tracking was negative in all three. Expenditure per student on non-teaching inputs (positive), age of building (negative), and educational innovation entered once each. The sums of the beta coefficients for school variables were .35, .80, and .47, in order.

When percent black was added to each equation, it was significant (negative) in two cases (except reading).

(b) Reading material in home, number of siblings, parents' education level, teachers' verbal ability, and presence of science laboratory facilities, average time spent in guidance, and days in session were all significant and positive. Regarding days in session as a community variable, the sum of the beta coefficients for school inputs was .32, very similar to the sum of school input beta coefficients in the TALENT reading equation.

Bowles then introduced student's control of environment and student's self-concept. Both were positive and very significant.

[11] Thomas G. Fox, "School System Resource Use in Production of Interdependent Educational Outputs" (mimeo), *The Joint National Meeting, American Astronautical Society and Operations Research Society*, Denver, Colorado, 1969.

UNIT OF ANALYSIS
School.

SAMPLE
39 Chicago schools.

DATA
Chicago school district records and the Census.

VARIABLES
Independent
1. Teacher man-years.
2. Auxiliary service man-years.
3. Total book expenditures (text and library).
4. Index of building utilization capacity.
5. Capacity of building, weighted by age.
6. Percent student class hours in vocational courses, weighted by number of students.
7. Median family income in attendance area, weighted by number of students.
8. Percent of students planning on college, weighted by number of students.
9. Number students employed part-time.

Dependent
1. Eleventh grade median reading stanine weighted by number of students.
2. Holding power (one minus dropout rate).

PROCEDURE
Two simultaneous equations were specified in double log form, one for each dependent variable. Each dependent variable enters the other dependent variable's equation as an independent variable. (The theory is that schools trade off between the two outputs.) Independent variable 8 (9) was deleted from the holding-power (reading) equation. Two-stage least squares (TSLS) was used to estimate the simultaneous system. Independent variable 4 was deleted (insignificant), and the reduced forms were calculated and estimated using ordinary least squares.

RESULTS
Holding power (positive) and total teacher man-years, total text and library book expenditures, and vocational class student hours (all negative) were significant in the TSLS equation for reading. Family income had a t-ratio below one. In the holding-power equation, reading, total teacher man-years, total book expenditures, and vocational class student hours were all positive and significant. Total auxiliary man-years, building capacity weighted by age, and total family income were

Appendix: Input-Output Studies

all negative and significant. No significance statistics were presented for the reduced-form equations. All variables were positive except book expenditures and building capacity-age code in the reduced-form reading equation. Only total students employed part-time was negative in the holding-power reduced-form equation.

[12]   Herbert J. Kiesling, *The Relationship of School Inputs to Public School Performance in New York State*, P-4211, The Rand Corporation, October 1969.

UNIT OF ANALYSIS
School District.

SAMPLE
97 school districts.

DATA
The dependent variable is the average for all 6th grade pupils who were in the same school and took the same test in the 4th grade. School resource and family background measures were drawn from district records.

VARIABLES
Independent
1. Teachers/pupil.
2. Principals and supervisors/pupil.
3. Special staff/pupil.
4. Expenditures/pupil for books and supplies.
5. Median teacher salary.
6. Average salary of teachers in top salary decile.
7. Index of occupation of family breadwinner of 5th grade pupils.
8. School district debt/pupil.
9. School district growth rate, 1950-1958.
10. ADA.
11. School property value/pupil.
12. Salary of superintendent of schools.
13. Mean salary of principals.

14. Expenditures/pupil for principals, assistant principals, and supervisors.
15. School district value of buildings/classroom.
16. School district value of furniture and equipment/classroom.
17. Median years teacher experience in school district.

Dependent
1. Composite score on Iowa test of basic skills.
2. Arithmetic score on Iowa.
3. Language score on Iowa.

Three variants of each dependent variable were used:
a. School district mean for 6th graders who were in the same school and took the same test in the 4th grade.
b. School district gain at the mean—4th grade to 6th grade (for all students present in both the 4th and the 6th grade, school district in 6th grade less school district mean in 4th grade).
c. School district mean for 6th graders who were present in the 4th grade with those pupils' mean score in the 4th grade entered as an independent variable.

The sample was stratified into five subsamples on the basis of the family breadwinner's occupation. For each subsample and for the total sample, the nine dependent variables were computed (that is, averaging over the pupils in each subsample). Thus the study included 54 dependent variables. Districts were then divided into two groups—urban and non-urban—and the 54 regressions were run for each group.

PROCEDURE

Factor analysis, *a priori* reasoning, and inspection of simple correlations were used to reduce the list of independent variables to six: index of occupation, teachers/pupil, expenditures/pupil for books and supplies, average salary of teachers in top salary decile, value of school district property/pupil, and expenditures/pupil for principals and supervisors. 108 regressions were then run.

RESULTS
Rural Sample

In the 54 regressions run on the sample of rural districts, only the occupation index was ever significant.

Appendix: Input-Output Studies   *211*

Urban Sample

The author claims (regression results are reported for 30 of the 54 regressions) that: (1) there are major differences in findings among the three variants of each dependent variable; (2) findings for all three test scores are basically the same; (3) the index of occupation is always positive and significant; (4) teachers/pupil and expenditures/pupil for books and supplies consistently related negatively to the dependent variable, often at an advanced level of significance (in the 30 reported regressions the teacher-pupil ratio was significant in 12 cases and expenditures per pupil was significant in 10 cases); and (5) none of the other three variables was uniformly important, although each was important at one time or another. (In 7 of the 30 reported regressions, none of the other three school variables was significant.)

[13]   Herbert J. Kiesling, *A Study of Cost and Quality of New York School Districts*, U.S. Department of Health, Education and Welfare, Office of Education, 8-0264, Washington, D.C., February 1970.

UNIT OF ANALYSIS
    School District.

SAMPLE
    Fifth and 8th grade pupils in 86 school districts in New York State. Eighth, and in some cases 5th, grade students in 273 schools in New York State.

DATA
    Ninety-nine school districts were chosen from among New York school districts that used the Iowa Test of Basic Skills in the 5th and 8th grades in the 1964-1965 school year. Usable information was obtained from 86 of them. Test scores and data concerning parents' occupations and education were obtained from the districts. School resources data were obtained from New York's Basic Educational Data System, which began collecting detailed data on New York schools in 1967.
    The selection of schools for the second part of the analysis is not described.

VARIABLES
Independent
1. Average teacher salary.
2. Average teacher experience.
3. Average teacher degree level.
4. Average teacher certification.
5. Pupils/classroom.
6. Pupils/laboratory.
7. Pupils/academic classroom.
8. Value of school-district-owned property/pupil.
9. Average salary of non-classroom professionals.
10. Principal's experience.
11. Principal's degree level.
12. Father's education level.
13. Mother's education level.
14. Father's occupation level.
15. Pupils/teacher.
16. Expenditures/pupil on central administration.
17. Principals and supervisors/pupil

Dependent
1. Score on Iowa mathematics test.
2. Score on Iowa verbal test.
3. Composite score.

PROCEDURE

All school variables were averaged over the school district. For each of the three dependent variables at each grade level (5th and 8th); the sample was divided into seven subsamples on the basis of the father's education. The dependent variable for each subsample was computed as the average score over all students in a district in the subsample. The design thus generated 42 regressions; but sample sizes were too small to support analysis in three cases. The sample was then restratified by seven categories of the father's occupation and the procedure was repeated. All 42 regressions were run. The independent variables in all 81 equations were mother's educational level (district average over all students in subsample), average (over entire district); teacher's salary, experience, degree level, and certification; pupils/teacher ratio; and expenditures/pupil on central administration.

Appendix: Input-Output Studies

An alternative model was formulated in which administrative expenditures/pupil was dropped from the regressions and the value of school-district-owned property and the number of pupils and supervisors (both on a per-pupil basis) were inserted. This model was run on the seven stratified-by-occupation 5th grade subsamples and the six stratified-by-education 8th grade subsamples. The composite score, averaged over the subsample, was the dependent variable in all cases.

A factor analysis of the independent variables suggested another alternative specification of the model. Mother's education level, average teacher's degree level, experience, and salary, the pupils/teacher ratio, administrative expenditures per student, and pupils/classroom ratio were the independent variables. Composite scores for six 5th grade and the seven 8th grade stratified-by-education subsamples were the dependent variables.

The sample of school districts was divided on the basis of population density into two groups—urban and rural. The original model (independent variables 1-4, 13, 15, and 16) was fitted for seven 5th grade urban district and six 5th grade rural district stratified-by-education subsamples. The dependent variables were average composite scores over all pupils in the subsamples.

The sample of districts was divided into two groups—within and outside the Standard Metropolitan Statistical Area. For the districts in each group, seven stratified-by-education regressions were run. The original set of independent variables (1-4, 13, 15, and 16) was used. The dependent variables were average composite scores for all 5th graders in each subsample.

Finally, data were collected on the level of the individual school. Eight subsamples were defined: schools in districts with six or more schools, schools in districts with five or fewer schools, all schools in Albany, Birmingham, Niagara Falls, Schenectady, and Syracuse, and all schools. The dependent variables were not defined.

RESULTS

The various stratification schemes add up to 127 regressions. The box-score is:

Variable	No. of Regressions in Which Variable is Entered	No. of Regressions in Which Variable is Significant With Positive Sign	No. of Regressions in Which Variable is Significant With Negative Sign
Mother's education level	127		48
Pupils/classroom	6		1
Teacher certification level	121	28	1
Teacher degree level	127	4	4
Teacher experience	127	18	4
Teacher salary	127	1	8
Pupils/teacher	127	3	3
Administrative expenditures/pupil	114	36	
Value of school-district property/pupil	13		2
Administrative personnel/pupil	13		

[14] Henry M. Levin, "A New Model of School Effectiveness," in *Do Teachers Make a Difference?*, U.S. Department of Health, Education and Welfare, Office of Education, Bureau of Educational Personnel Development, OE-58042, 1970, pp. 55-75.

UNIT OF ANALYSIS
School/individual.

SAMPLE
597 white 6th grade students in 36 schools in a large Eastern city who had attended no other school.

DATA
All data drawn from EEOS. School resources measured on school level; background factors measured on individual level.

VARIABLES
Independent
   1. Sex.
   2. Age.

Appendix: Input-Output Studies 215

3. Possessions in student's home.
4. Family size.
5. Real (or surrogate) mother in home.
6. Real (or surrogate) father in home.
7. Father's education.
8. Mother's employment status.
9. Attended kindergarten.
10. Teacher's verbal score.
11. Teacher's parents' income.
12. Teacher experience.
13. Whether teacher's undergraduate institution university or college.
14. Teacher's satisfaction with present school.
15. Percent white students.
16. Teacher turnover.
17. Library volumes per student.

Dependent
1. Student's attitude.
2. Parents' attitude.
3. Student's grade aspiration.
4. Student's verbal score.

PROCEDURE

One equation was specified for each of the dependent variables. The verbal score equation included the other three dependent variables and all independent variables except 5, 6, 8, 11, and 15. The student's attitude equation included verbal score and parents' attitude and independent variables 1-4, 6-8, 14, 16, and 17. The grade aspiration equation included verbal score and parents' attitude and all independent variables except 7, 10, 12, and 15-17. The parents' attitude equation included independent variables 1, 3-6, 8, 15, and 16. Ordinary least squares (OLS), two-stage least squares (TSLS), and reduced-form estimates (RFE) were calculated for dependent variables, 1, 3, and 4. OLS was used for the parents' attitudes equation.

RESULTS
Verbal Score

Student's attitude, parents' attitude, and grade aspiration were all significantly and positively related to verbal score in the OLS estimation. All were insignificant when TSLS was used. Age and family size (both negative) as well as possessions, father's education, teacher experience, and teacher's undergraduate institution (all positive) were significant in the OLS estimates. Only age (negative) and teacher experience (positive) were significant in the TSLS estimates.

Student Attitude

Verbal score, attended kindergarten, teacher's satisfaction (positive), and mother in home (negative) were significant in OLS estimates. TSLS yielded the same results except that mother's employment was also significant (positive).

Parents' Attitude

Possessions (positive) and family size, mother in home, and percent white students (all negative) were significant.

[15] Stephan Michelson, "The Association of Teacher Resourcefulness with Children's Characteristics," in *Do Teachers Make a Difference?*, U.S. Department of Health, Education and Welfare, Office of Education, Bureau of Educational Personnel Development OE-58042, 1970, pp. 120-168.

UNIT OF ANALYSIS
School/individual.

SAMPLE
597 white and 458 black 6th grade students in an unknown number of schools in a large Eastern city who had attended no other school.

DATA
All data were drawn from EEOS. School resources were measured on the school level. Teacher's attributes were averaged over teachers in the 3rd, 4th, and 5th grades. Background factors were measured on the individual level.

Apprendix: Input-Output Studies

VARIABLES
Independent
1. Sex.
2. Age.
3. Family size.
4. Possessions in student's home.
5. Father's education.
6. Attended kindergarten.
7. Real (or surrogate) mother in home.
8. Teacher's verbal ability.
9. Teacher's experience.
10. Teacher tenure.
11. Discrepancy between teacher's reported and desired percentage of white students.
12. Teacher's desired percentage of white students.
13. Whether teacher was academic major in college.
14. Whether school tracks (by ability groups).
15. Library books.
16. Whether school has auditorium, cafeteria, gymnasium.
17. Percent students in upper quartiles on test.
18. Size of school site (acres).
19-22. Four interaction terms crossing student socioeconomic status (SES), student-body SES, and level of school resources—the constructions of these variables are not clearly defined.
23. Father's occupation.
24. Mother's education.
25. Percent teachers white.
26. Teacher's parents' education.
27. Teacher's years of schooling.
28. Whether school has adequate texts ("adequate" not defined).
29. Age of school building.
30. Assignment (?).
31. Whether mother employed.
32. Teacher turnover.
33. Teacher's preference for another school.

Dependent
1. Verbal test score.
2. Reading test score.

3. Mathematics test score.
4. Student's attitude.
5. Student's grade aspiration.

PROCEDURE

The sample was stratified by race, and seven regressions—two each for dependent variables 1 and 3, three for dependent variable 2—were run for whites. Five regressions were run for blacks, two each for dependent variables 1 and 2 and one for dependent variable 3. Although there is considerable overlap, the set of independent variables entered into each regression differs between regressions within and between subsamples. A system of three simultaneous equations with the dependent variables verbal test score, student's attitude, and student's grade aspiration was specified and estimated using two-stage least squares for each of the racial subsamples. Specifications were the same in both cases.

RESULTS
Whites—Single Equation Model

Sex entered all seven white regressions and was significant in five of them. Its sign was positive when reading was the dependent variable, and negative when mathematics was the dependent variable. Age and family size were both significant and negative in each of the seven white regressions. Possessions and father's education were both significant and positive in each of the seven.

The remaining variables entered in each of the seven regressions (and their signs, if significant) were as follows:

Verbal 1:   6(+), 9(+), 11(-), 15(+), 16(+), 19(-), 20, 21, 22(-).
Verbal 2:   6(+), 8(+), 9(+), 12(+), 20(+), 22(-).
Reading 1:   9(+), 12(+), 20, 21.
Reading 2:   8(+), 9(+), 14, 16(+), 20(+).
Reading 3:   9, 10, 14, 16, 18(+), 20, 21(-).
Mathematics 1: 6(+), 7, 14(-), 15(+), 16(+), 17(+), 18(+), 19.
Mathematics 2: 6(+), 10(+), 11, 13(+), 14, 16(+), 18(+).

Blacks—Single Equation Model

Sex entered all five regressions, but was significant (+) only with respect to reading 2. Age was significant and negative in all five cases. Possessions also entered all five regressions, but was significant (+) only

Appendix: Input-Output Studies 219

in the two verbal equations. Family size entered the two verbal and the two reading equations, being negative and significant in all four.

The other variables (and their signs, if significant) in each regression were as follows:

Verbal 1:   10(-), 14(-), 24(+), 26(+), 28(+).
Verbal 2:   14(-), 15, 24(+), 26(+), 28(+), 29(-).
Reading 1:   5(+), 6(+), 7(-), 8, 13(-), 20(+), 23, 26.
Reading 2:   6(+), 7(-), 13(-), 20(+), 23, 25, 26(+).
Mathematics 1: 5(+), 23, 26, 27, 30(+).

Whites—Simultaneous Equation Model
The three dependent variables in the model were student's verbal test score, attitude, and grade aspiration. Attitude and grade aspiration were not significant in the verbal equation. Verbal score was significant and positive in the attitude and aspiration equations. Independent variables entered (and their sign, if significant) were as follows:

Verbal: 1, 2(-), 3, 4, 5, 6, 8, 9(+), 13(+), 15, 32.
Attitude: 1(+), 2, 3(-), 4, 5(+), 6, 7, 32(-), 33.
Aspiration: 1, 2, 3, 4, 5, 6, 7(-), 13, 31(+), 33(1).

Blacks—Simultaneous Equations Model
No measures of statistical significance were reported.

[16]   Eric Hanushek, *The Value of Teachers in Teaching*, RM-6362-CC/RC, The Rand Corporation, December 1970.

UNIT OF ANALYSIS
Individual.

SAMPLE
1,061 3rd grade students in a large California school system.

DATA
Student information was derived from cumulative school records, information on their teachers from a survey.

VARIABLES
Independent
   1. A student's 3rd grade teacher's experience.

2. A student's 3rd grade teacher's semester hours of graduate work.
   3. A student's 2nd grade teacher's experience.
   4. A student's 2nd grade teacher's semester hours of graduate work.
   5. Sex.
   6. Family income.
   7. Number of siblings.
   8. Number of absences.
   9. Percent Mexican-Americans in school.
   10. Average income in school.
   11. Student's score on Stanford Achievement Test in 1st grade.
   12. Student's score on Stanford Achievement Test in 2nd grade.
   13. Whether student repeated grade.
   14. Percent of time 3rd grade teacher spends on discipline.
   15. Third grade teacher's verbal facility.
   16. Years since most recent educational experience, 3rd grade teacher.
   17. Second grade teacher's verbal facility.
   18. Years since most recent educational experience, 2nd grade teacher.
   19. Whether father in clerical job.
   20. Years of experience teaching students of this SES level, 3rd grade teacher.
   21. Years of experience teaching students of this SES level, 2nd grade teacher.

Dependent
   1. Student's SAT score in 3rd grade.
   2. Student's SAT score in 2nd grade.

PROCEDURE

The records of all children in the 3rd grade in the system (2,445 students) were examined. Data on all independent variables were available for 1,061 students. Individual teachers were matched to individual students. This sample was divided into three subsamples: 323 whites whose fathers had non-manual jobs, 515 whites whose fathers had manual jobs, 140 Mexican-Americans whose fathers had manual jobs. A separate regression was run for each subsample and for an

Appendix: Input-Output Studies

"all-whites" subsample, the first dependent variable being regressed against the first 11 independent variables.

Then, for each of the three subsamples, 3rd grade SAT score was regressed on sex, 2nd grade SAT score, and a series of dummy variables T_{ij} where $T_{ij} = 1$ if the ith student has the jth teacher in the 3rd grade. These analyses were then repeated with 2nd grade SAT score, sex, 1st grade SAT score, and the teacher dummy variables as the dependent and three independent variables, respectively.

Last, stepwise regressions were run for the two white subsamples. The dependent variable in each case was 3rd grade SAT score. The complete set of independent variables considered is not given. The reported results list: for the white manual subsample, sex, 1st grade SAT score, and independent variables 13-18; and for the white non-manual subsample, 1st grade SAT score and independent variables 16, 18-21. The author states that rejected variables include: school composition in terms of occupational distribution, ethnic distribution, and achievement distribution; objective background characteristics of the teachers such as socioeconomic status, college major, and membership in professional organizations; and various measures of a teacher's attitudes toward his students.

RESULTS

The complete results of the first set of regressions mentioned above are not given. However, the teacher variables—3rd grade teacher's experience and advanced training, and 2nd grade teacher's experience and advanced training—were all insignificant in each of the four regressions.

For whites the hypothesis that the teacher dummy variables are identical was rejected at the 1 percent level. This was true for both the 2nd and the 3rd grade regressions and for both the manual and the nonmanual subsamples. However, for Mexican-Americans, the hypothesis that all teachers had an identical effect could not be rejected at either the 2nd or 3rd grade level.

In the last set of regressions, sex (+), whether grade repeated (-), 1st grade SAT score (+), time spent on discipline (-), 3rd grade teacher's verbal facility (+), and 2nd grade teacher's years since educational experience ( ) were significant for the white manual subsample. For the white nonmanual subsample only 1st grade SAT score (+) and whether father had clerical job (- if yes) were significant.

[17] Harvey Averch and Herbert Kiesling, "The Relationship of School and Environment to Student Performance: Some Simultaneous Models for the Project TALENT High Schools." The Rand Corporation, Santa Monica, 1972 (unpublished paper).

UNIT OF ANALYSIS
    a. School.
    b. School/individual.

SAMPLE
    a. About 5000 9th graders from 746 public comprehensive and college preparatory high schools.
    b. 820 9th graders randomly chosen from the above group.

DATA

All data were derived from Project TALENT. School variables were on the school level. In the first part of the analysis, individual achievement scores were averaged by school. In the second part, individual scores were the output measure.

VARIABLES
Independent
1. Socioeconomic index.
2. Perceived needs of staff.
3. Percent students to juvenile court.
4. Principal's degree level.
5. Number of tracks.
6. Average class size.
7. Percent teachers certified.
8. Average salary, male teachers.

Dependent
1. Percent teacher transfers.
2. Expected education.
3. Student achievement.

PROCEDURE

In the first part, a set of three simultaneous equations (one for each dependent variable) were estimated by two-stage least squares

Appendix: Input-Output Studies

techniques. Expected education, student achievement, percent students to juvenile court, and perceived needs of staff entered the teacher transfers equation as independent variables. Student achievement, socioeconomic index, and percent teacher transfers were the independent variables in the expected education equation. Independent variables 4 through 8, expected education, and percent teacher transfers were used to explain student achievement. Reduced-form estimates were computed and compared with ordinary least squares estimates.

Basically the same model for student achievement and expected education was then estimated on the level of the individual student. The percent teacher transfers equation was dropped. The results were compared with Levin's.

RESULTS
School Level System

School average student achievement was found to be significantly related to expected education (+), percent teacher transfers (-), male teacher's average salary (+), and the number of tracks in the school. Expected education was significantly related only to the socioeconomic index (+). Percent teacher transfers was significantly related to student achievement (-), expected education (+), and percent students to juvenile court.

In the ordinary least squares version of the student achievement and percent teacher transfer equations, all independent variables were entered into each. Socioeconomic index (+), class size (-), male teachers' average salary (+), and number of tracks (+) were significantly related to student achievement. Percent students to juvenile court (+) and class size (+) were significantly related to percent teacher transfers. Again, only the socioeconomic index was significantly related to expected education.

Individual Level System

Socioeconomic index (+) was the only significant predictor of educational expectations on the individual level. Expected education (+) and average salary of male teachers (+) were significantly related to student achievements.

[18]   James W. Guthrie, George B. Kleindorfer, Henry M. Levin, and Robert T. Stout, *Schools and Inequality*, M.I.T. Press, Cambridge, 1971, Ch. 4.*

UNIT OF ANALYSIS
Student/school.

SAMPLE
5,284 sixth-grade students in 89 Michigan elementary schools.

DATA
All data derived from the EEOS.

VARIABLES
Independent
1. School site size.
2. Building age.
3. Percent makeshift classrooms.
4. Library volumes/student.
5. School enrollment.
6. Percent students transferring.
7. Classrooms/1,000 students.
8. Teachers' experience.
9. Teachers' attitude toward teaching.
10. Teachers' attitude toward school.
11. Teachers' attitude toward other teachers in school.
12. Teachers' verbal ability.
13. Father's occupation.
14. Father's education.

Dependent
1. Score on reading test.
2. Score on mathematics test.
3. Score on verbal test.

*Guthrie *et al.* present the results of research into a number of educational problems. We are concerned here only with that segment of the report that deals with the relationship among school resources and background factors and student outcomes.

Appendix: Input-Output Studies

PROCEDURE

Each student was assigned an SES index by multiplying the 1960 Census estimate of income for his father's occupation by his father's education level. Students were then ranked by SES and divided into 10 deciles. For each decile a rank order coefficient was calculated between individuals' scores on a dependent variable and their scores on an independent variable. The procedure was repeated for all combinations of independent and dependent variables. Thus 360 rank order coefficients were calculated (3 dependent variables by 12 independent variables by 10 deciles).

RESULTS

Each independent variable was tested 30 times. Significant results are displayed below.

Independent Variable (sign)	1	2	3	4	5	6	7	8	9	10	11	12
	(+)	(-)	(-)	(+)	(-)	(-)	(+)	(+)	(+)	(+)	(+)	(+)
Number of times significant	5	22	5	14	13	18	14	2	23	23	17	18

It should be noted that each independent variable was tested individually with no control for influence of other independent variables. And many of the independent variables are highly correlated with one another.

[19] Marshall S. Smith, "Equality of Educational Opportunity: The Basic Findings Reconsidered," in F. Mosteller and D.P. Moynihan (eds.), *On Equality of Educational Opportunity*, Vintage Books, New York, 1972.

UNIT OF ANALYSIS
Individual/school.

SAMPLE
Northern 6th, 9th, and 12th grade subsamples from EEOS.

DATA
> EEOS.

VARIABLES
Independent
1. Urbanism of background.
2. Parents' education.
3. Integrity of family.
4. Family size.
5. Possessions.
6. Reading material in home.
7. Parents' interest.
8. Parents' educational desires.
9. Proportion own encyclopedia.
10. Student transfers.
11. Attendance.
12. Proportion in college preparatory curriculum.
13. Average hours homework.
14. Teacher perception of student's quality.
15. Instructional expenditures/pupil.
16. Library volumes/pupil.
17. Science laboratory facilities.
18. Extracurricular activities.
19. Accelerated curriculum.
20. Comprehensiveness of curriculum.
21. Tracking.
22. Movement between tracks.
23. School size.
24. School location.
25. Guidance counselor.
26. Promotion of slow learners.
27. Teacher's verbal achievement.
28. Teacher's degree level.
29. Teacher's socioeconomic status.
30. Teacher's preference for middle-class student.
31. Teacher's experience.
32. Teacher's localism.
33. Proportion teacher white.
34. Proportion students white.

Dependent
Verbal score.

PROCEDURE
This is a reanalysis of the Coleman report (see item 4, above) in the light of various errors, omissions, and controversial techniques alleged to be present in the original analysis.

RESULTS
Errors and Omissions
Smith argues that Coleman and his colleagues made two mechanical errors in creating their tables. First, two measures of home background—parents' education and urbanism of background—were inadvertently replaced in the analysis. Second, the student body composition variable called *proportion planning to attend college* is really a measure of the *proportion of students in the college track* in the school. Further, Coleman *et al.* made an error in their procedure for estimating the amount of school-to-school difference in achievement explained by individual home background. This error led to a serious overestimation of the possible unique effect that school variables might have.

Moreover, in their analysis and interpretation of the survey data, Coleman *et al.* completely overlooked the confounding effects that student assignment and self-selection practices might have on inferences about the relationships between school resources and student achievement. In particular, the Coleman data did not distinguish among trade, vocational, academic, and comprehensive high schools.

Background Factors
Measures of students' backgrounds bear a strong relationship to student achievement at all grade levels, both within and between schools. The two errors in the original analysis—leaving out two variables and underestimating the amount of between-school variance—led to a serious overestimation of the effect of school factors on achievement in the Coleman Report.

Student-body Effects
The Coleman Report's estimates of the amount of achievement variance uniquely explained by student-body variables (numbers 9-13)

are severely reduced when the intended background controls (including the two variables erroneously omitted) are used. The reduction is between 25 and 50 percent for whites and between 10 and 25 percent for blacks.

Furthermore, Coleman *et al.* thought that they had included the variable proportion of students planning to attend college, which they interpreted as a measure of the aspirations in the student body. Instead, however, they entered the variable *proportion* of students *in the college track*. This measure is essentially a direct measure selection in that those schools with large proportions of students in the college track are academic schools, whereas the schools with small such proportions are trade or vocational schools.

Finally, Smith performs a regression analysis for Northern blacks and whites in the 6th, 9th, and 12th grades—six regressions in all. All background and school resource variables are entered in each regression. The basic student-body variables 9-11 enter each equation. In addition, student-body variables 12 and 13 (14) enter each 9th and 12th (6th) grade equation. In these 28 cases (four student-body variables in each of two 6th grade equations, five student-body variables in each of two 9th and 12th grade equations), student-body variables are significant only three times. And in two of these cases—teacher perception of student-body quality (14) in both 6th grade regressions—the variable has the "wrong" sign (negative). Proportion in college track is significant and positive in only the 12th grade, Northern black equation.

In summary, Smith finds no evidence that characteristics of the student body have a strong independent influence on the verbal achievement of individual students.

School Facilities and Curriculum

Smith investigates the same 11 school facilities and curriculum variables (numbers 15-25) as did Coleman *et al.* He supports Coleman's original finding that the relationship between facilities and curriculum variables and student achievement is extremely slight. In the four full regressions, including all independent variables, for Northern blacks and whites in the 9th and 12th grade, facilities and curriculum measures are significant in only three of 48 cases—movement between tracks (-) for 9th grade blacks, comprehensive curriculum (-) for 9th grade whites, and school size (-) for 12th grade blacks.

Teacher's Characteristics

The teacher variables (numbers 27-33) are found to bear little relationship to between-school variations in student achievement. This is consistent with the overall conclusion reached in the EEOS report. In the four full regressions—9th and 12th grade Northern blacks and whites—no teacher characteristic appears to be significant in any regression.

[20] Byron W. Brown, "Achievement, Costs, and the Demand for Public Education," *Western Economics Journal,* 10, 1972, pp. 198-219.

UNIT OF ANALYSIS
School district.

SAMPLE
Fourth-grade students (all) in 520 Michigan school districts.

DATA
Test score and SES data collected and averaged by district by the Educational Testing Service for the Michigan Department of Education. Data on school districts obtained from Michigan Department of Education Files.

VARIABLES
Independent
1. Socioeconomic status scale.
2. Standard deviation, within district, of SES.
3. Number of fourth-grade students.
4. Students' attitudes toward school.
5. Students' attitudes toward selves.
6. Pupil/professional ratio.
7. Percent teachers with Masters.
8. Average teacher's experience.
9. State equalized valuation/pupil.
10. State school aid/pupil.
11. ESEA Title I aid/pupil.
12. Other federal aid/pupil.

13. Average teacher's salary.
14. Region of state.
15. Community type.

Dependent
Composite achievement test score.

PROCEDURE

Students' average test score by district regressed, two-stage least squares, on independent variables 1 through 8, 14, and 15, treating independent variables 9 through 13 as instrumental variables.

RESULTS

Coefficients of school inputs, variables 6, 7, and 8, are insignificant. Attitude measures are also insignificant. SES measure and most of the region and community type variables are significant.

[21] Lewis J. Perl, "Family Background, Secondary School Expenditure, and Student Ability," *Journal of Human Resources*, 8, 1973, pp. 156-180.

UNIT OF ANALYSIS
Individual/school/district.

SAMPLE

Twenty percent random sample of the 1960 high school seniors included in Project TALENT who responded to either the one-year or the five-year follow-up, about 3600 students.

DATA

Project TALENT. Students' family income estimated for parents' occupation, education, and age using Census data.

VARIABLES
Independent
1. Family income.
2. Father's occupation.
3. Mean income of students (high school).

Appendix: Input-Output Studies

4. Standard deviation of income (high school).
5. Average class size—science.
6. Average class size—nonscience.
7. Teachers' starting salary (B.A.).
8. Percent teachers with M.A.
9. Percent teachers with Ph.D.
10. Percent teachers male.
11. Percent teachers certified.
12. Average percent teachers' time spent in area of specialization.
13. Average teachers' experience.
14. Days in school year (district).
15. Age of building.
16. Books in library.
17. Enrollment.
18. Enrollment squared.
19. Expenditures/pupil (district).

Dependent
1. Ability measure 1.
2. Ability measure 2.

PROCEDURE

The TALENT aptitude and achievement test battery grouped into 22 composite scores and principal components estimated. First two principal components explain 70 percent of variance in 22 composite scores and used as dependent variables. Each dependent variable regressed on all 19 independent variables. Sample then stratified by income and each dependent variable regressed on all 19 independent variables for students above and below sample mean ($9,136).

RESULTS

Dependent variable: ability measure 1. For all students, variables 1-3, 7, 12, 16, and 19 are significant (all positive); for low-income students no variable is significant; for high-income students variables 8, 12, and 16 are significant (all positive).

Dependent variable: ability measure 2. For all students, variables 2, 3, 5, 10, 12, 14, 16, and 19 are significant. Variable 10 is negative and remainder have positive signs. For low-income students variables 6 (negative), 13 (negative), and 14 (positive) are significant; for high-income students variables 9, 16, and 18 are significant (all positive).

BIBLIOGRAPHY

Adams, J.F., *Learning to Lean on a Concept Attainment Task as a Function of Age and Socioeconomic Level,* Wisconsin University, Madison Research and Development Center for Cognitive Learning, No. UW-WRDCCL-TR-141, September 1970.

Adelson, J., "Personality," *Annual Review of Psychology,* 20, 1969, 217-252.

Allen, D.I., "Some Effects of Advance Organizers and Level of Questions on the Learning and Retention of Written Social Studies Material," *Journal of Educational Psychology,* 61, 1970, 333-339.

Allen, W.H., "Instructional Media Research: Past, Present and Future," *Audio-Visual Communications Review,* 29, 1971, 5-18.

Anastasi, A., "Psychology, Psychologists, and Psychological Testing," *American Psychologist,* 22, 1967, 297-306.

Anderson, James G., *Bureaucracy in Education,* Johns Hopkins Press, Baltimore, 1968.

Anderson, R.C., "Educational Psychology," *Annual Review of Psychology,* 18, 1967, 103-164.

Anderson, R.C., "How to Construct Achievement Tests to Assess Comprehension," *Review of Educational Research,* 42, 1972, 145-170.

Angoff, W.H., "Scales, Norms, and Equivalent Scores," in R.L. Thorndike (ed.), *Educational Measurement,* American Council on Education, Washington, D.C., 1971, 508-600.

Ashton-Warner, S., *Teacher,* Simon and Schuster, New York, 1963.

Ausubel, D.P., *The Psychology of Meaningful Verbal Learning,* Grune and Stratton, New York, 1963.

Ausubel, D.P., "An Evaluation of the Conceptual Scheme Approach to Science Curriculum Development," *Journal of Research in Scientific Teaching,* 3, 1965, 255-264.

Averch, Harvey and Herbert Kiesling, "The Relationship of School and Environment to Student Performance: Some Simultaneous Models for the Project TALENT High Schools," The Rand Corporation, Santa Monica, 1970 (unpublished paper).

Ball, Samuel and Gerry Ann Bogatz, *The First Year of Sesame Street: An Evaluation,* Educational Testing Service, Princeton, New Jersey, October 1970.

Ball, Samuel and Gerry Ann Bogatz, *The Second Year of Sesame Street: A Continuing Evaluation* (2 Vols.), Educational Testing Service, Princeton, New Jersey, November 1971.

Barbrack, Christopher R. and Della M. Horton, "Educational Intervention in the Home and Paraprofessional Career Development: A Second-Generation Mother Study with an Emphasis on Costs and Benefits," *DARCEE Papers and Reports,* 4, No. 4, 1970.

Barth, R.S., "So You Want to Change to an Open Classroom," *Phi Delta Kappan,* 53, 1971, 97-99.

Beller, E. Kuno, "The Evaluation of Effects of Early Educational Intervention on Intellectual and Social Development of Lower-class Disadvantaged Children," in E. Grotberg (ed.), *Critical Issues in Research Related to Disadvantaged Children,* Educational Testing Service, Princeton, 1969.

Benson, Charles et al., *State and Local Fiscal Relationships in Public Education in California,* Report of the Senate Fact Finding Committee on Revenue and Taxation, Senate of the State of California, Sacramento, March 1965.

Bereiter, C. and S. Engelmann, *Teaching Disadvantaged Children in the Preschool,* Prentice-Hall, Englewood Cliffs, 1966.

Bereiter, C. and S. Engelmann, *Academic Preschool, Champaign, Illinois,* "It Works" series, Preschool Programs in Compensatory Education I, Office of Education, 1969 (OE 37041).

Berg, Ivar, *Education and Jobs: The Great Training Robbery,* Praeger, New York, 1970.

Berger, Barbara, *A Longitudinal Investigation of Montessori and Traditional Prekindergarten Training with Inner City Children: A*

Comparative Assessment of Learning Outcomes. Three Part Study, Center for Urban Education, New York, 1969 (ED 034 588).

Bissell, Joan S., *The Cognitive Effects of Preschool Programs for Disadvantaged Children*, Ph.D. dissertation, Harvard University, 1970.

Bissell, Joan S., *Implementation of Planned Variation in Head Start: Part 1, First Year Report—Review and Summary*, Department of Health, Education and Welfare, Washington, D.C., 1971 (mimeo.).

Bloom, B.S., T.J. Hastings, and G.F. Madaus, *Handbook on Formative and Summative Evaluation of Student Evaluation of Student Learning*, McGraw-Hill, New York, 1971.

Bock, E.A. (ed.), *Essays on the Case Method*, Interuniversity Case Program, 1962.

Bormuth, J.R., *On the Theory of Achievement Test Items*, University of Chicago Press, Chicago, 1970.

Bowles, Samuel, *Educational Production Function*, Final Report, U.S. Department of Health, Education and Welfare, Office of Education, OEC-1-7-000451-2651, ED 037 590, Harvard University, Cambridge, February 1969.

Bowles, Samuel and Herbert Gintis, "IQ in the U.S. Class Structure," Harvard University, Cambridge, 1972 (mimeo.).

Bowles, Samuel and Henry M. Levin, "More on Multicollinearity and the Effectiveness of Schools," *Journal of Human Resources*, 3, No. 3, Summer 1968a, 393-400.

Bowles, Samuel and Henry M. Levin, "The Determinants of Scholastic Achievement—An Appraisal of Some Recent Evidence," *Journal of Human Resources*, 3, No. 1, Winter 1968b, 2-24.

Bracht, Glenn H., "Experimental Factors Related to Aptitude-Treatment Interactions," *Review of Educational Research*, 40, No. 5, December 1970, 627-645.

Bretz, Rudy, *Three Models for Home-based Instructional Systems Using Television*, R-1089-USOE/MF, The Rand Corporation, Santa Monica, October 1972.

Brophy, J.E. and T.L. Good, "Teacher's Communication of Differential Expectations for Children's Classroom Performance," *Journal of Educational Psychology*, 61, 1970, 365-374.

Brown, Byron W., "Achievement, Costs, and the Demand for Public Education," *Western Economics Journal*, 10, 1972, 198-219.

Brownell, W.A. and A.G. Moses, "Meaningful Versus Mechanical

Learning: A Study in Grade Three Subtraction," Duke University Research Studies in Education, No. 8, Duke University Press, Durham, 1949.

Bull, S.G., "The Role of Questions in Maintaining Attention to Text and Material," *Review of Educational Research,* 43, 1973, 83-88.

Burkhead, Jesse, Thomas G. Fox, and John W. Holland, *Input and Output in Large City High Schools,* Syracuse University Press, Syracuse, 1967.

Burton, B.B. and R.A. Goldberg, *The Effect of Response Characteristics in Multiple Life and Choice Alternatives on Learning During Programmed Instruction,* American Institute for Research, San Mateo, California, 1962.

Butler, A.L., *Current Research in Early Childhood Education,* E/K/N/E, NEA Center, Washington, D.C., 1970.

Cain, Glen and Harold Watts, *Problems in Making Policy Inferences from the Coleman Report,* 28-68, Institute for Research on Poverty, University of Wisconsin, Madison, 1968.

Campbell, D.T. and A. Erlebacher, "How Regression Artifacts in Quasi-experimental Evaluation Can Mistakenly Make Compensatory Education Look Harmful," in J. Hellmuth (ed.), *Disadvantaged Child,* Vol. 3, Brunner/Mazel, New York, 1970, 185-211.

Carpenter, M.B., *Case Studies in Educational Performance Contracting: Norfolk, Virginia,* R-900/2-HEW, The Rand Corporation, Santa Monica, December 1971.

Carpenter, M.B., A.W. Chalfant, and G.R. Hall, *Case Studies in Educational Performance Contracting: Texarkana, Arkansas; Liberty-Eylau, Texas,* R-900/3-HEW, The Rand Corporation, Santa Monica, December 1971.

Carpenter, M.B. and George R. Hall, *Case Studies in Educational Performance Contracting: Conclusions and Implications,* R-900/1-HEW, The Rand Corporation, Santa Monica, December 1971.

Carroll, J.B., "Reinforcement: Is It a Basic Principle, and Will It Serve in the Analysis of Verbal Behavior?" in R. Glaser (ed.), *The Nature of Reinforcement,* Academic Press, New York, 1971, 334-342.

Center for Educational Policy Research, "Education and Inequality," Harvard Graduate School of Education, Cambridge, 1971 (mimeo.).

Chomsky, N., "Review of Verbal Behavior," *Language*, 35, 1959, 26-58.
Chu, G.C. and W. Schramm, *Learning from Television*, Institute for Communication Research, Stanford University, Stanford, 1967.
Cicirelli, V.G. et al., *The Impact of Head Start: An Evaluation of the Effects of Head Start on Children's Cognitive and Affective Development*, Office of Economic Opportunity, Washington, D.C., 1969.
Coffman, W.E., "Essay Examinations," in R.L. Thorndike (ed.), *Educational Measurement*, American Council on Education, Washington, D.C., 1971, 271-302.
Cohen, D.K., "Politics and Research: Evaluation of Social Action Programs in Education," *Review of Educational Research*, 40, 1970, 213-238.
Cohn, Elchanan, "Economies of Scale in Iowa High School Operations," *Journal of Human Resources*, 3, Fall 1968, 422-434.
Coleman, James S., *The Evaluation of Equality of Educational Opportunity*, P-3911, The Rand Corporation, Santa Monica, August 1968.
Coleman, James S. et al., *Equality of Educational Opportunity*, U.S. Department of Health, Education and Welfare, Office of Education, OE-38001, Washington, D.C. 1966.
Corey, S.N., "The Nature of Instruction," in P.C. Lange (ed.), *Programmed Instruction*, University of Chicago Press, Chicago, 1967, 5-27.
Crain, R.L., *The Politics of School Desegregation*, Aldine Publishing Company, Chicago, 1968.
Cronbach, L.J., "The Two Disciplines of Scientific Psychology," *American Psychology*, 12, 1957, 671-684.
Cronbach, L.J., "The Logic of Experiments on Discovery," in L.S. Shulman and E.R. Keisler (eds.), *Learning by Discovery: A Critical Appraisal*, Rand McNally and Company, Skokie, Illinois, 1966.
Cronbach, L.J., *Essentials of Psychological Testing*, Harper and Row, New York, 1970.
Cronbach, L.J. and L. Furby, "How Should We Measure 'Change'—or Should We?" *Psychology Bulletin*, 74, 1970, 68-80.
Cronbach, L.J. and R.E. Snow, *Final Report: Individual Differences in Learning Ability as a Function of Instructional Variables*, Stanford University, Stanford, 1969.

Dahlstrom, W.G., "Personality," *Annual Review of Psychology,* 21, 1970, 1-48.
Deese, J., "Behavior and Fact," *American Psychology,* 24, 1969, 515-522.
Dellas, M. and E.L. Gaier, "Identification of Creativity: The Individual," *Psychology Bulletin,* 73, 1970, 55-73.
Denenberg, V.H. (ed.), *Education of the Infant and Young Child,* Academic Press, New York, 1970.
Dennison, George, *The Lives of Children,* Random House, New York, 1969.
DiLorenzo, Louis T., *Prekindergarten Programs for Disadvantaged Children,* New York State Education Department, Albany, Final Report to Office of Education, 1969 (ED 038 460).
Dreeben, Robert, *On What Is Learned in Schools,* Addison-Wesley Publishing Company, Reading, Massachusetts, 1968.
Education of the Disadvantaged: An Evaluation Report on Title I Elementary and Secondary Education Act of 1965, Fiscal Year 1968, U.S. Department of Health, Education and Welfare, Office of Education, Washington, D.C., 1970 (HE5-237:37013-68).
Elkind, D., "Piagetian and Psychometric Conceptions of Intelligence," *Harvard Educational Review,* 37, 1969, 318-337.
Elkind, D. and A. Sameroff, "Developmental Psychology," *Annual Review of Psychology,* 21, 1970, 191-238.
Engelmann, S., "The Effectiveness of Direct Instruction on IQ Performance and Achievement in Reading and Arithmetic," in J. Hellmuth (ed.), *Disadvantaged Child,* Vol. 3, Brunner/Mazel, New York, 1970.
Etzioni, A., "Essay Review of *Crisis in the Classroom* by C.E. Silberman," *Harvard Educational Review,* February 1971, 87-96.
Featherstone, J., "The British Infant Schools," in B. Gross and R. Gross (eds.), *Radical School Reform,* Simon and Schuster, New York, 1969.
Featherstone, J., *Schools Where Children Learn,* Liveright, New York, 1971.
Ferguson, G.A., "Human Abilities," *Annual Review of Psychology,* 16, 1965, 39-61.
Flavell, J.H. and J.P. Hill, "Developmental Psychology," *Annual Review of Psychology,* 20, 1969, 1-56.

Bibliography

Fleishman, E.A. and C.J. Bartlett, "Human Abilities," *Annual Review of Psychology*, 20, 1969, 349-380.

Fox, Thomas G., "School System Resource Use in Production of Interdependent Educational Outputs," The Joint National Meeting, American Astronautical Society and Operations Research Society, Denver, Colorado, 1969 (mimeo.).

Fresno, California, Preschool Program, "It Works" series, Preschool Programs in Compensatory Education I, Office of Education, 1969 (OE-37034).

Friedenberg, Edgar Z., *Coming of Age in America*, Random House, New York, 1963.

Gagné, R.M., "The Acquisition of Knowledge," *Psychological Review*, 69, 1962, 355-365.

Gagné, R.M., "Contributions of Learning to Human Development," *Psychological Review*, 75, 1968, 177-191.

Gagné, R.M. (ed.), *Learning and Individual Differences*, Merrill, Columbus, Ohio, 1967.

Gagné, R.M. and W.D. Rohwer, Jr., "Instructional Psychology," *Annual Review of Psychology*, 20, 1969, 381-418.

Garrett, M. and J.A. Fodor, "Psychological Theories and Linguistic Constructs," in T.R. Dixon and D.L. Horton (eds.), *Verbal Behavior and General Behavior Theory*, Prentice-Hall, Englewood Cliffs, 1968, 451-477.

Getzel, J.W. and P.W. Jackson, "The Teacher's Personality and Characteristics," in N.L. Gage (ed.), *Handbook of Research on Teaching*, Rand McNally, Chicago, 1963, 506-582.

Gintis, H., "Education, Technology, and the Characteristics of Worker Productivity," *The American Economic Review*, 61, 1971, 266-279.

Gittell, M. and T.E. Hollander, *Six Urban School Districts*, Praeger, New York, 1967.

Glaser, R., "Individuals and Learning: The New Aptitudes," *Educational Researcher*, 1, 1972, 5-13.

Glaser, R. and A.J. Nitko, "Measurement in Learning and Instruction," in R.L. Thorndike (ed.), *Educational Measurement*, American Council on Education, Washington, D.C., 1970.

Glaser, R. and L.B. Resnick, "Instructional Psychology," *Annual Review of Psychology*, 23, 1972, 207-276.

Glass, Gene V. et al., *Education of the Disadvantaged: An Evaluation*

Report on Title I, Elementary and Secondary Education Act of 1965, Fiscal Year 1969, University of Colorado, Boulder, 1970 (mimeo.).

Gollin, E.S. and M. Moody, "Developmental Psychology," *Annual Review of Psychology*, 24, 1973, 1-52.

Goodlad, J.I., "Curriculum: State of the Field," *Review of Education Research*, 39, 1969, 367-375.

Goodman, Paul, *Growing Up Absurd*, Vintage, New York, 1965.

Goodman, Paul, *The New Reformation*, Random House, New York, 1970.

Gordon, Edmund W., "Utilizing Available Information from Compensatory Education and Surveys," Final Report, Office of Education, 1971.

Gordon, Ira, *A Parent Education Approach to Provision of Early Stimulation for the Culturally Disadvantaged*, University of Florida, Gainesville, 1967 (ED 017 339).

Gordon, Ira, *Child Stimulation Through Parent Education*, Institute for the Development of Human Resources, University of Florida, Gainesville, Final Report to Children's Bureau, Department of Health, Education and Welfare, 1969 (ED 033 912).

Gotkin, L.G. and J.F. McSweeney, "Learning from Teaching Machines," in P.C. Lange (ed.), *Programmed Instruction*, University of Chicago Press, Chicago, 1967, 255-283.

Gough, H.G. and M.B. Fink, "Scholastic Achievement Among Students of Average Ability as Predicted from the California Psychological Inventory," *Psychology in the Schools*, 1, 1964, 375-380.

Gray, Susan W. and Rupert A. Klaus, "An Experimental Preschool Program for Culturally Deprived Children," *Child Development*, 36, No. 4, 1965, 887-898.

Gray, Susan W. and Rupert A. Klaus, "The Early Training Project," *Monographs of the Society for Research in Child Development*, 33, 1968.

Gray, Susan W. and Rupert A. Klaus, "The Early Training Project for Disadvantaged Children: A Report after Five Years," *Monographs of the Society for Research in Child Development*, 33, No. 4, 1968.

Gross, Beatrice and Ronald Gross (eds.), *Radical School Reform*, Simon and Schuster, New York, 1969.

Gross, N. and R.E. Herriott, *Staff Leadership in Public Schools*, John Wiley and Sons, Inc., New York, 1965.

Guilford, J.P., *The Nature of Human Intelligence*, McGraw-Hill, New York, 1967.
Guthrie, James W., George B. Kleindorfer, Henry M. Levin, and Robert T. Stout, *Schools and Inequality*, M.I.T. Press, Cambridge, 1971.
Hall, G.R. and M.L. Rapp, *Case Studies in Educational Performance Contracting: Gary, Indiana*, R-900/4-HEW, The Rand Corporation, Santa Monica, December 1971.
Hanley, E.M., "Review of Research Involving Applied Behavior Analysis in the Classroom," *Review of Educational Research*, 40, 1970, 597-625.
Hanushek, Eric, "The Education of Negroes and Whites," Ph.D. dissertation, Massachusetts Institute of Technology, 1968.
Hanushek, Eric, *The Value of Teachers in Teaching*, RM-6362-CC/RC, The Rand Corporation, Santa Monica, December 1970.
Harris, A.J., "The Effective Reading Teacher," *The Reading Teacher*, 23, 1969, 195-204.
Harris, C.W. (ed.), *Problems in Measuring Change*, University of Wisconsin Press, Madison, 1963.
Hartup, W.W. and A. Yonas, "Developmental Psychology," *Annual Review of Psychology*, 22, 1971, 169-392.
Havighurst, R.J., *The Public Schools of Chicago*, The Board of Education, Chicago, 1964.
Hawkridge, David G., Albert B. Chalupsky, and A.O. Roberts, *A Study of Selected Exemplary Programs for the Education of Disadvantaged Children*, American Institutes for Research, Palo Alto, California, Final Report to Office of Education, Parts I, II, 1968 (ED 023 776, ED 023 777).
Hawkridge, David G., P.L. Campeau, K.M. DeWitt, and P.K. Trickett, *A Study of Further Exemplary Programs for the Education of Disadvantaged Children*, American Institute for Research, Palo Alto, California, Final Report to Office of Education, 1969 (ED 036 668).
Heckhausen, H., *The Anatomy of Achievement Motivation*, Academic Press, New York, 1967.
Hellmuth, J. (ed.), *Disadvantaged Child*, Vol. 3, Brunner/Mazel, New York, 1970.
Henry, Jules, *Culture Against Man*, Random House, New York, 1963.
Herndon, James, *The Way Its Spozed to Be*, Simon and Schuster, New York, 1968.

Herndon, James, *How to Survive in Your Native Land,* Simon and Schuster, New York, 1971.
Heron, M.D., "The Nature of Scientific Enquiry as Seen by Selected Philosophers, Science Teachers, and Recent Curricular Materials," Ph.D. dissertation, University of Chicago, 1969.
Hodges. W., B. McCandless, and H. Spicker, *Diagnostic Teaching for Preschool Children,* Council for Exceptional Children, Arlington, Virginia, 1971.
Hodges, W., H. Spicker, and B. McCandless, "The Development and Evaluation of a Diagnostically Based Curriculum for Preschool Psycho-socially Deprived Children," Office of Education, Washington, D.C., 1966.
Hodges, W., H. Spicker, and B. McCandless, *The Development and Evaluation of a Diagnostically Based Curriculum for Preschool Psycho-socially Deprived Children,* Final Report to Office of Education, Washington, D.C., 1967.
Hodges, W., H. Spicker, and B. McCandless, *Diagnostically Based Curriculum,* Bloomington, Indiana, "It Works" series, Preschool Program in Compensatory Education, U.S. Office of Education, 1969 (OE 37024).
Hoepfner, Ralph (ed.), *CSE Elementary School Test Evaluation,* Center for the Study of Evaluation, UCLA Graduate School of Education, Los Angeles, 1970.
Holt, John, *How Children Learn,* Pitman Publishing Corporation, New York, 1967.
Holt, John, *What Do I Do on Monday?* E.P. Dutton & Co., New York, 1970.
Holtzman, W.H., "The Changing World of Mental Measurement and Its Social Significance," *American Psychologist,* 26, 1971, 546-553.
Hunt, J. McV., *Heredity, Environment and Class or Ethnic Differences in Assessment in a Pluralistic Society,* Educational Testing Service, Princeton, 1972, 3-36.
Illich, Ivan, *Deschooling Society,* Harper & Row, New York, 1971.
Inhelder, B. and J. Piaget, *The Growth of Logical Thinking,* Basic Books, New York, 1958.
James, H. Thomas, Excerpt from the preliminary report to the National Academy of Education's Executive Council meeting May 6, 1971 on the feasibility of an Academy task force to explore the reporting of performance by educational institutions.

James, H. Thomas, J.A. Kelly, and W.I. Garms, *Determinants of Educational Expenditures in Large Cities of the United States*, Cooperative Research Project 2389, Stanford University, Stanford, California, 1966.
Jamison, D. *et al.*, "Cost and Performance of Computer-assisted Instruction for Compensatory Education," National Bureau for Economic Research, Conference on Education as an Industry, June 1971.
Jencks, Christopher, "The Coleman Report and the Conventional Wisdom," in F. Mosteller and D.P. Moynihan (eds.), *On Equality of Educational Opportunity*, Vintage Books, New York, 1972.
Jencks, Christopher *et al.*, *Inequality*, Basic Books, New York, 1972.
Jensen, A.R., "How Much Can We Boost IQ and Scholastic Achievement?" *Harvard Educational Review*, 39, 1969.
Jensen, A.R., "Another Look at Culture Fair Testing," in J. Hellmuth (ed.), *Disadvantaged Child*, Vol. 3, Brunner/Mazel, New York, 1970, 53-101.
Kagan, J., "On Class Differences and Early Development," in V.H. Denenberg (ed.), *Education of the Infant and Young Child*, Academic Press, New York, 1970, 5-24.
Karnes, M., "Research and Development Project on Preschool Disadvantaged Children," Office of Education, Washington, D.C., 1969a.
Karnes, M., *The Ameliorative Preschool Program, Champaign, Illinois*, "It Works" series, Preschool Programs in Compensatory Education, U.S. Office of Education, 1969b (OE 37054).
Karnes, M., J.A. Teska, and A.S. Hodgins, "A Longitudinal Study of Disadvantaged Children Who Participated in Three Different Preschool Programs," University of Illinois, Urbana, 1970 (mimeo.).
Karraker, R.J. and L.A. Doke, "Errorless Discrimination of Alphabet Letters: Effects of Time and Method of Introducing Competing Stimuli," *Journal of Experimental Education*, 38, 1970, 27-35.
Katzman, Martin T., "Distribution and Production in a Big City Elementary School System," *Yale Economic Essays*, 8, Spring 1968, 201-256.
Keiser, R.H. *Some Relationships Between Concept Formation and Reading Achievement*, Rutgers University Graduate School of Education, New Brunswick, New Jersey, June 1971.

Kiesling, Herbert J., "Measuring a Local Government Service: A Study of School Districts in New York State," *Review of Economics and Statistics*, 49, No. 3, August 1967, 356-367.

Kiesling, Herbert J., *The Relationship of School Inputs to Public School Performance in New York State*, P-4211, The Rand Corporation, Santa Monica, October 1969.

Kiesling, Herbert J., *A Study of Cost and Quality of New York School Districts*, U.S. Department of Health, Education and Welfare, Office of Education, 8-0264, Washington, D.C., February 1970a.

Kiesling, Herbert J., *A Study of Successful Compensatory Education Programs in California*, The Rand Corporation, Santa Monica, 1970b (mimeo.).

Kiesling, Herbert J., *Input and Output in Compensatory Education Projects in California*, R-781-CC/RC, The Rand Corporation, Santa Monica, October 1971a.

Kiesling, Herbert J., *Multi-variate Analysis of Schools and Educational Policy*, P-4595, The Rand Corporation, Santa Monica, March 1971b.

Klein, G.S., H.L. Barr, and D.L. Wolitzky, "Personality," *Annual Review of Psychology*, 18, 1967, 465-560.

Klein, S.P., "The Uses and Limitations of Standardized Tests in Meeting the Demands for Accountability," *UCLA Evaluation Comment*, Center for the Study of Evaluation, 2, No. 4, January 1971.

Kohl, H., *36 Children*, New American Library, New York, 1967.

Kohl, H., "Can One Survive?" *The Teacher Paper*, October 1971, 10-11.

Kohlberg, L., "Early Education: A Cognitive-Developmental View," *Child Development*, 39, 1968, 1013-1062.

Kozol, Jonathan, *Death at an Early Age*, Houghton Mifflin, Boston, 1968.

Kozol, Jonathan, *Free Schools*, Houghton Mifflin, Boston, 1972.

Lambie, D.J. and D.P. Weikart, "Ypsilanti Carnegie Infant Education Project," in J. Hellmuth (ed.), *Disadvantaged Child*, Vol. 3, Brunner/Mazel, New York, 1970.

Leggett, T., "The Use of Non-Professionals in Large City Systems," in D. Street (ed.), *Innovation in Mass Education*, Wiley-Interscience, New York, 1969, 177-200.

Lennon, R.T., "Accountability and Performance Contracting," invited address to the American Educational Research Association, New York City, February 5, 1971.

Bibliography

Levien, Roger E., *National Institute of Education: Preliminary Plan for the Proposed Institute*, R-657-HEW, The Rand Corporation, Santa Monica, February 1971.

Levin, Henry M., *Community Control of Schools*, Brookings, Washington, D.C., 1970a.

Levin, Henry M., "A New Model of School Effectiveness," in *Do Teachers Make a Difference?* U.S. Department of Health, Education and Welfare, Office of Education, Bureau of Educational Personnel Development (OE-58042), 1970b, 55-75.

Levin, Henry M., "Concepts of Economic Efficiency and Educational Production," NBER Conference on Education as an Industry, June 4-5, 1971.

Light, Richard J. and Paul N. Smith, "Accumulating Evidence: Procedures for Resolving Contradictions Among Different Research Studies," *Harvard Educational Review*, 41, 1971, 429-471.

Los Angeles City Schools, "Evaluation ESEA Title I, 1969-1970," Technical Reports, 1970.

Macorie, Kenneth, *Up Taught*, Hayden, New York, 1970.

Maier, M. and P.B. Jacobs, "The Effects of Variations in a Self-instructional Program on Instructional Outcomes," *Psychology Reports*, 18, 1966, 539-546.

Martin, Ruby and Phyllis McClure, *Title I of ESEA: Is It Helping Poor Children?* Washington Research Project of the Southern Center for Studies in Public Policy and the NAACP Legal Defense and Educational Fund, Inc., 1969.

Mason, W.A., "Early Deprivation in Biological Perspective," in V.H. Denenberg (ed.), *Education of the Infant and Young Child*, Academic Press, New York, 1970.

Mayeske, George W. et al., *A Study of Our Nation's Schools*, Department of Health, Education and Welfare, Washington, D.C., 1969.

McCracken, Samuel, "Quackery in the Classroom," *Commentary*, June 1970.

Merrill, M.D., K. Barton, and L.E. Wood, "Specific Review in Learning a Hierarchial Imaginary Science," *Journal of Educational Psychology*, 61, 1970, 102-109.

Michelson, Stephan, "The Association of Teacher Resourcefulness with Children's Characteristics," in *Do Teachers Make a Difference?*, U.S. Department of Health, Education and Welfare, Office of

Education, Bureau of Educational Personnel Development (OE-58042), 1970, 120-168.

Miller, Louise B. and Jean L. Dyer, *Experimental Variation of Head Start Curricula: A Comparison of Current Approaches,* Child Development Laboratory, University of Louisville, Annual Progress Report to OEO, 1970 and 1971.

Milner, Murray, Jr., *The Illusion of Equality: The Effect of Education on Opportunity, Inequality, and Social Conflict,* Jossey-Bass, San Francisco, 1972.

Mollenkopf, William G. and S. Donald Melville, *A Study of Secondary School Characteristics as Related to Test Scores,* Research Bulletin RB-56-6, Educational Testing Service, Princeton, 1956.

Mort, P.R. and F.G. Cornell, *American Schools in Transition,* Teachers College, New York, 1941.

Mosbaek, E.J. et al., "Analyses of Compensatory Education in Five School Districts: Summary," TEMPO, General Electric Co., Santa Barbara, 1968 (mimeo.).

Mosteller, Frederick and Daniel P. Moynihan (eds.), *On Equality of Educational Opportunity,* Vintage Books, New York, 1972.

Nitko, A.J., "A Model for Criterion-Referenced Tests Based on Use," paper presented at the Annual Meeting of the American Educational Research Association, New York, February 4-7, 1971.

Oakland, California, Preschool Program, "It Works" series, Preschool Programs in Compensatory Education I, Office of Education, 1969 (OE 37057).

Office of Economic Opportunity, *An Experiment in Performance Contracting,* Washington, D.C., February 1972a.

Office of Economic Opportunity, *An Experiment in Performance Contracting,* Washington, D.C., June 1972b.

Perl, L.J., "Family Background, Secondary School Expenditure, and Student Ability," *Journal of Human Resources,* 8, 1973, 156-180.

Piccariello, Harry, "Evaluation of Title I," American Institute for the Advancement of Science, Washington, D.C. (n.d.) (mimeo.).

Popham, W. James (ed.), *Criterion-Referenced Measurement,* Educational Technology Publications, Englewood Cliffs, 1971.

Postman, Neil and C. Weingartner, *Teaching as a Subversive Activity,* Delacorte, New York, 1969.

Pressey, S.J., "Teaching Machines (and Learning Theory) Crises," *Journal of Applied Psychology,* 47, 1963, 1-6.

Project Head Start 1968: A Descriptive Report of Programs and Participants, Office of Child Development, U.S. Department of Health, Education and Welfare, 1970.

Rapp, M.L., *Case Studies in Educational Performance Contracting: Gilroy, California*, R-900/5-HEW, The Rand Corporation, Santa Monica, December 1971.

Rapp, M.L., M.B. Carpenter, S.A. Haggart, S.H. Landa, and G.C. Sumner, *Project R-3, San Jose, California: Evaluation of Results and Development of a Cost Model*, R-672-SJS, The Rand Corporation, Santa Monica, March 1971.

Raymond, Richard, "Determinants of the Quality of Primary and Secondary Public Education in Western Virginia," *Journal of Human Resources*, 3, No. 4, Fall 1968, 450-469.

Rist, R.C., "Student Social Class and Teacher Expectations: The Self-Fulfilling Prophecy in Ghetto Education," *Harvard Educational Review*, 40, 1970, 411-451.

Rogers, David, *110 Livingston Street: Politics and Bureaucracy in the New York Schools*, Random House, New York, 1968.

Rohwer, W.D., Jr., M.S. Ammon, N. Suzuki, and J.R. Levin, "Population Differences and Learning Proficiency," *Journal of Educational Psychology*, 62, 1971, 1-14.

Rombert, T.A., "Current Research in Mathematics Education," *Review of Educational Research*, 39, 1969, 473-492.

Rosenshine, B., "Evaluation of Instruction," *Review of Educational Research*, 40, 1970a, 279-300.

Rosenshine, B., "The Stability of Teacher Effects upon Student Achievement," *Review of Educational Research*, 40, 1970b, 647-662.

Rosenshine, B. and J. Furst, "Current and Future Research on Teacher Performance Criteria," in B.W. Smith (ed.), *Research on Teacher Education: A Symposium*, Prentice-Hall, Englewood Cliffs, 1971.

Rosenthal, R. and L. Jackson, *Pygmalion in the Classroom: Teacher Expectation and Pupils' Intellectual Development*, Holt, Rinehart and Winston, New York, 1968.

Rusk, Bruce A., *An Evaluation of a Six Week Head Start Program Using an Academically Oriented Curriculum: Canton, 1967*, Canton, Ohio, Public Schools, 1968 (ED 026 114).

Ryder, R.G., "Birth to Maturity Revisited: A Canonical Reanalysis," *Journal of Personality and Social Psychology*, 7, 1967, 168-172.

Saettler, P., *A History of Instructional Technology*, McGraw-Hill, New York, 1968.
Samuels, S.J., "Effects of Pictures on Learning to Read, Comprehension and Attitudes," *Review of Educational Research*, 40, 1970, 397-407.
Sarason, I.G. and R.E. Smith, "Personality," *Annual Review of Psychology*, 20, 1971, 393-446.
Scarr-Salapatek, Sandra, "Race, Social Class and IQ," *Science*, 174, December 24, 1971, 1285-1295.
Schaefer, Earl S. and May Aaronson, "Infant Education Project: Implementation and Implications of a Home Tutoring Program," in Ronald K. Parker (ed.), *Conceptualizations of Preschool Curricula*, 1971.
Schiller, J.S. and E.P. Murdoch, "Implications of Using Standardized Tests in Performance Contracting," in OEO, *An Experiment in Performance Contracting*, Washington, D.C., June 1972.
Schwartz, P.A., "Prediction Instruments for Educational Outcomes," in R.L. Thorndike (ed.), *Educational Measurement*, American Council on Education, Washington, D.C., 1971, 303-331.
Shulman, L.S., "Reconstruction of Educational Research," *Review of Educational Research*, 40, 1970, 371-396.
Shulman, L.S. and E.R. Keisler (eds.), *Learning by Discovery: A Critical Appraisal*, Rand-McNally, Skokie, Illinois, 1966.
Silberman, C.E., *Crisis in the Classroom*, Random House, New York, 1970.
Skeels, Harold M., "Adult Status of Children with Contrasting Early Life Experiences: A Follow-up Study," *Monographs of the Society for Research in Child Development*, 31, No. 3, Serial No. 105, University of Chicago Press, Chicago, 1966.
Skinner, B.G., *The Technology of Teaching*, Appleton-Century Crofts, New York, 1968.
Smith, H.A., "Curriculum Development and Instructional Materials," *Review of Educational Research*, 39, 1969, 397-414.
Smith, Marshall S., "Equality of Educational Opportunity: The Basic Findings Reconsidered," in F. Mosteller and D.P. Moynihan (eds.), *On Equality of Educational Opportunity*, Vintage Books, New York, 1972.
Snow, R.E., "Unfinished Pygmalion," *Contemporary Psychology*, 14, 1969, 197-200.

Snow, R.E., "Mental Abilities," *The Encyclopedia of Education*, Macmillan, Riverside, New Jersey, 1971.
Sontag, Marvin, Adina P. Sella, and Robert L. Thorndike, "The Effect of Head Start Training on the Cognitive Growth of Disadvantaged Children," *Journal of Educational Research*, 62, No. 9, 1969, 387-389.
Spicker, Howard H., Walter L. Hodges, and Boyd R. McCandless, "A Diagnostically Based Curriculum for Psycho-socially Deprived Preschool, Mentally Retarded Children, Interim Report," *Exceptional Children*, 33, 1966, 215-220.
Sprigle, H.A., *Learning to Learn Program, Jacksonville, Florida*, "It Works" series, Preschool Programs in Compensatory Education I, U.S. Office of Education, 1969 (OE 37056).
Sprigle, H.A. and V. Van De Riet, "The Learning to Learn Program," Report presented to the Carnegie Corporation of New York, 1968.
Spring, Joel H., *Education and the Rise of the Corporate State*, Beacon Press, Boston, 1972.
Stake, R.E., "Objectives, Priorities, and Other Judgmental Data," *Review of Educational Research*, 40, 1970, 181-212.
Stake, R.E., "Testing Hazards in Performance Contracting," *Phi Delta Kappan*, 12, 1971, 583-589.
Stanford Research Institute, *Longitudinal Evaluation Program*, Menlo Park, 1971a.
Stanford Research Institute, *Implementation of Planned Variation in Head Start: Part 2, Preliminary Evaluations of Planned Variations in Head Start According to Follow Through Approaches (1969-1970)*, Menlo Park, 1971b.
Stearns, Marian Sherman, "The Effects of Preschool Programs on Children and Their Families," 1971a (mimeo.).
Stearns, Marian Sherman, "Report on Preschool Programs: The Effects of Preschool Programs on Disadvantaged Children and Their Families," 1971b (mimeo.).
Stephens, J.M., *The Process of Schooling*, Holt, Rinehart and Winston, New York, 1967.
Stodolsky, S.S. and G. Lesser, "Learning Patterns in the Disadvantaged," *Harvard Review of Education*, 37, 1967, 546-548.
Sumner, G.C., *Case Studies in Educational Performance Contracting: Grand Rapids, Michigan*, R-900/6 HEW, The Rand Corporation, December 1971.
Thelen, H.A., "Programmed Materials Today: Critique and Proposal,"

The Elementary School Review, 64, 1963a, 189-196.
Thelen, H.A., "Programmed Instruction: Insight vs. Conditioning," *Education*, 83, 1963b, 416-420.
Thelen, H.A., *Classroom Grouping for Teachability*, John Wiley and Sons, New York, 1967.
Thomas, James Alan, "Efficiency in Education: A Study of the Relationship Between Selected Inputs and Mean Test Scores in a Sample of Senior High Schools," Ph.D. dissertation, Stanford University Library, 1962 (microf.).
Turner, Richard L., *Differential Association of Elementary Teacher Characteristics with School System Types, Final Report*, Project 2579, U.S. Office of Education, September 1968.
Turner, Richard L. and D.A. Denny, "Teacher Characteristics, Teacher Behavior, and Changes in Pupil Creativity," *Elementary School Journal*, 62, 1969, 265-270.
United Kingdom Ministry of Education, "Summerhill: Report of the British Government Inspectors," in B. Gross and R. Gross (eds.), *Radical School Reform*, Simon and Schuster, New York, 1969, 247-259.
U.S. Department of Health, Education and Welfare, Office of Education, *Education of the Disadvantaged: An Evaluative Report on Title I Elementary and Secondary Education Act of 1965, Fiscal Year 1968*, Washington, D.C., 1970.
Vandenberg, S.G., "Contributions of Twin Research to Psychology," *Psychology Bulletin*, 66, 1966, 327-352.
Van De Riet, Vernon, Hani Van De Riet, and Herbert Sprigle, "The Effectiveness of a New Sequential Learning Program with Culturally Disadvantaged Preschool Children," *Journal of School Psychology*, 7, No. 3, 1968, 5-14.
Vernon, P.E., "Ability Factors and Environmental Influence," *American Psychology*, 20, 1965, 723-733.
Wargo, M.J., P.L. Campeau, and G.K. Tallmadge, *Further Examination of Exemplary Programs for Educating Disadvantaged Children*, American Institutes of Research, Palo Alto, 1971.
Wei, Tham Thi Dang, *Piaget's Concept of Classification: A Comparative Study of Socially Disadvantaged and Middle Class Young Children*, Urbana College of Education, Illinois University, 1969.
Weikart, David P. (ed.), *Preschool Intervention: Preliminary Report of the Perry Preschool Project*, Campus Publishers, Ann Arbor, 1967.
Weikart, David P., *The Ypsilanti Preschool Curriculum Development*

Project 1968-71, High-Scope Educational Research Foundation, Ypsilanti, Michigan, 1971a.

Weikart, David P., "Early Childhood Special Education for Intellectually Subnormal and/or Culturally Different Children," prepared for the National Leadership Institute in Early Childhood Development, Washington, D.C., High-Scope Educational Research Foundation, Ypsilanti, Michigan, October 1971b.

Weikart, David P. and D.Z. Lambie, "Preschool Intervention Through a Home Teaching Project," in J. Hellmuth (ed.), *Disadvantaged Child*, Vol. 2, Brunner/Mazel, New York, 1969.

Welch, W.W., "Curriculum Evaluation," *Review of Educational Research*, 39, 1969, 429-444.

Wesman, A.G., "Writing the Test Item," in R.L. Thorndike (ed.), *Educational Measurement* (2nd ed.), The American Council on Education, Washington, D.C., 1971.

Westbury, I., "Curriculum Evaluation," *Review of Educational Research*, 40, 1970, 239-260.

Westinghouse Learning Corporation, *The Impact of Head Start, An Evaluation of the Effects of Head Start on Children's Cognitive and Affective Development: Vol. I, Text and Appendices A-E*, Ohio University, Report to OEO, Clearinghouse for Federal Scientific and Technical Information, 1969.

Wiggins, J.S., "Personality Structure," *Annual Review of Psychology*, 19, 1968, 293-350.

Wolff, Max and Annie Stein, "Head Start Six Months Later," *Phi Delta Kappan*, 48, March 1967, 349-350.

Wonnacott, R.S. and T.H. Wonnacott, *Econometrics*, John Wiley and Sons, New York, 1970.

Wrightstone, J. Wayne *et al.*, "Evaluation of the Higher Horizons Program for Underprivileged Children," New York City Board of Education, New York, 1964.

Yin, Robert K., *The Workshop and the World: Toward an Assessment of the Children's Television Workshop*, R-1400-MF, The Rand Corporation, Santa Monica, October 1973.

Zimiles, Herbert, "Has Evaluation Failed Compensatory Education?" in J. Hellmuth (ed.), *Disadvantaged Child*, Vol 3, Brunner/Mazel, New York, 1970.

INDEX

Achievement, 21
    cognitive, 21, 22, 25, 26, 27, 37, 147
    noncognitive, 22, 24, 25, 26, 36, 37, 52, 98
    standardized achievement tests, 26, 27, 28, 30, 31, 32, 33, 34, 36, 37, 47, 52, 150
    validity of, 31, 32
Alpha One, 142

Bereiter-Engelmann Programs, 137, 138, 139, 140
British infant schools, 8
    open classroom, 159-161

Children's Television Workshop, 118, 123
Coleman Report, 47, 48, 49
Compensatory education, 139-142, 144, 145
    costs, 139-142, 145
Conformity, 153, 154
Criterion-referenced tests, 33, 34

DARCEE, 138, 139

Educational effectiveness, 3, 5, 53, 182
    background, 3
    conclusions and policy implications, 171-175
    educational policy, 9, 10
    educational research, 9, 10, 12, 23

253

external validity, 11, 23
internal validity, 10, 11, 19, 20
measured by standardized tests, 8
Educational production function, 39, 40, 46
linear production function, 40
research problems, 52, 53
results, 46
student's outcome, 39, 40, 41, 42, 54, 55
variables, 43
background factors, 43, 50, 51, 53, 90
peer group influences, 43, 47-50, 55
school resources, 43, 50, 51, 53, 54, 55
Educational research, 170-182
methodological issues, 179-182
substantive issues, 175-179
different forms of education, 178-179
interaction, 177-178
non-school factors, 175-177
Educational technology, 8
audio-visual reinforcement, 9
cable television, 8, 9
computer-assisted instruction, 8, 128
programmed instruction, 9, 71, 72, 87, 88, 97, 99
research on teaching technology, 71
teaching machines, 71, 72, 97
television learning, 71, 97
Electric Company, 118
Elementary and Secondary Education Act of 1965, 6, 116
Title I, 6, 116, 117, 118, 119, 122, 126, 137, 139-141, 144
Title III, 6, 7
Title VII, 6
Title VIII, 6
Evaluation approach, 16, 17, 116-145, 169, 180
effects of poverty, 116
findings, 117, 126
compensatory education study, 126, 127, 169
Higher Horizons program, 118
New York City School System, 117, 118
TEMPO, 126

Index

      Westinghouse Report, 119, 120, 122, 143
    intervention studies, 128-131
      Bissell, 135, 136, 139
      DiLorenzo, 130, 139, 141, 144
      Gordon, 129
      Karnes, 129, 136, 139, 140
      Project Conquest, 130
      Stanford University, 128
    longitudinal analysis, 131-135
      achievement test findings, 134
      intelligence test findings, 131
      summary, 135
Experiential approach, 116-145
    conclusions and policy implications, 163-165
    defined, 146-147
    limitations of research, 151-152
    objectives and methods, 147-148
    results, 152-163
      learning environment, 155-159
      reformation: prescription for education, 157, 159-163, 164, 165, 169, 170, 180
      social values and educational objectives, 152-155
    variables, 148-151
      school-society, student-society relations, 148
      student-school relations, 148
      student-teacher relations, 148
      teacher-organization relations, 148

Federal government, 6
Follow Through program, 117, 120, 121

General intelligence tests, 35, 36
    IQ scores, 35

Head Start, 116, 117, 119, 120, 122, 136, 138, 143
    "Follow Through," 117, 120, 121, 138, 140
    OEO Study. *See* Westinghouse Report.
Higher Horizons 100 Project, 142

Input-output approach, 8, 12, 13, 23, 39-55, 100
    analytical problems, 44-46
        summary and discussion of findings, 166
            background factors, 166
            peer group influences, 166

Jensen model of intelligence, 35-36, 82, 83

Local school districts, 7

Montessori Method, 137, 138, 139
Multiple regression analysis, 42

National Institute of Education (NIE), 6
New York City Higher Horizons program, 121, 140
Normative scores, 29
    derivation and meaning, 29
    raw test scores, 29, 37
    sampling bias, 29, 30
    statistical problems, 32, 33

Organizational approach, 15, 16, 100-115, 168, 169, 180
    performance contracting evaluation, 112, 113
    research problems and methods, 101-105, 112, 113
        external validity, 105
        internal validity, 105
    results from case studies, 105-110, 168
        innovations, 110, 113, 168
        principals as leaders, 107-109, 114, 168
        rigidities in school system, effects, 107-109, 168
        school size, effects, 105-107, 168
    results from performance contracting studies, 110
        OEO, 110-112, 114, 115
        Rand approach, 110-112, 113, 114, 115

Process approach, 13, 14, 23, 56-99, 100
    attention factors in learning, 79
        paired-associate method, 80
    classroom studies, 56, 57

Index 257

    concept attainment, 89, 90
    creativity, 93, 94, 97
    curriculum, 66-70
    early development and learning, 94-96
    effects of instruction, 65, 66, 70, 96
    instructional psychology, 72-75, 95
    laboratory studies, 56, 57
    personality differences, 91
        overachievers, 92
        underachievers, 92
    reinforcement and feedback, 77-79
        behavior modification, 78
    results
        classroom, 167
        laboratory, 167, 168
    retention of learned material, 80, 81
    student characteristics, 81, 82, 84, 88, 97
        abilities and general intelligence, 82, 83
        aptitude-treatment interaction, 84-86
        attitude and motivation, 92, 93
        meaningfulness, 88, 89, 92, 93
        programmed instruction, 87
    student-teacher interactions, 64, 65
    teacher characteristics, 58-61
    teacher skills and effectiveness, 61-63, 96
    transfer of learning, 75
        "fading" or "vanishing," 77
        hierarchical organization, 75, 76
        lateral, 76
        vertical, 75, 76, 98
Progressive Education Association's Eight-Year Study, 22
Project Breakthrough, 141
Project Conquest, 142
Project Mars, 142
Public schools, 3-6
    costs, 5, 6
    functions, 3
        custodial, 3, 4
        encouragement of individual attributes, 3, 4

knowledge and skills training, 3, 4
socialization, 3, 5
sorting, 3, 5

Research approaches
　　evaluation, 16, 17, 116-145, 169, 180
　　experiential, 18, 19, 22, 146-165, 169, 170
　　input-output, 8, 12, 13, 23, 39-55, 100, 166, 167
　　limitations of available research, 170, 171
　　organizational, 15, 16, 100-115, 168, 169, 180
　　process, 13, 14, 23, 56-99, 100, 167, 168

Sesame Street, 9, 118, 123-125, 142
　　ETS study, 123-125
State governments, 7
Student learning, 21
　　acquisition of knowledge and cognitive skills, 21, 147
　　retention of subject matter, 21

Teacher grades, 27, 28
　　grading on the curve, 28
Tests
　　criterion-referenced, 33, 34, 142
　　general intelligence, 35, 36, 99, 129, 130, 142
　　standardized achievement (normative), 26, 27, 28, 30, 31, 32, 33,
　　　　34, 36, 37, 47, 52, 142

Westinghouse Report, 119, 120, 122, 143

RAND EDUCATIONAL POLICY STUDIES

John Pincus, Editor

PUBLISHED

Averch, Harvey A., Stephen J. Carroll, Theodore S. Donaldson, Herbert J. Kiesling, and John Pincus. *How Effective Is Schooling? A Critical Review of Research.* Englewood Cliffs, New Jersey: Educational Technology Publications, 1974.

Pincus, John (Ed.) *School Finance in Transition: The Courts and Educational Reform.* Cambridge, Mass.: Ballinger Publishing Company, 1974.

OTHER RAND BOOKS IN EDUCATION

Bretz, Rudy. *A Taxonomy of Communication Media.* Englewood Cliffs, New Jersey: Educational Technology Publications, 1971.

Bruno, James E., (Ed.) *Emerging Issues in Education: Policy Implications for the Schools.* Lexington, Mass.: D.C. Heath and Company, 1972.

Coleman, James S. and Nancy L. Karweit. *Information Systems and Performance Measures in Schools.* Englewood Cliffs, New Jersey: Educational Technology Publications, 1972.

Haggart, Sue A. (Ed.) *Program Budgeting for School District Planning.* Englewood Cliffs, New Jersey: Educational Technology Publications, 1972.